Everyday Information Practices

A Social Phenomenological Perspective

Reijo Savolainen

THE SCARECROW PRESS, INC.
Lanham, Maryland • Toronto • Plymouth, UK
2008

SCARECROW PRESS, INC.

Published in the United States of America
by Scarecrow Press, Inc.
A wholly owned subsidiary of
The Rowman & Littlefield Publishing Group, Inc.
4501 Forbes Boulevard, Suite 200, Lanham, Maryland 20706
www.scarecrowpress.com

Estover Road
Plymouth PL6 7PY
United Kingdom

British Library Cataloguing in Publication Information Available

Library of Congress Cataloging-in-Publication Data

Savolainen, Reijo.
  Everyday information practices : a social phenomenological perspective /
Reijo Savolainen.
     p. cm.
  Includes bibliographical references and index.
  ISBN-13: 978-0-8108-6111-4 (pbk. : alk. paper)
  ISBN-10: 0-8108-6111-9 (pbk. : alk. paper)
  1. Information behavior. I. Title.
ZA3075.S38 2008
025.5'24—dc22   2007050342

Contents

Preface

My major motive for writing this book originates from my enduring interest in the phenomena of everyday-life information seeking (ELIS). This refers to the ways in which people acquire information in non-work contexts, for example by monitoring daily events through the media or seeking information to solve specific problems at hand. In itself, this research area is not new, because the first surveys of citizen information needs and seeking were conducted in the United States in the 1970s. Even though the field of study has established itself fairly well since the 1990s, the overall picture of the phenomena of ELIS is still rather fragmentary. This is largely because most research findings are communicated through journal articles and conference papers. They elucidate individual issues but not the "big picture" of these phenomena.

Monographs serve this need better because they can provide a broader view. Unfortunately, few books have as yet focused on this area, most of them dating back to before the Internet. In this context is Patrick Wilson's seminal *Public Knowledge, Private Ignorance*[1] and *Second-Hand Knowledge: An Inquiry into Cognitive Authority*.[2] In the early 1980s, Ching-chih Chen and Peter Hernon presented the findings of a major U.S. survey in their *Information Seeking: Assessing and Anticipating User Needs*,[3] while Joan Durrance's *Armed for Action: Library Response to Citizen Information Needs*[4] characterized information seeking among citizen activists. The most recent monograph focusing on ELIS dates back to 1992 when Elfreda Chatman published her study *Information World of Retired Women*.[5]

Since that time, there has unfortunately been a major gap in this field as far as monographs are concerned. Even though some recent books, for example, Harry Bruce's *The User's View of the Internet*,[6] discuss many topics that are relevant to ELIS, their major focus is on specific issues, such as the use of networked sources. Thus, there seems to be a genuine need for a general book about everyday information practices characteristic of our time.

My first studies in this area date back to the early 1990s. At that time I explored the information-seeking practices of industrial workers and teachers, based on interviews conducted in Tampere, Finland. The main findings of this study were reported in an article published in *Library and Information Science Research*[7] in 1995. In the article, I proposed the concept of ELIS to stand for the research area previously known as citizen information needs and seeking. Later, it appeared that the concept of ELIS was quite widely accepted to denote a subfield of information-seeking studies and as contrasted with studies on work-related information seeking.

In the same study, mainly inspired by the idea of *habitus*[8] developed by Pierre Bourdieu, I proposed a model of ELIS that was conceptualized in the context of "way of life" and "mastery of life."[9] In this book, I will no longer use this model as a theoretical framework, even though many of the ideas proposed for the ELIS model are still relevant from the broader perspective of everyday information practices. One of the ideas I will develop is that everyday projects form a major context of ELIS. However, in contrast to the prior model, everyday projects will be discussed in the context of a life world, not any way of life in particular. This shift is due to my increased interest in the ideas of social phenomenology. Overall, social phenomenogy provides an intriguing framework in which to study how people perceive their information worlds and how they prefer or avoid certain information sources based on their interests. Another novel perspective of ELIS issues—closely connected to social phenomenology—is provided by so-called practice theories. They indicate that there is generally a more novel interest, in social sciences, to approaching the phenomena of everyday life from the viewpoint of everyday practices, habits, and routines.

Looking back at earlier studies, my shift toward the ideas of social phenomenology has been underway since around 2000. At that time I began to cooperate with my colleague, Dr. Jarkko Kari, in order to explore the ways in which the Internet had been incorporated in ELIS practices. My recent studies, discussed here, concentrate on two groups, that is environmental activists and unemployed people. At the same time, the perspective of ELIS studies has gradually been broadened to incorporate the issues of information use and information sharing. Given the relatively long span of empirical studies conducted since the early 1990s, it seems that the time is now ripe for drawing a broader picture of the ways people seek, use, and share information in everyday contexts. This suggests that we may extend the scope of ELIS issues to those of *everyday information practices*.

The major aim of the present book is to elaborate this novel concept and to elucidate the ways information practices manifest themselves in everyday contexts. I will address questions such as "How do we perceive the information world around us?" and "By which criteria do we accept or reject information in everyday contexts?" by drawing on empirical studies conducted between 2005 and 2006 and also using the findings of earlier studies to provide a comparative perspective.

NOTES

1. Patrick Wilson, *Public Knowledge, Private Ignorance: Toward a Library and Information Policy* (Westport, Conn.: Greenwood Press, 1977).

2. Patrick Wilson, *Second-Hand Knowledge: An Inquiry into Cognitive Authority* (Westport, Conn.: Greenwood Press, 1983).

3. Ching-chih Chen and Peter Hernon, *Information Seeking: Assessing and Anticipating User Needs* (New York: Neal-Schuman, 1982).

4. Joan C. Durrance, *Armed for Action: Library Response to Citizen Information Needs* (New York: Neal-Schuman, 1984).

5. Elfreda A. Chatman, *The Information World of Retired Women* (Westport, Conn.: Greenwood Press, 1992).

6. Harry Bruce, *The User's View of the Internet* (Lanham, Md.: Scarecrow Press, 2002).

7. Reijo Savolainen, "Everyday Life Information Seeking: Approaching Information Seeking in the Context of Way of Life," *Library and Information Science Research* 17, no. 3 (1995).

8. Pierre Bourdieu, *Distinction: A Social Critique of the Judgement of Taste* (London: Routledge, 1984).

9. Savolainen, "Everyday Life Information Seeking."

Acknowledgments

Some of the chapters of this book draw on reworked and extended versions of articles published in other forums. I am grateful to the publishers of my previous work for their permission to reuse material here in a new form and context.

Chapter 3 makes use of my article titled "Information Behavior and Information Practice: Reviewing the 'Umbrella Concepts' of Information Seeking Studies," published in *Library Quarterly*, vol. 77 (April 2007). Chapter 5 draws on "Information Source Horizons and Source Preferences of Environmental Activists: A Social Phenomenological Approach," published in *Journal of the American Society for Information Science and Technology*, vol. 58, no. 12 (2007), and "Source Preferences in the Context of Seeking Problem-Specific Information," published in *Information Processing and Management*, vol. 44, no. 1 (2008). Chapter 6 makes use of "Media Credibility and Cognitive Authority: The Case of Seeking Orienting Information," published in *Information Research*, vol. 12, no. 3 (2007), and "Filtering and Withdrawing: Strategies for Coping with Information Overload in Everyday Contexts," published in *Journal of Information Science*, vol. 33, no. 5 (2007). Finally, chapter 7 draws on "Motives for Giving Information in Non-Work Contexts and the Expectations of Reciprocity: The Case of Environmental Activists," a paper presented in the Annual Meeting of the American Society for Information Science and Technology, Milwaukee, Wisconsin, October 18–25, 2007.

In addition, I owe a special debt of gratitude to the interviewees who gave freely of their time and thoughts. Further, discussions in the sessions of the Research Group on Information Seeking (REGIS) at the Department of Information Studies, University of Tampere, Finland, provided valuable ideas for the development of the study.

Of course, this book would not exist without the support of the publishing team at Scarecrow Press. In particular, I wish to thank Martin Dillon. Martin's editorial skills and insightful comments made a real contribution. Finally, I'm indebted to the Academy of Finland for its financial support for the research project on everyday information practices.

Chapter One

Introduction

The issues of everyday life and everyday practices are enjoying something of a renaissance in contemporary social thought.[1] The circumstances in which people find themselves regarding their work and leisure time have been in a state of flux particularly since the 1990s. This is mainly due to major developments such as more flexible ways of defining the boundaries of work and leisure in times of an information-intensive global economy, and the growing use of the Internet in all spheres of daily life. Along with these developments, everyday life[2] in late modernity seems to be more complex and thus less predictable than in the traditional industrial society. In general, these transformations may be better understood by referring to *reflexive modernization*.[3] It stands for new modernity that is characterized by heightened insecurities and risks. They may originate, for example, from the side effects of industrial production that are now globalized and uncontrollable (e.g., climate change caused by global warming).

Reflexive modernization is also characterized by growing individualization, that is, by a tendency for individuals to make themselves the focus of their life experience. Thus, increasingly characteristic of everyday life in our age is the need to make choices in order to master one's destiny under these conditions. From the perspective of reflexive modernization, the use of information about the conditions of activity is a core means of regularly monitoring and redefining what that activity is.[4] In other words, the choices made by people are affected by the ways in which they seek and use information.

The development of reflexive modernization may seem familiar, and could be viewed as something natural or self-evident. Everyday life can also be characterized by the many paradoxes originating from the familiarity of mundane experiences. While it has been suggested that in itself everyday life is

1

unproblematic because "we all know" what is meant by it, once probed in detail, everyday life becomes ambiguous and elusive. Since the concept seems to defy any clear characterization, it is no wonder that the attempts to define everyday life and everyday practices may cause frustration among ordinary people as well as scholars. According to David Morgan, everyday life refers to events that are characterized as regular, repeated, familiar, quotidian, banal, and even boring.[5] However, such characterizations may not go beyond a commonsense understanding of mundane phenomena. Another paradox is that even though everyday life is an inescapable context of human action, this context is often seen as something trivial that is not worth talking about. Similar paradoxes seem to haunt the understanding of the phenomena of everyday practices, for example, housekeeping and cleaning. Because such practices are ubiquitous and self-evident, we tend to approach them without much reflection, simply as "ways of operating or doing things."[6]

The elaboration of these issues will continue in chapter 2. An attempt will be made to define the concept of practice in the context of everyday life. To elucidate the conceptual nature of practice, related concepts such as action, behavior, and habit are introduced. Chapter 2 ends with the introduction of a model of practice in the context of life world. The model draws on two major sources: the ideas of social phenomenology[7] and practice theory developed by Theodore Schatzki.[8] This is a starting point for a review of the concepts of information practice and everyday information practice that are discussed in chapter 3.

Similar to the categories of everyday life and practice, the issues of information practice are somewhat ambiguous. This is paradoxical since information practices are very familiar to most of us. Daily media habits refer to deeply ingrained ways in which activities such as reading newspapers, listening to the radio, and watching television are embedded within everyday activities. Media habits are also identified in the utilization of new media, as exemplified by the routine ways of checking e-mail. Due to the ubiquity of media habits, Bo Reimer has characterized media use as the "most common of practices," since activities such as watching television are carried out by most people in contemporary Western societies.[9] On the other hand, due to its extremely common nature, mass media use may be seen as a practice "without high merits." Nevertheless, such practices unite us because we share them daily.

The concept of information practice, or more specifically everyday information practice is new. Information practice may be understood as a set of socially and culturally established ways to identify, seek, use, and share the information available in various sources such as television, newspapers, and the

Internet. These practices are often habitual and can be identified both in job-related and non-work contexts.

Importantly, as Paul Solomon points out, such practices are part and parcel of something that people call "making sense of the everyday world and its events."[10] It is characteristic of everyday information practices that people seldom think of collecting, processing, or using information as something separate from the task or problem at hand. Information practices are embedded in everyday contexts; in addition, their self-evident nature make these practices "invisible" and difficult to see in greater detail. While information practices partially overlap in job-related and non-work settings, this book focuses on information practices accomplished in non-work contexts only. For clarity, such information practices are called everyday information practices. The non-work contexts in which they are accomplished include leisure activities such as hobbies, participation in the activities of civil society, and activities related to problem solving, for example, looking for a job.

The conceptual issues of information practice are focused on in chapter 3. The concept of information practice, or, more specifically everyday information practice is new. The issues of information seeking and use has been discussed under the umbrella of "information behavior" or "human information behavior." Tom D. Wilson—a distinguished proponent of the concept of information behavior—defines it as "the totality of human behavior in relation to sources and channels, including both active and passive information seeking, and information use."[11] Defined in this way, information behavior encompasses face-to-face communication with others, as well as the passive reception of information, without any intention of acting on the information given.

The concept of information behavior (or information-seeking behavior) suggests that information seekers are "needy" individuals hunting for information from various sources and channels.[12] It is assumed that individuals have information needs or "anomalous states of knowledge" that stem from problems encountered in the context of performing work tasks.[13] Naturally, problematic situations triggering information needs may also occur outside work contexts, for example, when an individual faces health problems. The concept of information behavior also assumes that information needs lead to information seeking, more specifically, the identification of various information sources and channels such as friends, Google, and the public library. Information-seeking behavior continues when an individual accesses and uses some of these sources.

One of the purposes of this book is to provide an alternative method to defining information behavior that doesn't use the concept of "needy" individuals.

The motivating factors involved in writing this book involve more than just clarifying the terminology used, but also the ways in which the phenomena of information seeking, use, and sharing are seen as socially and culturally sensitive phenomena.

Compared to information behavior, the major distinctive characteristic of the information practice approach is that it represents "a more sociologically and contextually oriented line of research."[14] Kimmo Tuominen and his colleagues point out that particularly from the constructionist perspective, the concept of information practice is preferred over that of information behavior.[15] The concept of information practice suggests that the processes of information seeking and use are constituted socially and dialogically, rather than based on the cognitive or mental models, needs, and motives of individual actors. All human practices are social, and they originate from interactions between the members of a community. This approach also emphasizes that knowledge is inherently social. Hence, the concept of "information practice" shifts the focus away from the needs and cognitive structures of individuals. Instead, attention is directed toward them as social actors, that is, members of various groups and communities that constitute the context of their everyday activities. Thus, the proponents of information practice emphasize the role of contextual factors that orient people's information seeking, use, and sharing as distinct from the individualist and often decontextualized approaches that are seen to be characteristic of the assumptions of "information behavior."[16] By drawing on these assumptions, this book takes the phenomena of practice as a starting point and prefers this concept to related concepts such as the concept of behavior.

Chapter 3 clarifies these issues by comparing the concepts of information practice, information behavior, and information action. Chapter 3 ends with the elaboration of the model of everyday information practices. There are three modes of everyday information practices: information seeking, information use, and information sharing. The model is based on the framework of practice in the context of life world discussed in chapter 2. Life world provides a general context in which everyday projects of diverse kinds are embedded. We may exemplify everyday projects by activities such as looking for a job and concern for the environment. Everyday information practices may serve as tools to achieve the goals of these projects. Further, it is proposed that the concept of information source horizon is central for the constitution of everyday information practices since this horizon indicates the ways in which people prefer information sources and thus navigate in the information world.

In order to substantiate the model of everyday information practices, an empirical study was conducted drawing on the social phenomenological[17] point of view. Why social phenomenology?[18] According to Michael Bull, this approach is particularly attentive to the way in which social meanings are embedded in individual forms of experience.[19] Social phenomenology also helps us to understand people's habitual activities and routines that are central to the constitution of everyday practices.

The empirical study of everyday practices has problems, though one may think that the research object, due to its ubiquitous nature and familiarity, would be easy to identify and study. However, if everyday practices are conceived of as the equivalent to normality, then one may run the risk of falling into naive empiricism. This approach means belaboring the obvious and describing just the surface of everyday phenomena as they appear to the researcher when he or she collects details of what people do in everyday contexts.[20] On the other hand, there is the risk of imbuing mundane practices with inappropriate complexity and/or significance. To navigate between these methodological rocks, the main question was shifted from "what are everyday information practices" to "how are they possible"? More specifically, the latter question refers to the research task to find out the ways in which people who accomplish everyday information practices construct them as meaningful.

To achieve this goal, everyday information practices have to focus on the ways in which people make their experiences and choices accountable to themselves (and the researcher) in the context of an interview. The accounts may cover, for example, the criteria by which they access (or avoid) information sources or share information with other people in life world contexts. Social phenomenology provides an appropriate methodological perspective that respects the individual viewpoint, that is, the ways in which the individual posits his or her preferences of seeking, using, and sharing information. In addition to individual variation, attention may be devoted to the common features people exhibit when they construct their information practices. The common features indicate the shared (social and cultural) characteristics of everyday information practices.

The empirical setting of the study will be elaborated on in greater detail in chapter 4. Primarily, the study draws on interviews with environmental activists and unemployed persons during the period between 2005 and 2006. In addition, earlier studies focusing on everyday-life information seeking (ELIS) will be used to compare the findings and to reflect whether information practices have changed since the 1990s.

Chapters 5–7 report the findings of the empirical study by discussing the practices of information seeking, information use, and information sharing. ELIS is a major component of everyday information practices, and is discussed in chapter 5. ELIS has two major aspects. Orienting information seeking serves the need to monitor everyday events through various sources, in particular the media. Another aspect is the seeking of problem-specific information, for example, to perform a task or to solve a problem. The distinction between orienting and practical information seeking serves analytic ends; in real acts of information seeking the dimensions of orienting and problem-specific information may be closely intertwined. However, the distinction is useful here, because it enables a more detailed analysis of ELIS practices.

There are a number of well-known examples of daily information seeking: reading newspapers in order to monitor current events, checking reference books in a library to check a fact, and consulting a doctor about health problems. In general, information seeking may be seen as a necessary part of meaningful action because without information seeking it is often impossible to interpret and make sense of one's daily world. The first ELIS studies date back to the late 1960s. In the 1970s and 1980s, extensive surveys were conducted in the United States to identify people's everyday information needs and the major information sources that were used to meet these needs.[21] Pioneering surveys such as these, as well as more focused studies discussing citizen information needs and seeking[22] made laudable efforts to posit information seeking in everyday contexts. On the other hand, the nature of information seeking as a routine practice was not elaborated on in detail.

The same applies to later ELIS studies, including Elfreda A. Chatman's major research project focusing on the information behavior of people living in "small worlds" such as a retirement home[23] and a prison.[24] Overall, Chatman's studies share many of the interests of this book, since her research approach is deeply contextualized in mundane settings. However, in contrast, Chatman mainly drew on the ideas of functionalist sociology by emphasizing the significance of group-specific norms and roles that tend to constrain information seeking. Although the importance of such binding factors is not denied here, a broader viewpoint will be adopted to explore how people seek information driven by their interests. A broader view of information seeking is also needed because it is obvious that in times of increasing individualization characteristic of reflexive modernization and the extensive availability of networked sources, people may be less subject to the norm-based pressures that direct information seeking.

In chapter 5, the ELIS practices will be investigated by discussing the practices of seeking orienting information and problem-specific information. In both cases, attention will be paid to the construction of information source horizons, that is, the criteria by which people prefer or avoid the sources available in the perceived information environment. The review of ELIS practices takes place in the context of everyday projects. This provides a novel approach to ELIS studies and opens new vistas for the elaboration of ELIS research.

Chapter 6 centers on the practice of information use. In general, it may be conceived of as a process that is preceded by information seeking. In information use, the usefulness of an information source is assessed and any information deemed valuable is absorbed, in order to solve a problem or make sense of a situation, for example.

Although the mundane processes of information utilization are ubiquitous, there is so far very little research knowledge on exactly how information is used. Indeed, information and media scientists have paid insufficient attention to questions of information use as a constituent of everyday life.[25] In particular, we lack qualitative research exploring how people make use of diverse information sources to further their everyday projects. However, such studies are vitally important, since information has no value in itself, information gains value when it is used.

Various disciplines, for example, cognitive science, communication studies, management science, and information studies explore the problems of information or knowledge use. The study of information use has emerged from several different traditions. The phenomena of information use are typically approached from the cognitive viewpoint by drawing on quasi-experimental research designs.[26] This approach assumes that information use manifests itself in the ways in which information, internalized by the individual, actually modifies his or her knowledge structures. Another way to look at information use would be the way in which knowledge thus gained is wielded in action.[27] Another influential approach to information use is that provided by the sense-making approach.[28] "Use" stands for the ways in which information that is obtained from various sources helped one create a new "sense" and to bridge a "gap." Empirical examples of "uses" include "got ideas, got understanding, kept going, got out of a bad situation, got pleasure, and got connected to others."[29] In a recent characterization of sense-making, Brenda Dervin approaches the phenomenon of information use more empathetically from the viewpoint of *verbing*.[30] Dervin defines verbing as the ways in which people make or use "cognitions, thoughts and conclusions; attitudes, beliefs and values; feelings, emotions and intuitions; and memories, stories and narratives."[31]

As the previous examples suggest, the phenomena of information use may be explored at varying levels of generality. On the one hand, information use may be approached at the micro level by focusing on the specific ways in which an individual's cognitive structures change when he or she processes information. In such micro-level studies, the main attention is devoted to the changes that can be identified in the conceptions of the information user, for example, a newspaper reader. These changes may be traced by using the "thinking aloud" method or collecting short narratives. These methods can be used to show—at least partly—how the internalized information has changed an individual's conceptions by adding new cognitive elements or deleting previous ones.[32] The phenomena of information use may also be approached at the macro level. Instead of focusing on real-time use processes in which the relevance of information is judged, the macro-level studies devote their main attention to the ways in which people interpret the value of information sources more generally. In such studies, questions worth closer examination include the value or relevance of everyday information, the criteria by which information from diverse sources is accepted or rejected, the credibility of information, the problems of information overload, as well as, the ways in which people may cope with everyday problems by making use of information.

Given the level of generality adopted in the study of ELIS practices, chapter 6 will concentrate on information use at the macro level. Two major issues of information use will be explored. First, media credibility and cognitive authority will be investigated in the context of using orienting information. Second, in the same context, the strategies by which people cope with information overload will be explored. These themes are important from the viewpoint of social phenomenology since they explain the ways in which people filter information in order to separate the wheat from the chaff when working on everyday projects. It is suggested that like information seeking, the actions that make up information use practices may become habitual. However, people do not perform actions such as filtering in a mechanistic way because they are also situationally sensitive.

The empirical review ends with the examination of the practice of information sharing (see chapter 7). Like information use, this issue has rarely been explored in detail in non-work contexts. Information seeking and use provide people with stocks of knowledge that may be "shared" with others because of such diverse motives as altruism or expectations of reciprocity in which help may be needed from others. Interestingly, the practice of information sharing may appear as a "less egoistic" practice compared to information seeking and use. This is due to the assumption that in everyday contexts people primarily seek and use information for their individual needs and interests at hand, in this context, the meeting of the needs of other people tends to remain secondary.

In communication studies, James W. Carey has evinced a useful distinction that helps to understand the nature of information sharing practices in everyday contexts.[33] He differentiates between the transmission and the ritual perspectives to communication; the former implies the sender-message-channel-receiver approach. From the perspective of the transmission model, the issues of information sharing remain secondary, because the model implies a one-way process in which information (as a representation of real world objects, events, and processes) is transported from the sender to the recipient. By contrast, the ritual perspective is characterized by expressions such as "sharing," "participation," "association," "fellowship," "communion," "community," and "the possession of a common faith."

Carey argues that the ritual view is directed not toward the extension of messages in space (as suggested by the transmission perspective) but toward the maintenance of society in time.[34] Thus, the focus is not on the act of imparting information but the representation of shared beliefs in the contexts of "community," for example, a local association of like-minded people. From the perspective of the ritual approach, reality is not given, but rather it is brought into existence, produced by communication, more specifically, by the construction, apprehension, and utilization of symbolic forms. This suggests that the idea of information sharing becomes more comprehensible in the context of the ritual or "communion" perspective than the framework provided by the transmission model.

The viewpoint of communion provides a starting point to thematize the practice of information sharing. The concepts of social capital[35] and strong versus weak ties[36] will also be used to make the phenomena of information sharing understandable. In chapter 7, the motives for information sharing are explored in order to identify the drivers of this practice. Another intriguing question concerns the degree to which information sharing may be based on the principle of "gift economy." Given that reflexive modernization increases individualization and thus the tendencies to emphasize the role of cost-benefit calculations, can cause problems with the idea of information sharing practices primarily based on a gift economy. However, as chapter 7 suggests, altruism is still a significant driver of information sharing, even though this motive may be primarily used to help people who are personally known.

In chapter 8, the major findings are discussed. The potential of this approach to everyday information practices is assessed, likewise the need to elaborate on it. Apparently, the major strength of the approach lies in the ways in which information seeking, use, and sharing are seen as deeply contextualized life world practices. They are constitutive of the maintenance and refinement of one's stock of knowledge that serves in furthering everyday projects of various kinds. The approach suggested in this book may be elaborated upon by scrutinizing conceptual and empirical questions concerning the relationships between factors that constitute life world, everyday projects, and information practices. Meeting these challenges would likely open a new path in the studies on information seeking, use, and sharing.

NOTES

1. David Chaney, *Cultural Change and Everyday Life* (Houndmills, Basingstoke, Hampshire, UK: Palgrave, 2002); Tony Bennett, "The Invention of the Modern Cultural Fact: Towards a Critique of the Critique of Everyday Life," in *Contemporary Culture and Everyday Life*, ed. Elizabeth B. Silva and Tony Bennett (Durham, UK: Sociologypress, 2004), 21–36; Rita Felski, "The Invention of Everyday Life," *New Formations* 39 (1999), 15–31; Michael E. Gardiner, *Critiques of Everyday Life* (London: Routledge, 2000).

2. Roger Silverstone, *Television and Everyday Life* (London: Routledge, 1994), 159–170. [Everyday life is a concept with a fairly long history in philosophy and social sciences. The prominent researchers of everyday life include, among others, Pierre Bourdieu, Michel de Certeau, Martin Heidegger, Jürgen Habermas, Agneta Heller, Henri Lefebvre, Georg Lukacs, and Alfred Schutz. Since this book centers on everyday information practices, not everyday life per se, it will not be discussed in greater detail from the general point of view. However, the issues of everyday life will be looked at in chapter 3, where life world projects are characterized as contexts of everyday information practices drawing on the social phenomenological ideas developed by Alfred Schutz.]

3. Ulrich Beck, Anthony Giddens, and Scott Lash, *Reflexive Modernization: Politics, Tradition and Aesthetics in the Modern Social Order* (Cambridge, UK: Cambridge University Press, 1994).

4. Chaney, *Cultural Change*, 24.

5. David Morgan, "Everyday Life and Family Practices," in *Contemporary Culture and Everyday Life*, ed. Elizabeth B. Silva and Tony Bennett (Durham, UK: Sociologypress, 2004), 37–38.

6. Michel de Certeau, *The Practice of Everyday Life* (Berkeley: University of California Press, 1984), xi.

7. Alfred Schutz, *Collected Papers 2: Studies in Social Theory*, ed. Arvid Brodersen (The Hague: Martinus Nijhoff, 1964); Alfred Schutz and Thomas Luckmann, *The Structures of the Life-World (Vol. 1)* (Evanston, Ill.: Northwestern University Press, 1973).

8. Theodore R. Schatzki, "Practice Mind-ed Orders," in *The Practice Turn in Contemporary Theory*, ed. Theodore R. Schatzki, Karin Knorr Cetina, and Eike von Savigny (London: Routledge, 2001), 42–55.

9. Bo Reimer, *The Most Common of Practices: On Mass Media Use in Late Modernity* (Stockholm: Almqvist & Wiksell International, 1994), 9.

10. Paul Solomon, "Discovering Information Behavior in Sense Making, Part 2: The Social," *Journal of the American Society for Information Science* 48, no. 12 (1997), 1125.

11. Tom D. Wilson, "Human Information Behaviour," *Informing Science* 3, no. 2 (2000), 49. http://www.inform.nu/Articles/Vol3/v3n2p49-56.pdf (10 May 2007).

12. Michael Olsson, "Beyond 'Needy' Individuals: Conceptualizing Information Behavior," in Proceedings of the Annual Meeting of the American Society for Infor-

mation Science and Technology, Charlotte, N.C., October 28–November 2, 2005 (CD-ROM). File:///Volumes/ASIST/papers/61/61_paper.html (10 May 2007).

13. Nicholas Belkin, N. R. Oddy, and H. M. Brooks, "ASK for Information Retrieval, Part 1: Background and Theory," *Journal of Documentation* 38, no. 2 (1982).

14. Sanna Talja, "The Domain Analytic Approach to Scholar's Information Practices," in *Theories of Information Behavior*, ed. Karen E. Fisher, Sanda Erdelez, and Lynne McKechnie (Medford, N.J.: Information Today, Inc., 2005), 123.

15. Kimmo Tuominen, Sanna Talja, and Reijo Savolainen, "The Social Constructionist Viewpoint to Information Practices," in *Theories of Information Behavior*, ed. Karen E. Fisher, Sanda Erdelez, and Lynne McKechnie (Medford, N.J.: Information Today, Inc., 2005), 328.

16. Christina Courtright, "Context in Information Behavior Research," in *Annual Review of Information Science and Technology*. Vol. 41, ed. Blaise Cronin (Medford, N.J.: Information Today, Inc., 2007), 289.

17. Martin Endress, "Introduction: Alfred Schutz and Contemporary Social Theory and Social Research," in *Explorations of the Life-World: Continuing Dialogues with Alfred Schutz*, ed. Martin Endress, George Psathas, and Hisashi Nasu (Dordrecht, The Netherlands: Springer, 2005), 2–4. [The research approach has also been labeled "phenomenological sociology" and "phenomenologically-based sociology." These concepts may be understood as more or less synonymous to social phenomenology. However, to emphasize the centrality of the conceptual and methodological issues of the study on how people perceive their daily life worlds and information environments, the present study prefers the concept of social phenomenology.]

18. Tom D. Wilson, "On User Studies and Information Needs," *Journal of Documentation* 37, no. 1 (1981); Tom D. Wilson, "Alfred Schutz, Phenomenology and Research Methodology for Information Behaviour Research," *The New Review of Information Behaviour Research* 3 (2002); Kwong Bor Ng, "Towards a Theoretical Framework for Understanding the Relationship between Situated Action and Planned Action Models of Behavior in Information Retrieval Contexts: Contributions from Phenomenology," *Information Processing and Management* 38, no. 5 (2002); John M. Budd, "Phenomenology and Information Studies," *Journal of Documentation* 61, no. 1 (2005). [So far, the ideas of social phenomenology have rarely been discussed in information studies. Tom D. Wilson is one of the earliest proponents of phenomenological ideas. Wilson's model of information-seeking behavior makes use of the construct of a "user's life world" as the totality of experiences centered upon the individual as an information user. Later, Wilson characterized the methodological principles of phenomenological sociology and developed a novel typology of methods with particular reference to information behavior research. Kwong Bor Ng has used the ideas of phenomenology, for example, a person's stock of knowledge to characterize the relationship between situated action and planned action models of behavior in information retrieval contexts. In most cases, the phenomenological studies have primarily focused on philosophical and methodological issues. For example, John M. Budd discussed the potential of the literature of phenomenology and showed that the close examination of central concepts such as perception, intentionality, and

interpretation is integral to individual activities related to searching for information and determining relevance.]

19. Michael Bull, *Sounding Out the City: Personal Stereos and the Management of Everyday Life* (Oxford, UK: Berg, 2000), 10.

20. Chaney, *Cultural Change*, 35.

21. Edward Warner, Ann D. Murray, and Vernon E. Palmour, *Information Needs of Urban Citizens: Final Report* (Washington, D.C.: U.S. Department of Health, Education and Welfare, Office of Education, Bureau of Libraries and Learning Resources, 1973); Brenda Dervin et al., *The Development of Strategies for Dealing with the Information Needs of Urban Residents, Vol. 1: Citizen Study* (Washington, D.C.: U.S. Department of Health, Education, and Welfare. Office of Libraries and Learning Resources, 1976); Ching-chih Chen and Peter Hernon, *Information Seeking: Assessing and Anticipating User Needs* (New York: Neal-Schuman, 1982).

22. Joan C. Durrance, *Armed for Action: Library Response to Citizen Information Needs* (New York: Neal-Schuman, 1984).

23. Elfreda A. Chatman, *The Information World of Retired Women* (Westport, Conn.: Greenwood Press, 1992).

24. Elfreda A. Chatman, "The Impoverished Life-World of Outsiders," *Journal of the American Society for Information Science* 47, no. 3 (1996).

25. Karen E. Pettigrew, Raya Fidel, and Harry Bruce, "Conceptual Frameworks in Information Behavior," in *Annual Review of Information Science and Technology.* Vol. 36, ed. Martha E. Williams (Medford, N.J.: Information Today, Inc., 2001); Reijo Savolainen, "Information Use as Gap-Bridging: The Viewpoint of Sense-Making Methodology," *Journal of the American Society for Information Science and Technology* 57, no. 8 (2006).

26. Ross J. Todd, "Utilization of Heroin Information by Adolescent Girls in Australia: A Cognitive Analysis," *Journal of the American Society for Information Science* 50, no. 1 (1999).

27. Charles T. Meadow and Weijing Yuan, "Measuring the Impact of Information: Defining the Concepts," *Information Processing and Management* 33, no. 6 (1997).

28. Brenda Dervin, *"An Overview of Sense-Making Research: Concepts, Methods and Results to Date"* (paper presented at the annual meeting of the International Communication Association, Dallas, Tex., May 1983); Brenda Dervin, "On Studying Information Seeking Methodologically: The Implications of Connecting Metatheory to Method," *Information Processing and Management* 35, no. 6 (1999); Brenda Dervin and Micheline Frenette, "Sense-Making Methodology: Communicating Communicatively with Campaign Audiences," in *Sense-Making Methodology Reader: Selected Writings of Brenda Dervin*, ed. Brenda Dervin and Lois Foreman-Wernet (Cresskill, N.J.: Hampton Press, 2003).

29. Dervin, *An Overview*, 17.

30. Dervin, "On Studying," 740.

31. Dervin and Frenette, "Sense-Making Methodology," 239.

32. Todd, "Utilization of Heroin Information."

33. James W. Carey, *Communication as Culture: Essays on Media and Society* (Boston: Unwin Hyman, 1989).

34. Carey, *Communication as Culture*.

35. Robert D. Putnam, *Bowling Alone: The Collapse and Revival of American Community* (New York: Simon & Schuster, 2000).

36. Mark Granovetter, "The Strength of Weak Ties," *American Journal of Sociology* 78, no. 6 (1973).

Chapter Two

Practice and Information Practice

Approaching the Major Concepts

Since everyday information practice is a novel concept, it is appropriate to elaborate its characteristics in more detail. Clarification is needed since the issues related to everyday practices can be ambiguous and researchers often talk about them in an unthinking way. Therefore, multiple meanings of the concept of practice and the related concepts such as action and behavior will be discussed first. Then an attempt will be made to outline a model of practice in the context of life world. This model serves as a starting point for the development of the model of everyday information practices discussed in chapter 3.

WHAT IS PRACTICE?

As in everyday life, practice is a paradoxical phenomenon: although people continually accomplish diverse practices in mundane contexts, the definition of practice has appeared to be a surprisingly difficult task in scientific research. Similar difficulties have been encountered with the definition of generic concepts such as culture, society, and time; ultimately, all of them seem to be opaque. The problems of defining everyday practices may be illustrated by looking at a mundane example such as driving a car.[1] A car and its driver are distinct entities in our perception and in much of our experience. While driving, however, the car becomes an instrument that has been absorbed into the practice of driving, just as the driver has been absorbed into the practice of driving. When driving, the driver is oriented to the street, the traffic, the direction, not to the car, unless it malfunctions and temporarily breaks down. Nor does the driver think herself or himself as separate from the immediate activity.

An additional challenge posed to the studies of practice is that practice manifests itself in a myriad of ways. Indeed, practices have many faces, and those seeking an unambiguous definition of practice are likely to be disappointed. For example, books with attractive titles such as *The Logic of Practice*,[2] *Understanding Practice: Perspectives on Activity and Context*,[3] and *The Practice of Everyday Life*[4] provide no easy solutions in this respect. The complexity of the phenomena of practice is exemplified by Ann Swidler.[5] She points out that practices can be the routines of individual actors—routines they know so well as to be able to improvise spontaneously without a second thought. Practices can also be transpersonal, embedded in routines that organizations use to process things. There is also the question of the relative significance (or triviality) of specific practices. Performing demanding work tasks such as brain surgery may be perceived to be a more interesting practice from the viewpoint of research, than say, highly mundane, though necessary and sometimes boring practices, such as tidying up the house.

The elusive nature of the phenomena of practices may lead to such questions as whether practices are researchable at all or if they are really worth closer examination. For example, Stephen Turner argues that practices seem to be "a vanishing point" in philosophy and in the domain of social theory, despite the fact that the use of the term "practice" is widespread.[6] This assumption is, however, too pessimistic. In recent years, issues of practice have attracted increasing attention in anthropology, sociology, philosophy, and science studies. For example, Theodore Schatzki believes that the development of "practice theory" would provide opportunities to defy the traditional duality formed by the two master concepts of social theory, that is, individuality and totality.[7] The former concept explains social phenomena departing from the actions and motives of individuals, while the latter draws on holistic ideas suggesting that the social is or is made up of wholes governed by specifiable principles.

The practice theory attempts to overcome this duality by suggesting that it is in practices that meaning is established in human life, and that social life may be best understood as a nexus of practice. Similarly, Carsten Østerlund and Paul Carlile believe that practice theories provide a novel approach to overcome the dichotomies between person and world, and subjectivism and objectivism; problems originating from these splits have long haunted the social sciences.[8] This belief is based on the assumption that in mundane practices, the subject and the world combine and interact repeatedly. A focus on social practices emphasizes the relational interdependencies between subject and object, person and world, individual and community.

Interestingly, the growing preoccupation with the issues of practice is epitomized in a recent book entitled *The Practice Turn in Contemporary Theory*.[9]

The interest in these phenomena is not totally new; a number of outstanding scholars, for example, Wittgenstein, Heidegger, Foucault, Giddens, and Bourdieu may be called "practice theorists," since they have reflected on central issues such as the philosophical and social scientific significance of human activity, the nature of subjectivity, rationality and meaning, and the organization, reproduction, and transformation of social life.[10] *The Practice Turn in Contemporary Theory* addresses such issues and provides a multifaceted picture of the potential of "practice theories." On the other hand, the writers pay attention to the difficulties inherent in these efforts. For example, Michael Lynch points out that the ethnomethodologists have identified problems that may be encountered when trying to capture the general "logic of practice."[11] Such attempts may lead to a theoretical delusion, since practices are produced locally; they are endogenous, naturally organized, and ongoing.

To exemplify the problems faced in the development of "general" theories of practice, we may briefly review the major ideas evinced by Pierre Bourdieu and Anthony Giddens (for a detailed comparison of their approaches, see Schatzki).[12] Both authors have made heroic attempts to identify the fundamental qualities of the complex phenomena called practice. Indisputably, they have identified questions that cannot be ignored in any practice theory.

Bourdieu tried to render the phenomena of practice comprehensible by an appeal to the embodied acquisition of preferences, perceptual schemes, and dispositions to react.[13] The central principle determining the production and reproduction of practice is *habitus*. It stands for a socially and culturally determined system of thinking, perception, and evaluation, internalized by the individual. Habitus is a relatively stable system of dispositions by which individuals integrate their experiences and evaluate the importance of different choices. More specifically, habitus refers to "systems of durable, transposable dispositions, structured structures predisposed to function as structuring structures, that is, as principles which generate and organize practices."[14] Therefore, on the one hand, habitus functions as a generative principle of objectively classifiable judgments (habitus as a "structuring structure" which organizes different dispositions). Habitus is a system of classification of these practices (habitus as a "structured structure" which divides things into different groups according to their value).

In this dual role, habitus manifests the incorporation of norms and social expectations within an individual; thus, habitus is more than an aggregation of "purely" personal dispositions. Importantly, the incorporation of the social is central to the formation of habitus; this occurs through processes of conditioning and social learning, forming the basis of that presence in the social world which is the assumption of successful social action.[15] As a socially and culturally intermediated system of classification, habitus renders a general direction to choices made in everyday life by indicating which choices are natural or desirable in relation to one's social class or cultural group. As a relatively stable system of dispositions, habitus "ensures the active presence of past experiences, which, deposited in each organism in the form of schemes of perception, thought, and action, tend to guarantee the correctness of practices and their constant over time."[16] This inertness preserves the constancy of practices, which the habitus seeks to ensure by fending off changes via its selections when given new information, for example, by rejecting information that could question the accumulated knowledge whenever it happens to come across it or cannot avoid it.[17]

As Schatzki points out, Bourdieu's governing intuition is that practices are self-perpetuating.[18] Practices are interwoven activities carried out in a specific domain or field. Although the concept of habitus has been highly influential in sociology, it has attracted criticism for the "rigidity" of habitus and the objectivist approach to practice implied by this concept.[19] According to critical views, habitus appears as a collective and stable force guiding one's behavior without the attention to the requirements of specific situations where human activities take place. Michel de Certeau also claims that as a single principle habitus tries to "explain everything," providing a total and dogmatic explanation of the ways in which everyday practices are produced and reproduced.[20]

Like Bourdieu, Giddens[21] characterizes practice in a broad manner in the context of structuration theory.[22] According to Giddens, practice incorporates the nature, conditions, and consequences of historically and spatiotemporally situated activities and interactions produced through the agency of social actors. In general, agency denotes the capacity for historically situated reflexive and purposive action. In this sense, practice refers to a continuous flow of social action that has both intended and unintended consequences: "out of social praxis is routinely constituted a social world."[23] In other words, agency refers to our capacity to act within the ongoing normality of everyday life.[24]

Giddens conceives of practice as a nexus of actions.[25] Practices form constellations called systems, whose structures encompass relations among the structures of practices. The structure that simultaneously organizes practices and governs actions is composed of sets of rules and resources. Rules (e.g., codes, norms) are generalized procedures of action implicated in the practical activities of daily life.[26] Resources, in turn, are the medium through which social power is exercised, where social power is the capacity to bring about changes when doing so depends on the actions of others.[27] In other words, rules and resources govern practices by establishing fields of possibility for constituent actions. Rules and resources also govern action as grasped in the practical consciousness that orients activity.[28] However, although rules and resources are constant determinants of action, they are not the sole factors orienting it. What people do can also depend on reasons and wants.[29] Reasons refer to the ground on which people tacitly and continuously understand their activity rests, while wants denote deep-seated motivations rooted in the unconscious. Many social practices are routine and repetitive in nature and are considered to be at the root of the constitution of both subject and object.

Compared to Bourdieu's habitus theory, Giddens's conception seems to provide a more flexible approach to practice. However, Giddens's conception has been criticized for the ambiguous assumptions by which rules are seen as "procedures of action."[30] Understanding rules as procedures of action are characterized by Giddens as practical consciousness. On the other hand, Giddens claims that what is characteristic of practical consciousness is its unformulability.[31] This assumption seems to render hollow and obscure Giddens's conception of practice because in this way, determinant content is denied these phenomena and their investigation is rendered inherently inadequate.

These approaches were reviewed in order to exemplify the discussion of major concepts constitutive of practice theories, therefore, we do not compare Bourdieu's and Giddens's views in more detail. This book does not primarily draw on their ideas on the approach to practice. However, the previous criticisms of Bourdieu and Giddens exemplify the fact that there is no consensus among researchers about the ways in which the issues of practice should be defined. Instead of a unifying practice theory, we have a number of competing approaches to practice. Given the generic nature of this concept, it is probable that a unifying practice theory will remain unattainable, likewise attempts to provide conclusive definitions of culture, power, and other generic concepts of sociology and social philosophy.

ACTION, ACTIVITY, BEHAVIOR, HABIT, OR PRACTICE?

As the previous discussion suggests, the concept of practice seems to defy any attempts at an exact definition. The problem is complicated by the fact that there are a number of closely related concepts such as action, activity, behavior, and habit referring to similar phenomena. As discussed in chapter 3, similar problems emerge in information studies since the researchers have to struggle with ambiguous concepts such as information action, information activity, and information behavior. To clarify the terminological issues, we briefly characterize the major qualities of the concepts of action, activity, behavior, and habit in relation to the concept of practice.

Action

The nature of (human) action is among the perennial issues of philosophy, psychology, and sociology. Hence, it is no wonder that there are a number of models and theories seeking to conceptualize this enormous topic at different levels of generality. In the widest sense, action may be defined as "the process or condition of acting or doing, the exertion of energy or influence; working, agency, operation."[32] George Wilson emphasizes that a characteristic of action is that something that an agent does is "intentional under some description."[33] Importantly, the concept of action thus defined opposes a mechanistic portrait of the human being because action denotes something that is meaningful from the perspective of the actor.[34] Many sociologists and social philosophers have devoted attention to the close connection between action and knowing. For example, Scott D. N. Cook and John Seely Brown suggest that information or knowledge and action are intricately intertwined: knowledge is used in action and "knowing is the epistemological dimension of action."[35] As Wilson notes, it is also important to the concept of "goal directed action" that agents normally implement a kind of direct control or guidance over their own behavior.[36]

The relationship between action and practice is open to multiple interpretations, and there is no consensus about this issue among researchers. However, Schatzki points out that many practice theorists, for example, Bourdieu and Giddens posit practices ontologically more fundamental than actions.[37] Thus, action is not rendered meaningful in itself but only in the context of practice. For example, Giddens conceives of practice as a nexus of actions.[38] By contrast, individualist theories accord priority to action. They tend to tie the identity of particular actions to properties of individuals who perform them; in addition, these theories devote the main attention to goals, intentions, and other mental states of the individual actors.

Activity

In general, "activity" may denote, among others, "the state of being active; the exertion of energy, action, and anything active; an active force or operation."[39] Again, drawing on dictionary definitions alone, one may encounter difficulties in trying to identify the specific meanings of this concept, as related to "act" and "action." In general, activity denotes the dynamic aspect of "doing things," and in this sense, it may be taken to be synonymous with act and action. Thus, at least at the level of dictionary definitions, act, activity, and action do not differ much from each other as they all refer to the processes of "doing things" in the broadest sense of the word.

While action is a concept primarily analyzed in philosophy, the phenomena of activity have mainly been analyzed in psychology. In this field, a specific "activity theory," or "cultural-historical activity theory" has been developed to characterize its specific features. Originally, this theory was developed as an alternative to behaviorism and psychoanalysis, and it drew on Marxian ideas.[40] Alexei Leontev defines activity as those processes "that realise a person's actual life in the objective world by which he is surrounded, his social being in all the richness and variety of its forms."[41] According to Leontev, activity is at the uppermost level in the conceptual hierarchy of activity, action, and operation.[42] Importantly, activity is collective in nature, and it is driven by object-related motives; there is no such thing as activity without a motive. In the middle level, there is action that is characteristic of individuals or groups. Actions are governed by their goals. Finally, at the bottom level, there are automatic operations that are governed by the conditions of the activity.

In Leontev's model, the basic components of separate human activities are the actions that realize activities while operations realize actions. However, human activity is not seen as an additive process in that actions would be separate things that are included in activity.[43] On the contrary, human activity is seen to exist as actions or chains of actions thus, actions are not special "units" that are included in the structure of activity.[44] If the actions that constitute activity are mentally subtracted from it, then absolutely nothing will be left of the activity. Finally, the action also has its operational aspect (how or by what means this can be achieved), which is determined not by the goal itself but by the objective-object conditions of its achievement.[45]

Depending on the definition of activity, its relation to practice can be understood differently. Practices may be seen as interwoven activities in a given social domain, for example, agriculture or politics.[46] On the other hand, the activity theory developed by Leontev[47] conceptualizes action as a component of activity, suggesting that human activity exists as actions or chains of actions. However, Leontev leaves open the question of how activity thus defined is related to practice. Researchers drawing on the ideas of social phenomenology maintain that action is not a component of activity as previously discussed. In their view, action is rendered meaningful in the context of an act or a project.[48] We return to this interpretation later on.

Behavior

Like action and activity, the generic concept of *behavior* is difficult to characterize in detail. Generally defined, the concept of (human) behavior refers to the "the potential and expressed capacity for physical, mental, and social activity during the phases of human life."[49] Overall, behavior denotes the complex and interrelated issues of motivation, emotion, perception, and personality. Complex phenomena such as attitudes, memory, and learning are also central to the study of behavior.

One of the problems encountered in the use of the concept of "behavior" is that it often reminds one of behaviorism, the mechanistic psychological paradigm. It emphasizes the importance of observing the person's outer performance.[50] This observation is utilized as the basis for drawing conclusions on his or her inner reality. Moreover, "behavior" is a passive term, as if an individuals functioning comprised solely of reacting to stimuli.[51] In addition, "behavior" does not convey any sense of intention, advancement, or process. According to George Graham, it has sometimes been said that "behave is what organisms do."[52] Behaviorism is built on this assumption, and it contends that psychology is the science of behavior, not the science of the mind. Secondly, this viewpoint suggests that behavior can be described and explained without making reference to mental events or to internal psychological processes. The sources of behavior are external (in the environment), not internal (in the mind). B. F. Skinner, the major exponent of "radical behaviorism," has advocated assumptions such as these.

However, the critics of radical behaviorism have claimed that we can never escape from using mental terms in the characterization of the meaning of mental terms.[53] Importantly, this suggests that mental discourse cannot be replaced by behavioral discourse. Currently, many philosophers and psychologists find the behaviorist approach hopelessly restrictive. Nevertheless, it is believed that the explanation of behavior cannot omit invoking an individuals representation of his or her world, and that psychological theorizing without reference to internal processing is impaired. Thus, behaviorism, not cognitive science or psychology offers a misleading account of what is "inside the head."[54]

To elucidate these issues, we must differentiate between "narrow and broad behavior."[55] Narrow behavior refers to "mere bodily motion, in abstraction from its causes and effects." Broad behavior is richer in that it incorporates phenomena characteristic of action in the sense of bodily movements caused by mental states or events.[56] This definition is illuminating, although it uncovers an additional difficulty, that is, drawing a clear distinction between behavior and action. In psychology, researchers use these concepts by giving them various meanings. For example, the theory of reasoned action developed by Martin Fishbein and Icek Ajzen applies "to behaviors under volitional control."[57] This suggests that intention is the immediate determinant of behavior.[58] Later, this theory was modified to include "perceived behavioral control" as an additional predictor of intention and action. Interestingly, reflecting this modification, this approach was renamed the "theory of planned behavior."[59]

Compared to action and activity as discussed previously, the relationships between behavior and practice seem even more ambiguous. Practice theorists have not considered this issue in more detail since they are more interested in the ways in which practices are composed of actions or activities. This may be due to the fact that the major concepts of behavior and practice imply opposite metatheoretical perspectives. The former stands for an individualist (psychologist) viewpoint while the latter draws on a more sociologically and contextually oriented perspective. In chapter 3, the concepts of information practice and information behavior will be characterized.

Habit

The concept of habit is often closely associated with that of practice. Again, there are different views on how to define the nature of *habits* and its relation to practice. As discussed previously, the issues of habits are relevant to Bourdieu's theory of practice, although he prefers the term habitus. The near kinship of habit and habitus is evident, since in general, habits are defined, more or less, as a self-actuating disposition or tendency to engage in a previously adopted or acquired form of action. Thus, it is central to the general definition of habit that it is produced by repetition and that forms of action that are frequently practiced over time become habitual.[60] A still broader usage of the term refers to the durable and generalized disposition that suffuses a persons action throughout his life. In this case, the term comes to mean a whole manner, turn, cast, or mold of the personality.[61] On the other hand, calling something "habitual" may imply a less positive evaluation than calling it "practical." This is due to the fact that practices tend to be associated with socially credited skills, whereas habits may also be perceived as marks of a defective character, for example, in the sense of "ossified habits" or outdated customs.[62]

Often, habits (or habitual action) are perceived to be constitutive of practices. On the other hand, they seem to refer to slightly different things, and thus, they are not totally synonymous. For example, Turner argues that there is neither foundation nor evidence for the belief in the existence of shared practice as a unitary object and no theory of cultural transmission and dissemination which allows us to understand how such an object could pass from person to person unchanged.[63] What we refer to as shared practice, is actually a composite, argues Turner. It is constituted of many separate individual habits—habits sufficiently alike for us to get along, but individual entities nonetheless, and not collective ones. Thus, practices without genuine sharing are simply habits—individual rather than shared.[64] According to Turner, habits are the part of the phenomenon described by the term "practices" that remains when the idea of people possessing the same shared thing is eliminated. We develop habits by performing activities at public occasions, for example, religious rituals or answering questions in first year law classes at university.[65] Thus, ultimately, public performances cause the habits (or habitual parts of practice).

Turner's view has been criticized for its individualistic overtones.[66] Barry Barnes disagrees with Turner's approach since it suggests that shared practice is actually nothing more than habituated individual behavior.[67] Barnes claims that practice at the collective level is not a simple summation of practices at the individual level (habits) because shared practice is a collective accomplishment.

COMPARATIVE NOTIONS OF THE MAJOR CONCEPTS

To summarize the previous discussion, we see that the concepts of action and activity can denote at the most abstract level, ways of "doing things," and often, these concepts are used synonymously. On the other hand, these concepts may also be given specific (non-synonymous) meanings, as exemplified by the activity theory. In comparison, the concepts of behavior and habit are more concrete than action and activity. This is because behavior can be defined by referring to various kinds of composite activities, while habits can be conceived of as repeated forms of action.

Action, activity, behavior, and habit can be understood differently in relation to practice. Ultimately, these definitional problems apparently arise because "practice" (or "practices") is one of the core words used when naming the primary generic "social thing."[68] In this sense, "practice" may be compared to terms such as "structure" and "meaning." Given the multiplicity of viewpoints on practice and related concepts, it is no wonder that there is neither a unified practice approach nor consensus about the ways in which concepts such as action, activity, behavior, and habit should be interpreted in relation to practice. Despite this diversity, it seems that most practice theorists understand practices as embodied, materially mediated arrays of human action (or activities), centrally organized around shared understanding.[69] The acceptance of such starting points means that the concept of practice is perceived as something that contrasts with the accounts of privileged individuals and their needs, as distinct from social contexts. This suggests that practice theorists take a critical view of the concept of behavior, particularly if it is looked at in a behaviorist fashion. Thus, it is central to practice theories that human actions or activities and habits, not "behaviors" are the main constituents of practices.

EVERYDAY PRACTICES IN THE CONTEXT OF LIFE WORLD

Given the myriad interpretations of the concept of practice, as well as, of related concepts of action, activity, and habit, no attempt will be made here to review them in great detail. This book is focusing mainly on information practices, not practice in general. In order to provide background for the elaboration of the concept of information practice to be discussed in chapter 3, an approach will be outlined by drawing on two conceptual frameworks that best serve the purposes of the present study. First, Schatzki—primarily inspired by the ideas of Wittgenstein—provides a relevant (general level) approach to practice.[70] Second, the social phenomenological approach[71] proposed by Alfred Schutz elucidates practices from the viewpoint of life world and the use of everyday knowledge. The ideas of social phenomenology are also useful because they serve as a bridge between the general level characterizations of practice discussed later and the elaboration of everyday information practices discussed in chapter 3.

The starting point adopted here is that practices are understood to be an organized composite of actions.[72] For example, "farming practices" may comprise actions such as building fences, harvesting grain, herding sheep, judging weather, and paying for supplies. According to Schatzki, the actions that compose a practice are either bodily doings or sayings, or the actions that these doings or sayings constitute. By "bodily doings and sayings" Schatzki means "basic actions" that people directly perform bodily and not by doing something else like, running, speaking words and writing them down exemplify basic actions of these kinds. In turn, the actions that these bodily doings and sayings constitute are exemplified by hurrying home, ordering someone to stand, and composing a poem.[73] To say that doings and sayings constitute actions means that the performance of doings and sayings amounts, in the circumstances involved, to the carrying out of actions. These actions and henceforth, practices are not merely individual accomplishments. The actions and practices are social, since they usually originate from interactions with other people and experiences of situated learning.

The ways in which practice is composed of actions may be further specified by drawing on the ideas developed within the tradition of social phenomenology. These ideas are particularly useful because they help to understand how actions, and thus practices, become meaningful in everyday contexts. In particular, Schutz has clarified the relationship between a person's goals and the specific steps (or actions) essential in achieving them.[74] One of Schutz's key assumptions is that a person is not motivated to do something unless it is meaningful for him or her.[75] According to Schutz, the goal provides the context within which each action is regarded as sensible.[76]

Further, action is tied to an awareness of how it fulfills some future project that is aspired to. In other words, action obtains its meaning from its goal, more specifically, the goal of the project pursued. This means that specific practices composed by actions (that are in turn constituted by doings and sayings) become meaningful in the horizon of everyday projects and their constituent acts. As we shall see later, the goals of these projects may also be referred to as "teleoaffective structures."

Everyday actions are not only directed by the specific goals of various projects; the actors knowledge base or stock of knowledge is important as well. To better understand the nature of this stock of knowledge, we may first characterize life world, that is, the major context in which everyday knowledge is used. Alfred Schutz and Thomas Luckmann broadly described life world as "that province of reality which the wide-awake and normal adult simply takes for granted in the attitude of common sense."[77] The everyday-life world also stands for "the province of reality in which man continuously participates in ways which are at once inevitable and patterned" and "the province of practice, of action." More specifically, life world refers to social reality that may be understood as

> the sum total of objects and occurrences within the social cultural world as ex-perienced by the commonsense thinking of men living their daily lives among their fellow-men, connected with them to manifold relations of interaction. It is the world of cultural objects and social institutions into which we are all born, within which we have to find our bearings, and with which we have to come to terms.[78]

In short, as a major context of everyday practices, life world is not a private world, but from the outset it is fundamentally intersubjective and thus a shared world.[79]

When people engage in action, they usually approach their life world by adopting a "natural attitude." In other words, this world is taken for granted, with people assuming they can go on as they always have and that they "can do it again."[80] Thus, habits and routines are assessed positively, they are not necessarily seen as "despotic mechanisms" or straitjackets that primarily con-strain everyday action.[81]

Natural attitude does not only represent a general approach by which peo-ple conceive of life world. This attitude also affects the way in which one's stock of knowledge is developed and used. In general, stock of knowledge stands for a cultural experience suggesting that one situation is different from another, that changes have occurred, or more commonly, that one situation is like another.[82] Therefore, this knowledge consists of a system of relevant typifications of typical solutions for typical practical and theoretical problems and of typical precepts of typical actions.[83]

Only a small fraction of the stock of knowledge at hand originates from the individual's own experience; most is socially derived and has been handed down to him or her by parents, teachers, and other significant persons as social heritage.[84] The sharing of stock of knowledge is therefore essential for day-to-day action. Everyday knowledge provides recipes for a variety of actions. Recipe knowledge is the product of sharing experience in particular times and places; it leads to common frameworks for seeing the world. Schutz and Luckmann propose that the explications based in one's stock of knowledge have the status of actionable directions: if things are thus and so, then an individual will act thus and so, and their continuous practical success guarantees their reliability for the actor, and they become habitual recipes.[85] As Kwong Bor Ng points out, such a focus may help us to understand the stability of structure of action, especially, the structure of habitual action.[86]

As noted previously, action (that draws on one's stock of knowledge) is also oriented by human *projects*.[87] *Acts* are experiences that derive their meaning from their relations to a human project. Acts are flows of experience that obtain their driving motive from the attainment of a goal projected in advance by the one who acts.[88] Primarily, action is a performance of consciousness because the final authority is the individual agent, however, this does not mean that one's consciousness is not socially constructed.[89] Most importantly, action is an experience planned in advance; the person who acts knows that he or she is doing so. Action refers to the step-by-step performance of an act, while the finished chain of the action history stands for the completed act.[90] Actions (and therefore acts) are preceded by a project, for example, climbing a mountain or earning a master's degree in a university. In this sense, the projects are conditioned by the biography of the actor, but they may also be triggered by specific lived experiences, such as by hobbies. In any case, the projects do not occur by themselves but are chosen in situations that are perceived as problematic in some sense.[91] On the other hand, every project stems from an interest that has a prior history formed in the context of the persons biography.

In an everyday project, the individual steps of the act related to this goal are prepared for in advance.[92] The individual projects are structured temporally, that is, they are future oriented. The projects may incorporate daily or weekly plans that can be structured hierarchically according to their importance or the urgency of each individual (competing) project. In addition, the practicability of the projects is considered. Some projects may be feasible, while others are associated with daydreaming and are not necessarily actionable. Some projects are unproblematic in that the steps leading to the goal have been taken often, becoming habits, and so there is no specific need for "project planning." However, the goal of a project may be unclear and the steps of action may be problematic for the actor. Or a project may be discontinued or postponed, due to other projects that are given priority.[93] Finally, it may also appear that the completed act does not perfectly coincide with the projected one. However, perfection is rarely necessary in the everyday-life world, and it suffices in most cases if a "good enough" performance can be made to coincide with the goal of the project.

This framework can be further specified by assuming that a practice (as a set of meaningful actions) is organized in the context of life world by two additional factors:[94] a set of social rules and something that Schatzki calls "teleoaffective structure."[95] These factors are important since it is obvious that practical intelligibility of what people are doing in everyday contexts is not merely determined by cognitive factors, that is, the structure of one's stock of knowledge. In general, social rules denote explicit formulations that enjoin or school particular actions.[96] More specifically, social rules may be understood as a generic phrase that refers to the cognitive criteria used by societal members to organize their daily affairs.[97] Rules are sometimes highly formalized and codified, as in legal and bureaucratic settings. Rules may also be relatively informal, taken-for-granted features of commonsense or recipe knowledge within a given culture, such as the appropriate rules for being a parent.[98] In the context of this book, rules of this type of "commonsense or recipe knowledge" are most relevant. They form an integral part of the actors stock of knowledge. Since they are mainly learned from others, and used by members of mundane societal groups such as family, they may be called social rules.

The third factor making practices and constitutive actions understandable is "teleoaffective structure"; it stands for a mix of teleology and affectivity.[99] Teleology is oriented toward ends, while affectivity is how things matter. What makes sense to a person largely depends on why he or she is prepared to act, on how he or she will proceed to achieve or possess these things, and how things matter to him or her. These issues are related to his or her ends, the projects and tasks he or she will carry out for the sake of those ends given his or her beliefs, hopes, and expectations, and his or her emotions and moods. Values are also important in this context. In general, values refer to something that is desirable and desired. On this basis, values may be classified, for example, as religious and secular, materialist and postmaterialist.[100] Based on one's set of values, one may turn toward some act or project rather than others. People are assumed to act on the basis of individually held, but socially grounded values.[101] On the other hand, people's values may clash with each other, at least occasionally, and people may find it difficult to reconcile, for example, pleasure with a feeling of duty, since these values may conflict in specific situations.

Schutz crystallizes the same idea by maintaining that the objects of the everyday world capture a person's attention through his or her interests: "it is our interest at hand that motivates all our thinking, projecting, acting, and therewith establishes the problems to be solved by our thought and the goals to be attained by our actions."[102] Thereby, practical intelligibility is teleologically and affectively oriented. Schatzki proposes that taking teleology and affectivity as a clue, this dimension of the organization of practice can be specified as a normative "teleoaffective structure."[103] It refers to a range of acceptable or correct ends, acceptable or correct tasks to carry out these ends, acceptable or correct beliefs, and acceptable or correct emotions that prompt action. For example, farming practices embrace a range of acceptable or correct combinations of such ends, such as preserving the land, feeding one's family, and building fences, and such beliefs that barns should be built in certain forms. The major ideas of this approach to everyday practices are illustrated in figure 2.1.

Figure 2.1 suggests that practices, understood as a set of routine or nonroutine actions (more specifically: doings and sayings) are accomplished in the context of daily life world. Practices are not valuable in themselves; they

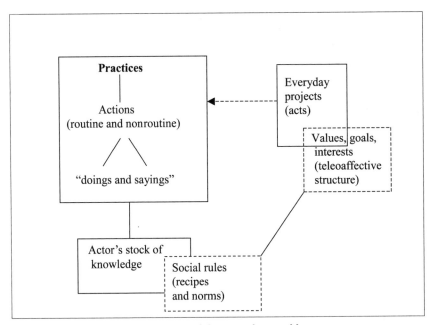

Figure 2.1.   Practices in the Context of the Everyday World.

are given meaning as tools that are used to attain the values, goals, and interests attached to everyday projects. Thus, it is characteristic of practices that they are project-oriented, more specifically, oriented by the teleoaffective structure of the projects. In general, practice and project stand for the different sides of the same coin; practice refers to "how," that is, the ways in which things are done, while project denotes "why," that is, the goals of this doing.

Practice is a generic concept; specific everyday practices in non-work contexts may include, for example, childcare, cooking, shopping, and information seeking (we discuss the features of specific practices such as information seeking in the subsequent chapters). Further, as suggested by figure 2.1, practices draw on the actors stock of knowledge. In addition, practices make use of a set of internalized social rules and norms that are incorporated in the stock of knowledge. These rules and norms are not stable; they may undergo changes, due to their reinterpretation, as the actor pursues everyday projects. On the other hand, experiences obtained from the furtherance of everyday projects may affect the ways in which practices are accomplished in the future, as illuminated by the dashed arrow in figure 2.1.

The framework illustrated in figure 2.1 suggests that even though many practices tend to change relatively slowly—due to the continuities inherent in the basic stock of knowledge and social rules, as well as values and interests—practices are not stable sets of habitual actions. Not just the doings and sayings involved, but the stock of knowledge, rules, and teleoaffectivities that organize them, can change over time in response to contingent events and different life world situations. In this respect, we may agree with Karin Knorr Cetina's assumption that practices do not necessarily need to be rigid and static, bound to deeply ingrained habits or dispositions and dependent on mechanistic adherence to rules or iterative procedural routines.[104] Practices may also be creative and constructive ways of doing things differently. Finally, practices—routine or creative—can also draw on affective factors such as the pleasurability of doing things and emotional involvement with objects of everyday action.

NOTES

1. Karin Knorr Cetina, "Objectual Practice," in *The Practice Turn in Contemporary Theory*, ed. Theodore R. Schatzki, Karin Knorr Cetina, and Eike von Savigny (London: Routledge, 2001), 178.

2. Pierre Bourdieu, *The Logic of Practice* (Cambridge, UK: Polity Press, 1984).

3. Jean Lave, "The Practice of Learning," in *Understanding Practice: Perspectives on Activity and Context*, ed. Seth Chaiklin and Jean Lave (Cambridge, UK: Cambridge University Press, 1993).

4. Michel de Certeau, *The Practice of Everyday Life* (Berkeley: University of California Press, 1984).

5. Ann Swidler, "What Anchors Cultural Practices?" in *The Practice Turn in Contemporary Theory*, ed. Theodore R. Schatzki, Karin Knorr Cetina, and Eike von Savigny (London: Routledge, 2001), 74–75.

6. Stephen Turner, *The Social Theory of Practices: Tradition, Tacit Knowledge and Presuppositions* (Cambridge, UK: Polity Press, 1994), 1–2.

7. Theodore R. Schatzki, "Practices and Actions: A Wittgensteinian Critique of Bourdieu and Giddens," *Philosophy of Social Sciences* 27, no. 3 (1997), 283–84.

8. Carsten Østerlund and Paul Carlile, "Relations of Practice: Sorting through Practice Theories in Knowledge Sharing in Complex Organizations," *The Information Society* 21, no. 2 (2005), 92.

9. Theodore R. Schatzki, Karin Knorr Cetina, and Eike von Savigny, eds., *The Practice Turn in Contemporary Theory* (London: Routledge, 2001).

10. Schatzki, "Practices and Actions"; Theodore R. Schatzki, "Introduction: Practice Theory," in *The Practice Turn in Contemporary Theory*, ed. Theodore R. Schatzki, Karin Knorr Cetina, and Eike von Savigny (London: Routledge, 2001), 1.

11. Michael Lynch, "Ethnomethodology and the Logic of Practice," in *The Practice Turn in Contemporary Theory*, ed. Theodore R. Schatzki, Karin Knorr Cetina, and Eike von Savigny (London: Routledge, 2001), 146–47; Michael Lynch, "Theorizing Practice," *Human Studies* 20, no. 2 (2001).

12. Schatzki, "Practices and Actions."

13. Pierre Bourdieu, *Distinction: A Social Critique of the Judgement of Taste* (London: Routledge, 1984), 170–175; Bourdieu, *The Logic of Practice*.

14. Bourdieu, *The Logic of Practice*, 54.

15. Wolfgang Wagner and Nicky Hayes, *Everyday Discourse and Common Sense: The Theory of Representations* (Houndmills, UK: Palgrave, 2005), 268–69.

16. Bourdieu, *The Logic of Practice*, 54.

17. Wagner and Hayes, *Everyday Discourse*, 269–70.

18. Schatzki, "Practices and Actions," 298.

19. Anthony King, "Thinking with Bourdieu against Bourdieu: A 'Practical' Critique of the Habitus," *Sociological Theory* 18, no. 3 (2000); Laurent Thévenot, "Pragmatic Regimes Governing the Engagement with the World," in *The Practice Turn in Contemporary Theory*, ed. Theodore R. Schatzki, Karin Knorr Cetina, and Eike von Savigny (London: Routledge, 2001), 58, 71.

20. de Certeau, *The Practice of Everyday Life*, 59–60, 63.

21. Anthony Giddens, *The Constitution of Society: Outline of a Theory of Structuration* (Cambridge, UK: Polity Press, 1984).

22. Schatzki, "Practices and Actions," 290–93.

23. Giddens, *The Constitution of Society*, xxii.

24. Roger Silverstone, *Television and Everyday Life* (London: Routledge, 1994), 169.

25. Giddens, *The Constitution of Society*.

26. Giddens, *The Constitution of Society*, 21.

27. Giddens, *The Constitution of Society*, 93.

28. Schatzki, "Practices and Actions," 293.

29. Giddens, *The Constitution of Society,* 5–6, 376.

30. Schatzki, "Practices and Actions," 291.

31. Giddens, *The Constitution of Society*, 19–22; Schatzki, "Practices and Actions," 300.

32. Oxford English Dictionary, "Action," http://dictionary.oed.com (10 May 2007).

33. George Wilson, "Action," in *Stanford Encyclopedia of Philosophy.* http://plato .stanford.edu/entries/action (10 May 2007).

34. Tim Dant, *Knowledge, Ideology and Discourse: A Sociological Perspective* (London: Routledge, 1991).

35. Scott D. N. Cook and John Seely Brown, "Bridging Epistemologies: The Generative Dance between Organizational Knowledge and Organizational Knowing." *Organization Science* 10, no. 4 (1999), 387.

36. Wilson, "Action."

37. Schatzki, "Practices and Actions," 285–86.

38. Giddens, *The Constitution of Society*.

39. Oxford English Dictionary, "Activity," http://dictionary.oed.com (10 May 2007).

40. Tom D. Wilson, "A Re-Examination of Information Seeking Behaviour in the Context of Activity Theory," *Information Research* 11, no. 4 (2006). http://InformationR .net/ir/11-4/paper260.html (10 May 2007).

41. Alexei N. Leontev, "Activity and Consciousness," in *Philosophy in the USSR: Problems of Dialectical Materialism* (Moscow: Progress Publishers, 1977). http:// www.marxists.org/archive/leontev/works/1977/leon1977.htm (10 May 2007).

42. Alexei N. Leontev, *Activity, Consciousness, and Personality* (Englewood Cliffs, N.J.: Prentice-Hall, 1978). http://www.marxists.org/archive/leontev/works/1978/ index.htm (10 May 2007).

43. Wilson, "A Re-Examination."

44. Leontev, *Activity, Consciousness, and Personality*.

45. Leontev, *Activity, Consciousness, and Personality*.

46. Schatzki, "Practices and Actions," 285.

47. Leontev, "Activity and Consciousness."

48. Alfred Schutz, *The Phenomenology of the Social World* (Evanston, Ill.: Northwestern University Press, 1967); David L. Altheide, "The Sociology of Alfred Schutz," in *Existential Sociology*, ed. Jack D. Douglas et al. (Cambridge, UK: Cambridge University Press, 1977).

49. Encyclopedia Britannica Online, "Human Behaviour," http://search.eb.com/ eb/article-9110429 (10 May 2007).

50. Gernot Wersig and Gunter Windel, "Information Science Needs a Theory of "Information Actions," *Social Science Information Studies* 5, no. 1 (1985).

51. Dant, *Knowledge, Ideology and Discourse*.

52. George Graham, "Behaviorism," in *Stanford Encyclopedia of Philosophy.* http://plato.stanford.edu/entries/behaviorism/ (10 May 2007).

53. Graham, "Behaviorism."

54. Graham, "Behaviorism."

55. Alfred R. Mele, *Springs of Action: Understanding Intentional Behavior* (Oxford, UK: Oxford University Press, 1992), 18.

56. Richard P. Bagozzi, Zeynep Gürhan-Canli, and Joseph H. Priester, *The Social Psychology of Consumer Behavior* (Buckingham, UK: Open University Press, 2002), 68–69.

57. Martin Fishbein and Icek Ajzen, *Belief, Attitude, Intention and Behavior: An Introduction to Theory and Research* (Reading, Mass.: Addison-Wesley, 1975).

58. Bagozzi, Gürhan-Canli, and Priester, *The Social Psychology*, 69.

59. Bagozzi, Gürhan-Canli, and Priester, *The Social Psychology*, 72.

60. Charles Camic, "The Matter of Habit," *American Journal of Sociology* 91, no. 5 (1986), 1044.

61. Camic, "The Matter of Habit," 1046.

62. Lynch, "Theorizing Practice," 337.

63. Turner, *The Social Theory of Practices*; Barry Barnes, "Practices as Collective Action," in *The Practice Turn in Contemporary Theory*, ed. Theodore R. Schatzki, Karin Knorr Cetina, and Eike von Savigny (London: Routledge, 2001), 22.

64. Stephen Turner, "Throwing Out the Tacit Rule Book: Learning and Practices," in *The Practice Turn in Contemporary Theory*, ed. Theodore R. Schatzki, Karin Knorr Cetina, and Eike von Savigny (London: Routledge, 2001), 120.

65. Stephen Turner, "Bad Practices: A Reply," *Human Studies* 20, no. 2 (1997), 353.

66. Theodore R. Schatzki, "Practice Mind-ed Orders," in *The Practice Turn in Contemporary Theory*, ed. Theodore R. Schatzki, Karin Knorr Cetina, and Eike von Savigny (London: Routledge, 2001), 49.

67. Barnes, "Practices as Collective Action," 22–23.

68. Schatzki, "Introduction: Practice Theory," 1.

69. Schatzki, "Introduction: Practice Theory," 2.

70. Schatzki, "Practices and Actions," 300–306; Schatzki, "Practice Mind-ed Orders."

71. Schutz, *The Phenomenology of the Social World*; Alfred Schutz and Thomas Luckmann, *The Structures of the Life-World (Vol. 1)* (Evanston, Ill.: Northwestern University Press, 1973).

72. Schatzki, "Practice Mind-ed Orders," 48.

73. Schatzki, "Practice Mind-ed Orders," 48.

74. Schutz, *The Phenomenology of the Social World*; Altheide, "The Sociology of Alfred Schutz," 139.

75. Schutz, *The Phenomenology of the Social World*; Altheide, "The Sociology of Alfred Schutz," 135–36.

76. Schutz, *The Phenomenology of the Social World*.

77. Schutz and Luckmann, *The Structures of the Life-World (Vol. 1)*, 3, 18; Alfred Schutz and Thomas Luckmann, *The Structures of the Life-World (Vol. 2)* (Evanston, Ill.: Northwestern University Press, 1989), 1–21.

78. Alfred Schutz, *Collected Papers 1: The Problem of Social Reality*, ed. Maurice Natanson (The Netherlands, The Hague: Martinus Nijhoff, 1962), 53; Jochen Dreher,

"The Symbol and the Theory of the Life-World: The Transcendences of the Life-World and Their Overcoming by Signs and Symbols," *Human Studies* 26, no. 2 (2003), 141–63.

79. Schutz and Luckmann, *The Structures of the Life-World (Vol. 1)*, 4.

80. Schutz, *Collected Papers 1*, 224; Schutz, *Collected Papers 3: Studies in Phenomenological Philosophy*, ed. Ilse Schutz (The Netherlands, The Hague: Martinus Nijhoff, 1966), 116.

81. Tony Bennett, "The Invention of the Modern Cultural Fact: Towards a Critique of the Critique of Everyday Life," in *Contemporary Culture and Everyday Life*, ed. Elizabeth B. Silva and Tony Bennett (Durham, UK: Sociologypress, 2004), 30–31.

82. Altheide, "The Sociology of Alfred Schutz," 136.

83. Dreher, "The Symbol and the Theory," 155.

84. Alfred Schutz, "Appendix: The Notebooks," in *The Structures of the Life-World (Vol. 2)* (Evanston, Ill.: Northwestern University Press), 288.

85. Schutz and Luckmann, *The Structures of the Life-World (Vol. 1)*, 15.

86. Kwong Bor Ng, "Towards a Theoretical Framework for Understanding the Relationship between Situated Action and Planned Action Models of Behavior in Information Retrieval Contexts: Contributions from Phenomenology," *Information Processing and Management* 38, no. 5 (2002), 615.

87. Schutz and Luckmann, *The Structures of the Life-World (Vol. 2)*, 21–45.

88. Schutz and Luckmann, *The Structures of the Life-World (Vol. 2)*, 4.

89. Schutz and Luckmann, *The Structures of the Life-World (Vol. 2)*, 6–7.

90. Schutz and Luckmann, *The Structures of the Life-World (Vol. 2)*, 14.

91. Schutz and Luckmann, *The Structures of the Life-World (Vol. 2)*, 29.

92. Schutz and Luckmann, *The Structures of the Life-World (Vol. 2)*, 18–19.

93. Schutz and Luckmann, *The Structures of the Life-World (Vol. 2)*, 33–34.

94. Schatzki, "Practice Mind-ed Orders," 50–51. [In this context, Schatzki discusses a third factor, that is, "a pool of understandings." They link the actions composing practices; the understandings are construed as abilities that pertain to those actions. Interestingly, the concept of "a pool of understandings" comes close to the category of "stock of knowledge" discussed previously. This is obvious, since, according to Schatzki, a key ability is knowing how to perform an individual action, that is, knowing which of the doings and sayings of which one is capable would constitute the performance of an action in the current circumstances. For example, a person knows "how to build a fence, when he or she knows which actions such as hammering, lifting a board, eyeing the fence line, and inserting a post into a hole would constitute building a fence in the immediate circumstances." Two other major abilities are knowing how to identify performing certain actions and knowing how to prompt as well as to respond to performing them.]

95. Schatzki, "Practice Mind-ed Orders," 50.

96. Schatzki, "Practice Mind-ed Orders," 51.

97. John M. Johnson, "Ethnomethodology and Existential Sociology," in *Existential Sociology*, ed. Jack D. Douglas et al. (Cambridge, UK: Cambridge University Press, 1977), 165–71.

98. Johnson, "Ethnomethodology and Existential Sociology," 165–71.

99. Schatzki, "Practice Mind-ed Orders," 52.

100. Bo Reimer, *The Most Common of Practices: On Mass Media Use in Late Modernity* (Stockholm: Almqvist & Wiksell International, 1994), 43–50.

101. Reimer, *The Most Common of Practices*, 56–57.

102. Schutz, *Collected Papers 2*, 124.

103. Schatzki, "Practice Mind-ed Orders," 52–53.

104. Knorr Cetina, "Objectual Practice."

Chapter Three

Conceptualizing Everyday Information Practices

The framework depicted in figure 2.1 serves as a starting point to characterize information practice in general and everyday information practices in particular. Tentatively, information practice may be defined as an umbrella concept that qualifies the ways in which people seek, use, and share information in work-related and non-work contexts. In this chapter, we first discuss the major features of information practice. In order to elucidate the specific features of information practice and to give sufficiently detailed reasons for the terminological preference adopted in this study, we also present some comparative notions on two related concepts, that is, information behavior and information action/information activity. Then the conceptual framework of everyday information practices will be outlined. In this context, we discuss in greater detail, life world projects, the nature of everyday knowledge, and the characteristics of information source horizons and information pathways. This chapter concludes with a model of everyday information practices that serves as the point of departure of the empirical study.

APPROACHES TO INFORMATION PRACTICE

The concept of information practice appears randomly in the information-seeking literature as early as the 1960s and 1970s. However, a more detailed discussion on the nature of this concept was only started recently and major articles on this topic began appearing in the early 2000s. Interestingly, this discussion may be seen as an indication for the need to find an alternative to the dominating concept of information behavior to be discussed later.

In the context of information seeking, concepts closely related to "information practice" were used as early as the mid-1960s. For example, Thomas

J. Allen emphasized the need to examine the ultimate impact that various "information-gathering practices" have on the quality of the research being conducted.[1] In information studies accomplished in the 1970s and 1980s, the phrase information practice was seldom used. In Robert S. Taylor's seminal *Value-Added Processes in Information Systems*, he discusses "the praxis of information."[2] However, the concept was not defined in more detail. Taylor simply referred to the need to develop an overall model of the practices of organizing, storing, manipulating, retrieving, analyzing, evaluating, and providing information. In Taylor's vocabulary, "the praxis of information" primarily denotes the phenomena of information organization, processing, and provision, not the issues of information seeking, use, and sharing.

Perhaps the most prominent proponent of the concept of information practice is Pamela McKenzie. She advocates a constructionist approach to information practices, focusing on the ways in which people construct descriptions of cognitive authority in discourses.[3] Drawing on the empirical studies conducted in the early 2000s, she developed a model of information practices for everyday-life information seeking (ELIS) in particular. The main idea is that the individual may flexibly use various modes of information practices—depending on the contextual needs and requirements. The model describes four modes of information practices, that is, active seeking, active scanning, nondirected monitoring, and obtaining information by proxy.[4]

Active seeking can be defined as the most systematic and purposeful mode of information practice. Consulting a previously identified source, for example, a family physician, reading an article in an encyclopedia, or conducting a systematic known-item search in a medical database exemplify active seeking. *Active scanning* is a less systematic mode of information practice and focuses on certain themes. This mode may manifest itself as semi-directed browsing or scanning in likely locations, for example, looking at medical books in a bookstore or web pages discussing diabetes. Information may also be sought for future needs; a new book identified in the bookstore may be purchased later on if there appears to be information related to issues discussed in that book. Active scanning may also be based on opportune questioning, that is, presenting spontaneous questions to the family doctor during a consultation, for example. *Nondirected scanning* involves a serendipitous encounter with information sources, for example, incidentally getting a useful idea from a TV program on how to stop smoking. Finally, *obtaining information by proxy* refers to cases where "instances in which helpful or unhelpful information comes or is given without the initiative or actions of another agent."[5] For example, friends and colleagues may deliver information, based on the anticipated information needs of the recipient or the knowledge of his or her current interests. In this case, a friend interested in stopping smoking may refer to new web pages related to this topic and recommend them to the information seeker. Alternatively, the colleague may have bought a new book on this topic and he or she lends it to the information seeker.

Differing from McKenzie's approach, Sanna Talja and Preben Hansen emphasize that information practices are firmly embedded in work and other social practices and that these practices draw on the social practice of a community of practitioners, a sociotechnical infrastructure, and a common language.[6] More specifically, information practice denotes "practices of information seeking, retrieval, filtering, and synthesis."[7] Talja and Hansen devote particular attention to collaborative information behavior (CIB) and the outlining of a social practice approach to CIB research. They assume that "information seeking and retrieval are dimensions of social practices and that they are instances and dimensions of our participation in the social world in diverse roles, and in diverse communities of sharing. Receiving, interpreting, and indexing information . . . are part of the routine accomplishment of work tasks and everyday life."[8]

Except for these studies, the phrase information practice has been adopted without deeper reflection on its ultimate meaning. For example, Gloria Leckie refers both to information practices and to information-related practices but the ultimate differences between these phrases are not discussed.[9] Eric Thivant exemplifies a liberal way of concept usage: in an empirical study focusing on the "information seeking and use behaviour" of economists and business analysts, hybrid concepts such as "information activity practices" are referred to.[10] Christina Courtright reflects on the "labeling problem" in a major review of context in information behavior research, but leaves the question open: terms such as information behavior, information practices, and information activities are employed interchangeably.[11]

In a study discussing organizations as "cultures of information seeking and use," Chun Wei Choo tackles this problem by providing a fairly clear definition: "practices are repeated patterns of behavior that affirm organizational roles, structures, and forms of interaction."[12] Furthermore, he points out that information practices are "revealed in the activities by which people find, use, and share information to do their work and sustain their identities."[13] This characterization is well founded. However, an intriguing question remains concerning the nature of information practices: what does it mean to say that information practices are "revealed" in the activities of information seeking, use, and sharing? Are information practices somehow "hidden" in these composite activities, that is, are these practices observable through their constituent elements only?

Interestingly, Elena Prigoda and Pamela McKenzie also come up against this conceptual issue in a study focusing on "human information behavior"

(HIB) in a knitting group. They suggest that HIB (e.g., information seeking and use) "takes place within a broader set of information practices, linguistic, and conversational constructions . . . that are produced within existing discourses."[14] Further, in the same study they argue that the "HIB taking place within the knitting circle becomes information practice as it takes several kinds of social action related to . . . meanings producing textile handwork in a group setting."[15] This suggests that HIB stands for a set of activities performed by individuals. However, if these activities are performed in a group (or in a discourse community like a knitting circle in which meanings are constructed), the same "behavioral" activities are transformed into collectivistic entities, that is, information practices. The idea of "behavior + social = practice" is intriguing. However, it seems that, particularly in the context of information sharing, the individualistic category of HIB is unnecessary since information sharing is essentially social in nature. More generally, this suggests that the individualistic vocabulary of HIB may not cohere well with the collectivist approaches that capture information seeking, use, and sharing in terms of information practices.

Timothy Hogan and Carole Palmer's study exemplifies similar problems encountered in the characterization of information practice in relation to neighboring concepts. Drawing on the ideas of Juliet Corbin and Anselm Strauss,[16] Hogan and Palmer introduce the concept of "information work" that is characterized as "broader than information seeking but narrower than information behavior."[17] According to them, information work[18] is firmly contextualized in mundane activities and it is a necessary component of "the work of living."[19] Information work emerges from this framework as "something essential, dynamic, ongoing and social that intermixes with, complements, supports, and is supported by other kinds of work" or "everyday-life work," for example, coping with a chronic illness.[20] Information work is dealing with purposive, conscious, and intended actions. It focuses on the "actual labor—the time, effort, resources, and outcomes necessary in finding and using information."[21] The accounts of information work articulated in interviews may deal with "what is done with information after it is sought and found, whether it is assimilated, passed on to a peer, or just filed away for future reference."[22] As information work covers the whole spectrum of locating, gathering, sorting, interpreting, assimilating, giving, and sharing information, it comes close to information practices as defined by McKenzie.[23] Unfortunately, Hogan and Palmer do not discuss information work in relation to information practices. The relationships between these terms remain ambiguous, as exemplified by casual expressions such as "the practice of information work."[24]

The studies mentioned previously indicate the problems faced in the definition of the content and scope of information practice. Jenny Fry approaches information practices from the particular viewpoint of domain analysis.[25] The concept of information practices covers a number of activities such as information seeking, searching, and use, as well as formal and informal communication. One of the strengths of this approach is that the problems associated with drawing the boundaries between information seeking and communication can be avoided. However, given the scope of information practice there is a danger that the discriminatory power of this concept will be impaired.

Wanda Orlikowski outlines a perspective on "knowing in practice" by highlighting the essential role of human action in knowing.[26] Knowledge and practice are understood as reciprocally constitutive: it does not make sense to talk about either knowledge or practice without the other.[27] Since Orlikowski explored the issues of knowing in practice empirically, she had to define the major terms in more detail. Activities comprising the practice of "interacting face to face" include "gaining trust, respect, credibility, and commitment," "sharing information," and "building and sustaining social networks."[28] These definitions are illuminating, although again, we face the problem that both practices and activities refer to broad concepts in the meaning of "doing things in general." Thus, it is not easy to specify whether some practice is more general than the activity that constitutes it. For example, "sharing information" may also be understood as a specific practice having different constitutive activities such as "sharing information by e-mail" (cf. chapter 7 of the present volume).

Olof Sundin and Jenny Johannison provide a final example of the problems faced in the definition of the concept of information practice.[29] In a pioneering study they advocate the concept of "social practice," drawing on neopragmatist ideas. From a neopragmatist viewpoint, information seeking — including the shaping of information needs and relevance assessments — may be understood as a social practice. A social practice is defined as an institutionalized activity that consists of more or less formal sets of rules concerning, among other things, what should be considered "proper" information seeking. The institutionalization of social practices takes place in different "communities of justification." This is where the sets of rules are negotiated and become formalized.

This definition is well grounded, although we may ask how well it would work outside professional contexts that do not necessarily incorporate communities of justification. What kind of communities of justification may be found in non-work contexts? Probably, these contexts are without clear boundaries, ill defined and devoid of specific communities of justification setting rules and criteria for information seeking and daily communication. Naturally, there may also be information habits in non-work contexts, but probably there are not many activities that are "institutionalized." For example, the reading of the morning newspaper may not be defined as an "institutionalized" activity, although it clearly meets the criteria of a habitual activity.

The concept of information practice was occasionally mentioned as early as the 1960s but was paid more systematic attention before the early 2000s. So far, there is no consensus among researchers about the scope of this concept. It is also apparent that advocates of the concept of information practice have not reflected in greater detail about what is meant by "practice" in this context; more or less, the concept of practice is taken as given. In most cases, information practice is understood to denote activities and processes such as seeking, use, and sharing of information. In addition, information retrieval, filtering and synthesis, and informal communication have been referred to as components of information practice. Despite the different definitions of the scope of information practice, most researchers agree that a significant characteristic of the concept of information practice is the central role of social and cultural factors qualifying information seeking, use, and sharing. Overall, however, the concept of information practice has remained somewhat ambiguous, and researchers have encountered difficulties in trying to draw clear boundaries with related concepts, such as information work and information behavior.

INFORMATION BEHAVIOR

We may continue the elaboration of the conceptual characteristics of information practice by comparing the ways in which the issues of information seeking and use have been approached from the perspective of information behavior. In recent years, this concept has become popular as an umbrella concept. Case gathered citations for the review of studies on information behavior and identified more than 2,000 potentially relevant documents published between January 2001 and December 2004.[30] However, despite its popularity, the content of information behavior has remained ambiguous, for example, there is not much discussion on what exactly is meant by behavior in the context of information behavior. On the other hand, the encounter with this problem is not surprising since the definition of the concept of behavior seems to challenge psychologists and philosophers (cf. chapter 2).

In view of the ambiguous nature of the concept of behavior, the proponents of information behavior have adopted a straightforward and optimistic ap proach to terminological issues. For example, Karen Fisher and her colleagues, referring to Donald O. Case's[31] textbook on information behavior believe that information behavior "is a term whose time has come, largely because it captures a broader range of information related phenomena."[32] Further, in the preface of the monograph entitled *Theories of Information Behavior*, Fisher and her colleagues legitimated the central position of this concept by noting that in "the mid and late 1990s a flurry of theoretical activity coincided with emerging consensus about the name of this sub-discipline within library and information science."[33]

In information studies, the concept of information behavior has been referred to since the mid-1960s. In the 1970s, the concept of "information behavior" gradually began to establish its position in the vocabulary of researchers focusing on information needs, seeking, and use. So far, perhaps the most influential advocate of the concept of information behavior is Tom D. Wilson. In a study focusing on information needs, Wilson developed a model of "factors affecting needs and information-seeking behavior."[34] Distinct from earlier studies, Wilson emphasized the significance of investigating information-seeking behavior rather than the user's need for information. In this context, a central task is to find out "why the information user behaves as he or she does."[35]

The concept of information behavior consolidated its position as an umbrella concept in the 1980s. For example, James Krikelas defined information-seeking behavior as "any activity of an individual that is undertaken to identify a message that satisfied a perceived need."[36] Information was understood as "any stimulus that reduces uncertainty," while "need" was defined as a "recognition of the existence of this uncertainty in the personal or work-related life of an individual."[37] Similar to Wilson's model, needs were seen as central triggers of information-seeking behavior. However, Krikelas was more eager to share the traditional behaviorist vocabulary when referring to information as a "stimulus." On the other hand, it was not a question of a schematic stimulus-response model focusing on observable behavior, because "a stimulus that reduces uncertainty is an internalized process that cannot be observed."[38] As Krikelas astutely pointed out, this dilemma had already been identified in user studies, where some researchers speculated on the nature of the unobservable factors, that is, needs triggering behavior.[39] However, most researchers had omitted this issue and concentrated on the observable behavior, that is, information seeking manifesting itself as accessing diverse information sources.

Later, Wilson revised the model of information-seeking behavior and extended it into a general model of "information behavior."[40] In this model, information behavior includes four modes of information seeking; that is, passive

attention, passive search, active search, and ongoing search, as well as information processing and use. Wilson suggests that a number of contextual factors
affect information behavior; they include psychological, demographic, and environmental factors. In an article drawing together the major ideas received
from the development of the models of information behavior research, Wilson
defined information behavior as "the totality of human behavior in relation to
sources and channels, including both active and passive information seeking,
and information use."[41] Thus defined, information behavior would encompass face-to-face communication with others, as well as the passive reception
of information, without any intention to act on the information given. In this
framework, information-seeking behavior, information-searching behavior, and
information-use behavior are conceived as constituents of information behavior. Information behavior thus defined covers a broad area, but human communication behavior represents something even more extensive, and the former
may be conceived as a part of it.

The growing popularity of the concept of information behavior does not
mean that all researchers accept this phrase without reservations. For example, in a debate on this concept in the listserv JESSE in 1999, it was argued that as a phrase, information behavior is less felicitous because it may
be associated too closely with the behaviorist paradigm in psychology.[42] It
was also noted that the term information behavior is incorrect, grammati-
cally speaking, because "information does not behave"; only people do.
Thus, for example, "information-related behavior" would be a more appropriate phrase.[43]

Recently, Case has pointed out that the problem with broadening the scope
of information behavior is that the importance of this concept is undermined.[44] If all aspects of searching, seeking, and using information are placed
under the umbrella of information behavior, is there any topic in information
studies that has nothing to do with information behavior? The definitional
problems are aggravated further when the nature of "cognitive behavior" is
explored. In itself, this expression is less felicitous, since it is difficult to specify how we might characterize, for example, thinking as a particular mode of
"behavior," at least if the discourse on behavior is burdened with the customary connotations of "observable" or "narrow behavior."[45]

Given the formidable challenges related to the reliable characterization of
the interaction between "internal" and "external" components of information
behavior there is a danger that the concept of "information behavior" remains
somewhat hollow. In fact, these problems had already been discussed in the
mid-1980s, in a critique of the traditional system-centered approach to information seeking. Brenda Dervin and Michael Nilan pointed out that this traditional approach had stuck to "externals" and "observables," while one of the

characteristics of the new user-centered approach is that it addressed the issues of "cognitive behavior" and "internals."[46] One of the problems of the studies of information behavior seems to be that they stress the importance of studying quantifiable phenomena measured in variables at an individual level while the issues of unobservable cognitive behavior[47] are given only secondary attention.

As defined by Wilson,[48] the concept of information behavior provides a sufficiently broad context where information needs, seeking, and use can be reviewed as a whole. Although information behavior is a popular phrase, the reflective discourse on information behavior has remained fragmentary, and the concept is used indiscriminately. Except for Tom D. Wilson's studies, information researchers have not reflected in greater detail on the ways in which information behavior represents a "behavioral" approach and how it is related to behavioral research more generally.

INFORMATION ACTION AND INFORMATION ACTIVITY

Similar to information behavior, *information action* is an umbrella concept that describes the ways in which people "deal with information." Generally, information action may be understood as a process in which the "individual performs meaningful deeds in relation to information and knowledge in order to achieve something."[49] Compared to information behavior, "information action" has attracted fewer advocates, and has seldom been referred to in information-seeking studies. There are very few empirical studies drawing on this concept.[50]

One of the reasons for preferring information action to information behavior may be the fact that behavior is reminiscent of behaviorism. It focuses on "narrow behavior" as mere bodily motion, that is, the mechanistic psychological paradigm in which only the person's outer performance is observed, and this concept is utilized as the basis for drawing conclusions on his or her inner reality.[51] From this critical viewpoint, behavior is a passive term, as if the individuals functioning were merely reacting to stimuli.[52] As discussed in chapter 2, behavior can also be understood in the sense of "broad behavior," or as action, more specifically, bodily movements caused by mental states or events.[53] Naturally, definitions such as these blur the boundary line between behavior and action, making it difficult to characterize the specific nature of action. On the other hand, researchers drawing on phenomenological sociology favor the concept of action instead of behavior, in order to emphasize that human action is intentional in nature. This terminological preference is also reflected in information studies. For example, Kwong Bor Ng refers to "information-seeking action" instead of "information-seeking behavior," in order to emphasize the intentional aspects of human action.[54]

The concept of information action[55] was introduced into the international debate in the mid-1980s by Gernot Wersig and Gunter Windel. They argued for an action-oriented approach to researching informational phenomena in order to understand the underlying meanings that people attribute to information seeking and its context. One of the motives for introducing a novel concept was the critique of the concept of "information man."[56] This concept assumes that information behavior is rationally motivated and organized and that it remains relatively stable over time. Thus, information behavior of this kind would appear to be an analogy to the "economic man" developed by modern economics. However, as Wersig and Windel pointed out, information man is a complex and differentiated animal guided by rational and nonrational motives and behavior.[57] The assumption that information man is primarily a psychological construct seems to be one-sided because all social, economic, and cultural factors have been omitted.

Wersig and Windel proposed an alternative model in which information processes and information behavior are described, analyzed, and understood as being segments of an underlying factor or problem.[58] It can be defined as a state of dissatisfaction about any object in the world or universe. Information is seen as being only one element, though an important one, contributing to coping with that problem. Wersig and Windel emphasized that the individual (or group) in the need state and the possible external mechanisms of information provision have to be conceived of as an action system in which information activities form only one aspect which is embedded in a much larger context. Information science should develop a kind of "theory of action" which allows one to localize and describe information action more clearly.[59]

The main idea of their programmatic approach is that action and behavior are closely related concepts, but are used for different purposes. In the case of behavior, the focus lies on what is observable, while the concept of action suggests that behind the action there is an intention of the actor to achieve something, and this intention makes the action "meaningful," at least for the actor. Wersig and Windel made an important contribution by clearly differentiating the concepts of behavior and action, thus paving the way for an alternative approach.

Similar to information behavior, the scope of the concept of information action appears hard to define in detail. An example of this is provided by J. David Johnson's "Comprehensive Model of Information Seeking" (CMIS) where one of the components is information-seeking actions.[60] These actions may result from the impetus provided by the foregoing set of factors in the CMIS such as an individual's beliefs about the outcomes of information seeking or the personal experience received from the use of a specific information source. Information action may be rendered comprehensible by referring to various ways in which information seekers select and use various kinds of sources and channels. Although Johnson employs the concept of information actions, it is not qualified in more detail.

Some researchers, for example Anders Hektor, prefer the concept of information activity instead of information action. Hektor defines activity as action taken by an agent; meaning the performance of some physical or mental process.[61] More specifically, Hektor understands information activity as a set of behaviors that people display in their interactions with information.[62] However, information activities have a social connotation, as they are mainly concerned with information that is external to the individual. Information activities involve elements of physical manipulation but are also concerned with the manipulation of signs and symbols.

Hektor identifies four different "forms" of information behaviors, that is, seeking, gathering, communicating, and giving.[63] Eight different information activities related to these behaviors are also specified. These activities are as follows: search and retrieve and browse (these are primarily related to information seeking); monitor and unfold (primarily related to information gathering); exchange and dress (primarily related communicating); and finally, instruct and publish (primarily related to information giving). Jenna Hartel has also used Hektor's ideas in her empirical study focusing on the information practices of hobbyist cooks.[64] Jenna Hartel identifies information activities such as imagining, reading, browsing, talking, experiencing, searching, seeking, use, and reuse. She also suggests that, for example, the use and reuse of culinary documents are information practices.[65] Overall, Hektor's and Hartel's studies indicate that the field of information behaviors and activities is fairly broad, ranging from information seeking to communicating. The boundaries between the concepts are elusive. For example, information seeking may denote information behavior composed of information activities such as searching and browsing (Hektor) as well as an individual information activity (Hartel).

Information action may be primarily conceived of as a "counterconcept" to information behavior that is seen to be plagued by the mechanistic and positivistic connotations of behaviorism. To avoid these shortcomings, the concept of information action emphasizes the intentional (nonmechanistic) character of human action. As with information behavior, information action has not been defined in sufficient detail. Upon closer consideration, information action seems to incorporate similar components referred to in the context of information behavior, such as, information seeking and use, browsing and reading. The conceptual setting is complicated if information activity is used for information action without reflecting on how these concepts may differ from each other. Overall, this suggests that the boundaries between these concepts are elusive, and that so far, the proponents of information action have not succeeded in profiling it as an umbrella concept.

INFORMATION PRACTICE, INFORMATION BEHAVIOR, AND INFORMATION ACTION

Information practice, information behavior, and information action stand for umbrella concepts whose meaning has seldom been discussed in detail in studies on information needs, seeking, and use. Overall, the discussion about the nature and scope of these concepts has been fragmentary, and in most cases, the attempts to define them have been based on monologue rather than dialogue between their advocates. Interestingly, the proponents of the concept of information practice have been more active in this sense.[66] This is understandable because they have attempted to challenge the dominating discourse on information behavior by proposing an alternative viewpoint.

One of the barriers encountered on the way toward more specific definitions of information practice, information behavior, and information action is the fact that the major concepts of *behavior, action,* and *practice* are subject to multiple meanings not only in the vocabularies of philosophy, psychology, and sociology but also in the discourses of information-seeking studies (cf. chapter 2). Given these complexities, it is no wonder that most information scientists tend not to analyze the concepts of behavior, action, and practice fully. Obviously, most researchers see no specific need to open up generic concepts such as these because it is assumed that everyone knows—at least roughly—what is meant by behavior, action, or practice in everyday contexts.

Ultimately, the major concepts of behavior, action, and practice apparently denote the same phenomena: they deal with the ways in which people "do things." On the other hand, information behavior, information action, and information practice apparently refer to the ways in which people "deal with information" or "do things with the help of information." The major difference is that within the discourse on information behavior, the "dealing with information" is primarily seen to be triggered by an individual's needs and motives. From the viewpoint of information action, the main driver is an individual's intention. Finally, within the discourse on information practice, dealing with information is primarily driven by socially and culturally shaped values and interests. In this way, the concept of information practice has much in common with ideas of information action, particularly with regard to the idea that human action is intentional and that it is directed by one's goals and interests. Hence, the concept of information action will be employed here. However, information action will not be referred to as an umbrella concept; instead, it will be used to specify constituents of everyday information practice such as identifying information sources and judging the value of information content.

TOWARD A CONCEPTUAL FRAMEWORK OF EVERYDAY INFORMATION PRACTICES

To clarify the conceptual issues and to put the major issues of this book in a broader context, we have characterized everyday practice and information practice. This chapter continues the conceptual elaboration by focusing on everyday information practices, at the same time, background is provided for the empirical part of the study (see chapters 5–7). The main components of everyday information practices are specified in figure 3.1.

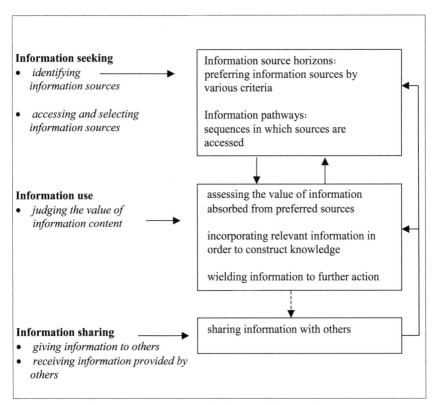

Figure 3.1.   Major Components of Everyday Information Practices.

As suggested in figure 3.1, three major everyday information practices may be identified: *information seeking, information use,* and *information sharing.* Drawing on the terminology discussed in chapter 2, it is proposed that individual practices are composed of actions (more specifically, "doings and sayings"), and that similarly, information practices are constituted by specific information actions. Figure 3.1 also specifies a few information actions such as identifying and accessing information sources, judging the value of information content, and giving information to others. Like any other everyday practice, information practices take place in the context of life world, and they serve as tools for the furtherance of everyday projects in this major context.

The ways in which people identify and access information sources are oriented by their *information source horizons,* that is, the ways in which information sources are perceived to be available in different situations such as monitoring daily events or solving specific problems. The preference (or avoidance) of information sources is based on such perceptions. Further, information seeking is affected by the nature of *information pathways,* that is, the sequence in which the (preferred) sources are accessed.

It is characteristic of information use that the value of the information available in the preferred sources is judged by various criteria. Information is incorporated in order to construct knowledge, and knowledge may be wielded to further action, for example, solving a current problem. Finally, knowledge constructed in the process of information use may be shared with other people by drawing on various criteria, for example, the degree to which other people are expected to reciprocate. Finally, as the dashed arrows on the right side of figure 3.1 suggest, experiences perceived from the sharing of information may affect the information source horizons and information pathways and thus, modify people's source preferences.

The review of the concepts of information behavior and information action showed that the discriminatory power of these concepts may be impaired if their scope is loosely defined. The same dilemma concerns the concept of everyday information practices. To avoid this problem, some limitations are necessary to define the scope of everyday information practices in a realistic way.

First, the phenomena of communication are included in everyday information practices only to the extent they deal with information sharing, more specifically, personally giving information to others. A sharp focus is well founded because incorporating communication of all kinds would result in an excessively broad scope. A loose approach would mean that, for example, media (use) practices such as watching soap operas on television and going to the cinema should be discussed under the label of everyday information practices.[67] Admittedly, entertainment may also serve the ends of information seeking, use, and sharing, and in individual cases, there may be no need to draw sharp boundaries between entertainment and factual news material. However, to profile the concept of information practice, the main focus is devoted to the seeking, use, and sharing of material that may be primarily employed for serious (informational, not solely frivolous) purposes, for example, to monitor everyday events and to solve everyday problems.

Second, to retain the discriminatory power of the concept, phenomena related to information production (e.g., journalistic work), as well as the organization of information (e.g., classification and indexing of printed and electronic material in libraries) are excluded. Thus, the activities characteristic of professional intermediaries such as librarians, information specialists, and reporters fall outside the scope of the concept of everyday information practices. Ultimately, these limitations are due to the fact that everyday information practices are reviewed from the perspective of ordinary citizens living in mundane non-work contexts.

LIFE WORLD PROJECTS AS CONTEXTS OF EVERYDAY INFORMATION PRACTICES

As suggested in chapter 2, the most general level context of everyday practices is one's life world.[68] From the subjective viewpoint of everyday information practices, the life world is formed by the totality of experiences obtained from the realization of mundane projects of various kinds. Importantly, life world also incorporates transindividual and social characteristics because it represents a shared context for intersubjective action. Structural and material factors determine the degree of freedom of action, as people pursue their everyday projects. Such factors include, for example, income level, the length of the workday which determines the amount of daily leisure time, and the nature of their dwelling place (e.g., urban vs. rural area). The existence of life world as the totality of experiences and shared context of action presupposes the maintenance of the "material substratum" of this world.[69] This suggests that from the perspective of the structural factors, life world manifests itself to people in an "order of things," that is, a relatively well-established constellation of work and non-work activities taking place in specific spatiotemporal contexts. Therefore, one easily takes this constellation as the most natural or normal way to organize his or her everyday practices in the context of life world.

These factors apparently also have direct implications with respect to the social and cultural nature of everyday information practices. For example, the practice of reading the newspaper in the morning in order to seek orienting information is dependent on structural factors such as the regular publishing of the newspaper. On the other hand, there are spatiotemporal qualifiers of everyday practices: the fact that the newspaper subscribed to is delivered to the mailbox early in the morning in order for the paper to be read before leaving for work. Similarly, television may be taken for granted as part of the seriality and spatiality of everyday life, because broadcast schedules can markedly define the structure of the households' day.[70] Reading the morning paper at the breakfast table or watching television news at 8.30 p.m. in the living room refer to routine information practices occurring at "ritual times" and in "ritual spaces."[71] Ultimately, however, these routines in themselves may be less interesting than the meanings that people attach to them.[72]

Naturally, the fact that most people can participate in such ritualistic information practices is by virtue of mass production. There are always structural factors behind these practices, for example, the agreement between the newspaper printing house and the reader.[73] The subscription to a newspaper binds the company and the reader together in that the former regularly provides news worth reading to the latter who has paid for this service. The continuity of this agreement forms the basis for the reproduction of the practice of newspaper reading. However, subjective and situational factors may affect the ways in which this practice manifests itself in reality. For example, on workday mornings, the reader may occasionally be very busy and he or she has to be satisfied with a hasty glance at the paper, while on the weekends he or she may have time enough to read the whole paper.

This suggests that through their choices, people have practically engaged in a certain order of things, and it is in their interest to keep that order as long as they find it meaningful. One might see this as an indication of inherent conservatism of everyday-life world[74] but basically there is nothing unnatural in it. Although people often seek variation in life, particularly in leisure time, the recreational elements are usually sought in "managed" ways; totally uncontrolled action just for a change is an exception. Thus, at least implicitly, most people seek an internal coherence of everyday things because it gives them a better chance to plan their choices and act meaningfully. In general, the ways in which the order of things are organized in one's daily life is culturally conditioned. The culture, with its specific values, directs habits and attitudes to working life as well as to how people are spending their leisure time, for example, whether reading a book or watching television.

Therefore, everyday practices (in general) begin to establish themselves in a natural order,[75] being perceived as self-evident. As to the development of everyday information practices, the concrete examples received at home and school influence this developmental process. In this way, individuals receive experiences concerning the usefulness of different information sources while monitoring daily events and solving everyday problems. These experiences may affect the informational orientation of the individual and lead to certain information-seeking habits. Therefore, a profile of informational orientation will be developed, that is, a set of attitudes and dispositions toward information seeking and use in certain problem situations. The habits of information seeking and use are often rooted at an unconscious level and they are not wholly subject to reflection. According to Anthony Giddens, these practices exist as a part of practical consciousness.[76]

Elfreda A. Chatman discusses the unquestionable starting points of everyday information seeking by referring to the concept of "life in the round."[77] In general, it denotes a dynamic everyday world based largely on approximation.[78] It is a world where imprecision is largely accepted and inexactitude tolerated and where "members move in and out of the round depending on their need for more systematic, precise, and defined information."[79] Understanding life in the round results when information is clear enough to impart sensible meaning to things. The most important consequence of this construct for the practices of everyday information seeking is that life in the round adversely affects information seeking in day-to-day situations; people will not search for information if there is no need to do so. Thus, from the perspective of life in the round, the actual context shapes an individual's definition of information as well as appropriate ways of seeking information and using it. As Paul Solomon points out, "roundness" is the way by which we simplify the world sufficiently so that we can accomplish what we need to accomplish.[80] In a positive sense, roundness permits people to cope with their daily lives and to deal with information overload. Thus, rounding is important in helping people focus on doing what needs to be done and making order out of chaos.

Daily practices are not, however, rooted in the life world in an abstract way; these practices are anchored in everyday projects that are oriented to the future. In other words, one's life world consists of many different projects with varying temporal and spatial perspectives or horizons. Everyday information practices are constitutive of these projects and ultimately these projects give information practices their meaning.

In the tradition of social phenomenology, everyday projects are approached at a general level as human projects that provide a meaningful context of action.[81] Thus, human action is perceived as project-oriented and perspectivist. Action implies past, present, and future; action is rooted biographically, it takes place at the present moment, and it reaches toward the future. Action is shaped by this temporal dialectic: the ways in which things have been done in the past (implying habitual action), the ways in which it can be performed at the moment (implying the actual constraints of action), and the ways in which it is projected to continue in the future.

We may concretize the idea of human projects by drawing on the ideas proposed by Hektor.[82] According to him, there are two major kinds of everyday projects, that is, generic and specific. *Generic projects* such as household care or monitoring everyday events are understood to be common for all members of society or the community while the *specific projects* may be characteristic of a particular life situation, for example, pregnancy. Specific projects may manifest themselves in two ways. First, they may be understood as *change projects* that are dealing with managing transitions in life, for example, moving from a rural village to a major city to get a new job. Projects of these kinds often presuppose the active seeking of problem-specific information (for details, see chapter 5). On the other hand, we may identify *pursuit projects* that are less dependent on immediate needs.[83] These projects are continually present, furthering a general interest, for example, a hobby of familiarizing oneself with the great classic works of world literature by making use of the public library. It is characteristic of the pursuit projects that opportunities are acted upon where valued information is encountered. Change projects require a certain level of attention to the activities and they are probably often related to conscious strategies, while pursuit projects tend to be related to minimally conscious practices in the course of everyday life.

Such everyday projects form broad contexts for information practices. The contextual nature of everyday projects, for example, their temporal features, vary. Generic projects such as regularly monitoring everyday events through the media may begin as a teenager and continue until old age. Naturally, in this case, it may be difficult to articulate the totality of these activities in terms of a "project" because of their routine nature and the broad repertoire of topics involved in monitoring everyday events. Similarly, coping with a chronic disease such as type one diabetes exemplifies lifelong everyday projects. Specific projects such as acquiring a new job or buying a new car may exemplify another end of the temporal continuum because in some cases projects such as these may take only a couple of days and their temporal, as well as topical boundaries are fairly well defined.

Independent of the endurance of everyday projects, they may be broken down further into individual tasks whose performance may entail problems to be solved in order to further the project. From the temporal point of view, the performance of these tasks occurs in *episodes*; an episode may be understood as an incident or event that is a part of a progression or a larger sequence of actions comprising the everyday project. Episodes may last only a couple of minutes but in some cases, they may take several hours or even days. Hartel describes cooking episodes in her study focusing on the information seeking and use habits of hobbyist cooks.[84] An episode may last just a few minutes for a simple and singular preparation, such as "swiss chard." On the other hand, the preparation for a major party with multiple courses may require several days of effort. This episode entails a number of tasks such as planning the menu, obtaining the necessary ingredients, cooking, and serving. On the other hand, the project of acquiring a new job may incorporate episodes like visiting an employment agency and checking the employment section of the want ads when reading newspapers. It is characteristic of everyday projects of various kinds that they are furthered in parallel ways within a period of time, for example, a day or a week. For example, the projects of searching for a new job in another city, planning the practicalities related to moving, and taking care of the diet required in coping with diabetes may run parallel. In addition, work-related and non-work projects and tasks may follow each other or partly overlap.

Diane Kelly exemplifies the occurrence of such task performance in her study based on the examination of online information seeking during a 14-week period.[85] The numbers and kinds of tasks identified by the study participants varied considerably. For example, one of the participants (a Ph.D. student) reported the following 12 tasks specifically giving rise to online information seeking during the 14-week period: (1) travel; (2) applying for fellowships, grants, and awards; (3) submitting papers to conferences; (4) staying in touch with people; (5) shopping for material possessions; (6) writing the dissertation; (7) legal trouble/conflict; (8) weather; (9) development as a scholar; (10) teaching instruction; (11) additional teaching gigs; and (12) housing options.[86]

As the previous examples indicate, everyday information projects are deeply embedded in spatial and temporal contexts. These contexts suggest specific kinds of temporal "orders" for the furtherance of the projects and their constituent tasks or problems (e.g., travel or solving a legal problem), as well as specific information sources to be used in problem-solving and the monitoring of everyday events. For example, a person may have deeply ingrained routines to monitor weather forecasts by checking a newspaper in the morning. Interestingly, the monitoring activity not only provides encounters with information but also reaffirms the normality of the situation from the viewpoint of "ontological security," as theorized by Giddens.[87]

Ultimately, ontological security is an emotional, rather than cognitive phenomenon and is rooted in the unconscious. Ontological security refers to the confidence that most human beings have in the continuity of their self-identity and in the constancy of the surrounding social and material environments of action. Thus, ontological security is sustained through the familiar and the predictable. It draws on a sense of reliability of persons and things, and is offered by the generally trustworthy, unchanging, and predictable format of, for example, printed newspapers. In itself, the monitoring of everyday events through media always implies some time horizon, because monitoring may be focused on both the immediate past, present, and also on the immediate future, as exemplified by most people's interest in watching weather forecasts on television. Not all information is received through systematic monitoring of everyday events through the media because useful information may be encountered incidentally, for example, when listening to other people chatting in a clinic waiting room.[88]

These ideas suggest that information practices such as monitoring daily events can be conceived of as a lifelong activity focused on everyday matters. In this light, the reading of a newspaper in the morning exemplifies a (habitual) task that is rendered meaningful because it serves the ends of the generic project of keeping up-to-date. To keep things in meaningful order and to adjust them as required, it is necessary to continuously monitor various events occurring in the life world because the conditions of daily activity may not necessarily remain the same. It is necessary to ascertain that radical changes affecting internal and external conditions of daily routines are noticed. Thus, a considerable part of this monitoring activity largely goes on in an unconscious fashion, following familiar tracks from day to day.

In the daily life world, the nature of the lived experience is affected, by the degree of alertness or spontaneity; the degree to which one's thinking may be characterized as realistic or only daydreaming; and whether the problems at hand are reflected on individually or together with other people.[89] The objects in the everyday world capture a person's attention through his or her *interests*. Ultimately, these interests also direct the pursuit of the everyday project. As Alfred Schutz emphasizes, "it is our interest at hand that motivates all our thinking, projecting, acting, and therewith establishes the problems to be solved by our thought and the goals to be attained by our actions."[90] The individual's interest determines the direction of the judgments as to what elements from the ontological structure of the available world—as represented in the individual's stock of knowledge—are to be seen as relevant with regard to the definition of a situation and possible action.

It is characteristic of the furtherance of everyday projects that the major part of the flow of experiences obtained in this context goes on in routine ways. In most cases, the perceptions made of the objects available in the environment are compatible with the expectations of the individual and thus, these perceptions indicate that the stock of knowledge at hand so far is sufficient and relevant to master the situations encountered.[91] From this perspective, the stock of knowledge may be perceived as a tool to deal with everyday occurrences. Therefore, this knowledge consists less of considered elements of knowledge, than of various layers of unconscious and unconsidered routine knowledge.[92]

According to the ideas of social phenomenology, sedimentation is the process by which elements of knowledge, their meaning, and significance are integrated into an actor's stock of previously acquired knowledge. The structure of sedimentation of experience depends on the relevance and typicality of the experience. More specifically, the "social stock of knowledge" contains typifications of various situations, various motives or acts, goals, and courses of action by different kinds of actors.[93] This suggests that the sedimentations of the stock of knowledge provide a necessary basis for everyday information practices to further everyday projects. However, the stock of knowledge is not solely acquired on the basis of the individual's experiences, but mainly adopted from the social stock of knowledge. This is because "my life-world is not my private world, but rather, is intersubjective; the fundamental structure of its reality is that it is shared by us."[94] Finally, it is important to note that such stocks of knowledge do not remain the same but undergo gradual changes, as people seek, use, and share information.

THE HORIZONS OF EVERYDAY INFORMATION PRACTICES

Given that everyday projects are driven by one's interests, or more generally, his or her teleoaffective structure, everyday information practices serving the ends of these projects are also oriented by future-oriented factors. The varying importance of interests as driving forces of action may be characterized by drawing on a spatial metaphor of regions of relevance. The metaphor is based on the assumption that people are not equally interested in all provinces of the life world. More specifically, it may be assumed that "plan-determined and situationally related interest . . . organizes the world in strata of greater and lesser relevance."[95] From this perspective, it is probable that people devote most of their attention to things that come close to everyday affairs, for example, home, family, work, and major hobbies.[96] Interest in events occurring beyond these affairs may vary occasionally; the interest may depend, for example, on how dramatically these events are reported in the media.

By drawing on a topographical metaphor, Schutz proposes that interest structures the objects of life world by opening within the actor's horizon into various regions or zones of relevance and operation.[97] Because the interest at hand gives a general direction to thinking and provides a horizon for action, the interest also articulates the problems that may be solved by means of thinking and action.[98] Ultimately, the interest at hand implies selection, and thus, preference, even though the interest does not always refer to the conscious weighing of alternatives and the selecting of someone or something over another or others.[99] Schutz assumes that the requirements of the accuracy and relevance of knowledge vary in the zones of operation. The major regions of relevance may be differentiated as follows.[100]

The World within Actual Reach

This region represents a specific part of the life world that is directly at hand and where actions serving the needs of everyday projects, as well as daily or life plans, primarily takes place. Hence, this world has essentially the temporal character of the present. The world within actual reach embraces actually perceived objects as well as objects that can be perceived through attentive advertence. This region arranges itself spatially and temporally with the actor as its center; it is the place where the actor finds him- or herself, his or her actual "here."

Thus the world within actual reach also stands for the region of primary relevance with regard to thinking and action because this part of our life world can be observed immediately, and it can also be changed and rearranged by our actions, at least partly. Due to this opportunity for direct action, the world within actual reach may also be characterized as a zone of operation. Apparently, by virtue of the qualities of primary relevance and the opportunity to affect the objects of primary relevance, this region of life world is most important from the viewpoint of one's everyday practices.

The World within Potential Reach

The everyday-life world also encompasses objects of interest that are not directly at hand or that cannot be mastered, but that may be accessed if needed. These objects of interest may lie within restorable or potential reach. The former case can be exemplified by referring to a book that was left at home in haste. For this reason, it does not belong to the world within actual reach at the moment when the actor is driving to work. However, the book lies within restorable reach because it is highly probable that it can be found at home upon returning and thus brought into actual reach. The restorability within potential reach bears the temporal character of the remembered past, while another dimension of the world within potential reach, that is, attainable reach, is characterized by the temporal character of the future. A world that was never within the reach of the actor can be brought within it. For example, the actor can climb Mount Everest, given that specific conditions (economic, technical, health, etc.) can be met.

Thus, the prospects of the attainability of the planned acts may vary situationally, depending on the resources at the disposal of the actor. The chances tend to decrease in relation to the increasing social, temporal, and spatial distance from the center of the actual present world of the actor. Due to these characteristics, the world within potential reach stands for the region of secondary relevance and a secondary (or potential) zone of operation. In most cases, it suffices if the actor is broadly familiar with this region of secondary relevance in relation to the region of primary relevance. Along with the development of technology, in particular information and communication technology,[101] the world within potential reach tends to be broadened, and thus, one's dependence on an immediately available physical and cultural environment constitutive of world within actual reach diminishes.

Relatively Irrelevant Regions

For the time being, these areas have no connection with our immediate interests. These regions can be taken for granted as long as no changes occur within them that might cause unexpected changes or risks in the previously discussed regions.

Absolutely Irrelevant Regions

Finally, there are regions of the life world that have no relevance whatsoever from the viewpoint of the actor primarily because he or she cannot in practice influence things or processes to be found in this area.

From the perspective of social phenomenology it is apparent that everyday information practices are strongly directed by an individual's interests that structure the life world into regions of decreasing relevance. As discussed in more detail later, the idea of regions of decreasing relevance can be applied in the study of information source preferences. More generally, as Alfred Schutz and Thomas Luckmann point out, "the arrangement of the life-world into various provinces of reality with finite meaning-structure is of decisive importance for the continuation . . . (and interruptions) of the acquisition of knowledge."[102] We may think that in addition to information seeking, the idea of regions of decreasing relevance may be employed to understand the ways in which people filter information in order to cope with information overload (see chapter 6) or the ways they prefer people with whom they share information (chapter 7).

INFORMATION SOURCE HORIZONS
AND INFORMATION PATHWAYS

The zones of the life world discussed previously provide the major context in which the issues of everyday information practices may be reviewed in detail. In particular, the idea of regions of relevance is useful for the study of information source preferences. This assumption is based on the view that overall, everyday information practices are significantly directed by one's *information source horizons*. In particular, these horizons affect the selection of information sources, that is, the source preferences while seeking information.

The concept of information source horizon originates from information-seeking studies conducted by Diane Sonnenwald.[103] She approaches information seeking as an activity that is located in specific contexts and situations. Sonnenwald[104] proposes that within a context and situation there is an "information horizon"[105] in which we can act. According to her, an information horizon may consist of a variety of information resources such as colleagues, librarians, books, documents, information retrieval tools, and web pages.

Empirical illustrations of information horizons are discussed by Sonnenwald and her associates.[106] Eleven undergraduate students participated in a study where they were interviewed about their ways to seek information for the needs of university course work. After the interview, they were asked to draw a picture describing their information horizon. First, the informant located him- or herself on the map.[107] However, in the study, they were not asked to reflect their potential as an information source, that is, as eventual users of their own knowledge but actors who identify various information sources which they deemed relevant, for example, for the current course work. Some of the informants' also specified relationships between the sources indicating, for example, which sources were accessed first or which were most peripheral for the needs of the course work.

Inspired by the ideas proposed by Schutz, Reijo Savolainen and Jarkko Kari adopted a phenomenological perspective to Sonnenwald's ideas.[108] They approached the concept of information horizon differently because in their view material objects such as books and libraries do not per se constitute an information horizon. Importantly, a horizon of this kind draws on a spatial metaphor. Savolainen and Kari defined horizon as an imaginary field that opens before the "mind's eye" of the onlooker or information seeker.[109] He or she may position information sources in this field so that sources deemed most significant are placed nearest to the onlooker, the less significant ones farther on, and the least central ones closest to the horizon line indicating the outmost boundary of his or her area of interest. A field of this kind opening toward the horizon line enables the actor to position information sources with regard to their assumed or perceived relevance in situations where they make sense of the everyday world or solve specific problems. Taking this viewpoint, we may speak about the concept of *information source horizons*.

These horizons are created in a broader context which may be defined as a *perceived information environment*.[110] This construct refers to a set of information sources of which the actor is aware and of which he or she may have obtained use experiences over the years. Because the perceived information environment indicates a general picture of the sources available in the everyday world, it changes quite slowly. When construing an information source horizon, the actor judges the relevance of information sources available in the information environment and selects a set of sources, say to clarify a problematic issue that is important to the everyday project. Thus, due to the selective approach to information sources, the horizon covers only a part of the actual information environment. Finally and most importantly, the selected information sources are positioned preferentially within the horizon so that the most relevant ones will be placed closest to the actor and the least relevant farther on.

Apparently, the construction of information source horizons is a result of a complex interplay of judgments about how well diverse sources would be able to meet the interests that drives the furtherance of the everyday project. It is assumed that judgments of this kind will enable people to put information sources in their "own" place in the information source horizon. Obviously, information source horizons will affect the strategies of information seeking because the horizons suggest which sources should be preferred or avoided. The concept of information source horizon is illustrated in figure 3.2. (Source: Savolainen and Kari [2004, 420]. Reprinted with permission from "Placing the Internet in Information Source Horizons: A Study of Information Seeking by Internet Users in the Context of Self-Development," *Library and Information Science Research*, vol. 26, no. 4, p. 420. Copyright: Elsevier, Inc. 2004.) In figure 3.2, the following legend is used:

Zone 1 = Most strongly preferred information sources
Zone 2 = Information sources of secondary importance
Zone 3 = Peripheral information resources

Shapes such as the rectangle illustrate various types of information sources; however, the individual shapes are selected arbitrarily and thus, they do not stand for specific types of sources like printed media.

As exemplified by the arrow in figure 3.2, the horizon indicates the direction of looking: before the mind's eye, a field opens, offering space for information sources to be positioned in various "zones" according to their significance. For illustrative purposes, only three zones of preference are depicted in figure 3.2. Naturally, the number of zones may differ, depending on the valuations of information seekers. The information sources that are felt most relevant are placed closest to the actor (Zone 1), while sources of secondary importance are located farther on (Zone 2). Finally, sources of least importance

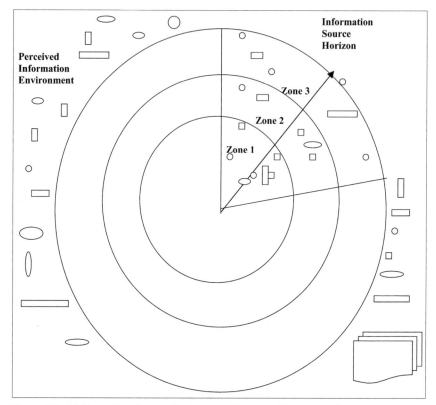

Figure 3.2.   Information Source Horizons and Zones of Source Preferences.

are placed in the periphery (Zone 3). As suggested, information source horizons stand for a construct that indicates the selection of information sources within a perceived information environment, and positioning them in the horizon according to their potential to meet the actor's interest at hand. Depending on the nature of the interest, the information source horizon may be constructed differently. For example, if the everyday project aims at monitoring daily events, television and newspapers may be preferred more strongly and located to Zone 1, as compared to projects that deal with solving specific problems. In the context of the latter projects, the Internet may be preferred and broadcast media such as television may be located in the periphery (Zone 3). We return to these issues more concretely in chapter 5.

Since the interest at hand indicates the general preference for information in terms of its content (e.g., football rather than sports in general), the selection and positioning of individual sources may be based on the use of specific criteria such as specificity of information content and easy accessibility of the source (we return to these criteria in chapter 5). Overall, the information source horizons may be of two types: first, relatively stable horizons indicating the ways in which people tend to value information sources across situations and second, dynamic, that is, problem- or situation-specific horizons, sensitive to the unique requirements of a task or project at hand. Thus, the horizons may change (broaden or narrow) when experiences of the use of alternative sources are obtained. Similarly, the individual sources, for example, colleagues or web pages may be located differently in the preference zones, depending on the nature of information needed. Finally, there may be partially overlapping horizons with shared information sources.

The concept of *information pathways*[111] proposed by J. David Johnson and his associates provides a useful approach to elaborate on the information source horizon, since information pathways indicate the sequences in which people intend to access (or have actually accessed) information sources placed in the information horizon. This is a welcome elaboration since in itself, the concept of an information source horizon may suggest a fairly static approach in that it stands for the constellation of source preferences. Thus, the concept of information pathways may complement the conceptual setting, and yield a more dynamic picture of the construction of source preferences particularly in the context of seeking problem-specific information (for a more detailed discussion, see chapter 5).

The concept of information pathways[112] stems from the elaboration of the concept of *information fields* proposed by Johnson.[113] According to Johnson, information fields provide a "rich infrastructure" and the starting point for information seeking. In short, information fields represent the typical arrangement of information stimuli to which an individual is exposed daily.[114] Further, the information field embedded within the individual may be one of the constraints affecting information seeking. Individuals are embedded in a physical world that involves recurring contacts with an interpersonal network of, for example, coworkers. On the one hand, physical context in organizations serves to stabilize an individual's information field; on the other hand, it largely determines the nature of information that individuals are exposed to on a regular basis.

The picture of information fields is not necessarily deterministic since Johnson and his colleagues emphasize that people can, if they so desire, arrange the elements of their information fields to maximize their surveillance of information.[115] In a sense, individuals are embedded in a field that acts on them, but they also make choices about the nature of their fields, and the types of media they attend to. This assumption is a major characteristic of the concept of information pathways.[116] Individuals can pursue their information seeking within information fields by using different kinds of pathways, for example, consulting a friend, using a search engine, or checking a printed encyclopedia in a library.

The concept of information pathways differs from that of information fields (or information source horizons) in that the former is more dynamic and active, focusing on an individual's actions in selecting information sources over time. In brief, an information pathway may be understood as the route someone follows in the pursuit of answers to questions within an information field. The individual may choose whether he or she wants to be involved with a particular topic, which information to accept or reject, and whether to continue the journey within an information field. However, not all pathways are necessarily unique because sometimes individuals may follow habitual pathways within the field.

THE MODEL OF EVERYDAY INFORMATION PRACTICES

We may end the conceptual review by setting everyday information practices in the broader context of everyday practices and projects. Figure 3.3 presents a model that crystallizes the major ideas discussed in chapters 2 and 3.

Information seeking, information use, and information sharing are modes of everyday information practices accomplished in the context of daily life world. This context refers to the totality of experiences (individually perceived life world) and the shared context of intersubjective action that is determined by social, cultural, and economic factors. In addition to general level contextual factors such as these, there are specific contextual factors like the relative significance of an everyday project and the lack of time constraining information use. These factors may affect the seeking, use, and sharing of information, and thereby shaping everyday information practices.

Information practices are composed of specific information actions such as identifying information sources (in the case of information seeking) and judging the value of information (in the case of information use). Information actions, in turn, are composed of "doings and sayings," as suggested in chapter 2. For example, in the specific context of identifying information sources, "doings" stand for bodily activities such as clicking hyperlinks while searching on the web or browsing a printed journal in the library. "Sayings" refer to mental and discursive activities like asking a librarian for help to find a book. As components of information practices, information actions may be routine (habitual) or nonroutine.

Information source horizons and information pathways are constitutive of the practice of information seeking, since these constructs orient the ways in which information sources are set in preferential order and accessed with re-

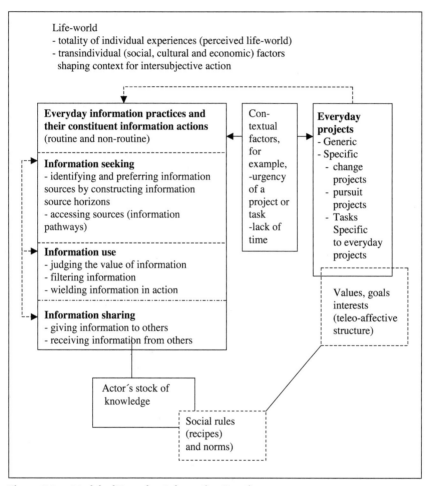

Figure 3.3. Model of Everyday Information Practices.

gard to their potential usefulness (for details, see chapter 5). The practice of information use is oriented by the judgment of the value of information. From this perspective, information is filtered to identify the most relevant content that may be wielded in the furtherance of everyday projects; these issues are explored in chapter 6. Finally, the practice of information sharing is constituted by actions that stand for giving information to others, and receiving information given by others. The issues of information sharing will be investigated in chapter 7.

From the schematic point of view provided in figure 3.3, information seeking precedes information use and information use precedes information sharing. In reality, however, the modes of everyday information practices are interdependent. For example, information sharing through a networked forum such as mailing lists may enhance the opportunities of information seeking because access to novel human sources is provided. Experiences received from information use may affect the construction of information source preferences and thereby information seeking, since a novel source that was used may be found very helpful for the purposes of finding facts about health issues, for example.

Similar to practices in general, information seeking, use, and sharing draw on the stock of knowledge for suggestions on how to proceed in typical situations. In most cases, the actions serving the practices of information seeking, use, and sharing do not occur randomly. These actions are directed by social rules (or recipe-like cues) and norms suggesting what information sources are acceptable and potentially useful and what should be avoided in seeking, using, and sharing information. Importantly, one's stock of knowledge forms a necessary basis for information practices since the ways in which information is sought, used, and shared draws on this resource. Information seeking, use, and sharing becomes more refined as the actor gains new experiences and constructs novel typifications of the occurrences of the life world. However, the ultimate meaning of everyday information practices does not lie in the refinement of the stock of knowledge per se. Everyday information practices are not valuable in themselves; they become meaningful as tools that serve the furtherance of everyday projects of various kinds, both generic and specific.

NOTES

1. Thomas J. Allen, *The Differential Performance of Information Channels in the Transfer of Technology* (Cambridge: Massachusetts Institute of Technology, 1966).

2. Robert S. Taylor, *Value-Added Process in Information Systems* (Norwood, N.J.: Ablex, 1986), 2–3.

3. Pamela J. McKenzie, "A Model of Information Practices in Accounts of Everyday Life Information Seeking," *Journal of Documentation* 59, no. 1 (2003), 19–40.

4. McKenzie, "A Model of Information Practices."

5. McKenzie, "A Model of Information Practices," 38.

6. Sanna Talja and Preben Hansen, "Information Sharing," in *New Directions in Human Information Behavior*, ed. Amanda Spink and Charles Cole (Berlin: Springer, 2005), 113–34.

7. Talja and Hansen, "Information Sharing," 113.

8. Talja and Hansen, "Information Sharing," 125.

9. Gloria J. Leckie, "General Model of Information Seeking of Professionals," in *Theories of Information Behavior*, ed. Karen E. Fisher, Sanda Erdelez, and Lynne McKechnie (Medford, N.J.: Information Today, Inc., 2005), 159.

10. Eric Thivant, "Information Seeking and Use Behaviour of Economists and Business Analysts," *Information Research* 10, no. 4 (2005). http://InformationR.net/ir/10-4/paper234.html (10 May 2007).

11. Christina Courtright, "Context in Information Behavior Research," in *Annual Review of Information Science and Technology*. Vol. 41, ed. Blaise Cronin (Medford, N.J.: Information Today, Inc., 2007), 275.

12. Chun Wei Choo, "Information Seeking in Organizations: Epistemic Contexts and Contests," *Information Research* 12, no. 2 (2007). http://InformationR.net/ir/12-2/paper298.html (10 May 2007).

13. Choo, "Information Seeking."

14. Elena Prigoda and Pamela J. McKenzie, "Purls of Wisdom: A Collectivist Study of Human Information Behaviour in a Public Library Knitting Group," *Journal of Documentation* 63, no. 1 (2007), 90.

15. Prigoda and McKenzie, "Purls of Wisdom," 105.

16. Juliet M. Corbin and Anselm L. Strauss, *Unending Work and Care: Managing Chronic Illness at Home* (San Francisco, Calif.: Jossey-Bass Publishers, 1998).

17. Timothy P. Hogan and Carole P. Palmer, "'Information Work' and Chronic Illness: Interpreting Results from a Nationwide Survey of People Living with HIV/AIDS," in Proceedings of the Annual Meeting of the American Society for Information Science and Technology, Charlotte, N.C., October 28–November 2, 2005 (CD-ROM). Volumes/ASIS05/papers/150/150_paper.html (10 May 2007).

18. Carole L. Palmer and Laura J. Neumann, "The Information Work of Interdisciplinary Humanities Scholars: Exploration and Translation," *Library Quarterly* 72, no. 1 (2002); Carole L. Palmer, "Structures and Strategies of Interdisciplinary Science," *Journal of the American Society for Information Science* 50, no. 3 (1999), 248–49. [Palmer and Neumann also refer to "information work" in their study focusing on the ways in which interdisciplinary humanities scholars extend their knowledge base. To characterize information work of this kind, they differentiate two general types of boundary-crossing research work that is, exploration and translation. The former draws on activities such as scanning, eclectic reading and anchoring, while the latter incorporates activities like consulting, apprenticing, and converting. In an earlier study focusing on interdisciplinary scientists, Palmer specified three types of information practices: gathering, finding, and probing. *Gathering* was understood as drawing together background information and new literature on a topic, whereas *finding* was referred to as locating specifics, with a range from finding a paper recommended by a colleague to finding out how to apply a new method. In turn, *probing* denotes exploratory searching for the unknown, also in unfamiliar domains. These categories are relevant and they make sense in the context of this study. However, the conceptual nature of information practices is not discussed in more detail and the relationships between knowledge strategies and information work (and its constitutive elements) remain rather ambiguous.]

19. Hogan and Palmer, "Information Work," 3.

20. Hogan and Palmer, "Information Work," 4, 15.

21. Hogan and Palmer, "Information Work," 3.

22. Hogan and Palmer, "Information Work," 3.

23. McKenzie, "A Model of Information Practices."

24. Hogan and Palmer, "Information Work," 4.

25. Jenny Fry, "Scholarly Research and Information Practices: A Domain Analytic Approach," *Information Processing and Management* 42, no. 1 (2006).

26. Wanda J. Orlikowski, "Knowing in Practice: Enacting a Collective Capability in Distributed Organizing," *Organization Science* 13, no. 3 (2002).

27. Orlikowski, "Knowing in Practice," 250.

28. Orlikowski, "Knowing in Practice," 256.

29. Olof Sundin and Jenny Johannison, "The Instrumentality of Information Needs and Relevance," in *CoLIS 2005*, ed. Fabio Crestani and Ian Ruthven (Berlin: Springer, 2005).

30. Donald O. Case, "Information Behavior," in *Annual Review of Information Science and Technology*. Vol. 40, ed. Blaise Cronin (Medford, N.J.: Information Today, Inc., 2006).

31. Donald O. Case, *Looking for Information: A Survey of Research on Information Seeking, Needs and Behavior* (San Diego, Calif.: Academic Press, 2002).

32. Karen E. Fisher, Joan C. Durrance, and Marian B. Hinton, "Information Grounds and the Use of Need-Based Services by Immigrants in Queens, New York: A Context-Based, Outcome Evaluation Approach," *Journal of the American Society for Information Science and Technology* 55, no. 8 (2004), 754.

33. Karen E. Fisher, Sanda Erdelez, and Lynne McKechnie, "Preface," in *Theories of Information Behavior*, ed. Karen E. Fisher, Sanda Erdelez, and Lynne McKechnie (Medford, N.J.: Information Today, Inc., 2005), xix.

34. Tom D. Wilson, "On User Studies and Information Needs," *Journal of Documentation* 37, no. 1 (1981), 3.

35. Wilson, "On User Studies," 7.

36. James Krikelas, "Information-Seeking Behavior: Patterns and Concepts," *Drexel Library Quarterly* 19, no. 6 (1983), 6.

37. Krikelas, "Information-Seeking Behavior," 6.

38. Krikelas, "Information-Seeking Behavior," 7.

39. Krikelas, "Information-Seeking Behavior," 7–8.

40. Tom D. Wilson, "Information Behaviour: An Interdisciplinary Perspective," in *Information Seeking in Context*, ed. Pertti Vakkari, Reijo Savolainen, and Brenda Dervin (London: Taylor Graham, 1997).

41. Tom D. Wilson, "Human Information Behaviour," *Informing Science* 3, no. 2 (2000), 49. http://www.inform.nu/Articles/Vol3/v3n2p49-56.pdf (10 May 2007).

42. JESSE, "Listserv Discussion on Information Behavior, December 1999." http://listserv.utk.edu/cgi-bin/wa?A1=ind9912&L=jesse (10 May 2007).

43. Karen E. Pettigrew, Raya Fidel, and Harry Bruce, "Conceptual Frameworks in Information Behavior," in *Annual Review of Information Science and Technology*. Vol. 36, ed. Martha E. Williams (Medford, NJ: Information Today, Inc., 2001).

44. Case, "Information Behavior," 315–16.

45. Alfred R. Mele, *Springs of Action: Understanding Intentional Behavior*. (Oxford, UK: Oxford University Press, 1992), 18.

46. Brenda Dervin and Michael Nilan, "Information Needs and Uses," in *Annual Review of Information Science and Technology.* Vol. 21, ed. Martha E. Williams (White Plains, N.Y.: Knowledge Industry Inc., 1986), 15–16.

47. Peter Ingwersen and Kalervo Järvelin, *The Turn: Integration of Information Seeking and Retrieval in Context* (Dordrecht, The Netherlands: Springer, 2005), 261–62, 385. [Many researchers drawing on the cognitive viewpoint, are critical of ambiguous concepts such as "cognitive behavior," even though they accept the umbrella term "information behavior." For example, Ingwersen and Järvelin define information seekers as "cognitive actor(s)" while elaborating the issues of interactive information seeking, retrieval, and behavioral processes. These actors interact with information objects (documents), information technology (e.g., retrieval engines), interfaces, and the organizational-social-cultural context. More specifically, information interaction, not information behavior, is the key phrase to characterize the specific behavioral processes of information seeking and retrieval. Information behavior, in turn, denotes general level phenomena "dealing with generation, communication, use and other activities concerned with information, such as information seeking and interactive information retrieval."]

48. Wilson, "Human Information Behaviour," 49.

49. Jarkko Kari, *Information Seeking and Interest in the Paranormal: Toward a Process Model of Information Action* (Tampere, Finland: University of Tampere, 2001), 38. http://acta.uta.fi/pdf/951-44-5134-1.pdf (10 May 2007).

50. Kari, *Information Seeking.*

51. Jarkko Kari and Reijo Savolainen, "Toward a Contextual Model of Information Seeking on the Web," *The New Review of Information Behaviour Research* 4 (2003), 162.

52. Tim Dant, *Knowledge, Ideology and Discourse: A Sociological Perspective* (London: Routledge, 1991).

53. Richard P. Bagozzi, Zeynep Gürhan-Canli, and Joseph H. Priester, *The Social Psychology of Consumer Behavior* (Buckingham, UK: Open University Press, 2002), 68.

54. Kwong Bor Ng, "Towards a Theoretical Framework for Understanding the Relationship between Situated Action and Planned Action Models of Behavior in Information Retrieval Contexts: Contributions from Phenomenology," *Information Processing and Management* 38, no. 5 (2002), 614.

55. Gernot Wersig and Gunter Windel, "Information Science Needs a Theory of 'Information Actions,'" *Social Science Information Studies* 5, no. 1 (1985).

56. Wersig and Windel, "Information Science," 12.

57. Wersig and Windel, "Information Science," 12.

58. Wersig and Windel, "Information Science," 13.

59. Wersig and Windel, "Information Science," 18.

60. J. David Johnson, *Information Seeking: An Organizational Dilemma* (Westport, Conn.: Quorum Books, 1996).

61. Anders Hektor, *What's the Use? Internet and Information Behavior in Everyday Life* (Linköping, Sweden: Linköping University, 2001), 68.

62. Hektor, *What's the Use? Internet*, 80.

63. Hektor, *What's the Use? Internet*, 81.

64. Jenna Hartel, "Information Activities and Resources in an Episode of Gourmet Cooking," *Information Research* 12, no. 1 (2006). http://InformationR.net/ir/12-1/paper282.html (10 May 2007).

65. Hartel, "Information Activities."

66. McKenzie, "A Model of Information Practices."

67. Bo Reimer, *The Most Common of Practices: On Mass Media Use in Late Modernity* (Stockholm: Almqvist & Wiksell International, 1994); Roger Silverstone, *Television and Everyday Life* (London: Routledge, 1994).

68. Roy Elveton, "Lebenswelt (Lifeworld)," in *The Literary Encyclopedia*. http://www.litencyc.com/php/stopics.php?rec=true&UID=1539 (10 May 2007); Alfred Schutz, *Collected Papers 2: The Problem of Social Reality* (The Hague, The Netherlands: Martinus Nijhoff, 1964); Timothy M. Costelloe, "Between the Subject and Sociology: Alfred Schutz's Phenomenology of the Life-World," *Human Studies* 19, no. 3 (1996); Martin Endress, "Reflexivity, Reality and Relationality: The Inadequacy of Bourdieu's Critique of the Phenomenological Tradition in Sociology," in *Explorations of the Life-World: Continuing Dialogues with Alfred Schutz*, ed. Martin Endress, George Psathas, and Hisashi Nasu (Dordrecht, The Netherlands: Springer, 2005); Michael E. Gardiner, *Critiques of Everyday Life* (London: Routledge, 2000), 5, 198–99; Jürgen Habermas, *The Theory of Communicative Action Part 2; Lifeworld and System: A Critique of Functionalist Reason* (Cambridge, UK: Polity Press, 1992). [The concept of life world originates in the phenomenology of Edmund Husserl, and it emphasizes the centrality of perception for human experience. This experience is multidimensional and includes the experience of individual things and their contextual or perceptual fields, the embodied nature of perceiving consciousness, and the intersubjective nature of the world as it is perceived, especially our knowledge of other subjects, their actions, and shared cultural structures. The experience of the life world is temporally and spatially structured. Husserl distinguished between "nearby space" (*Nahraum*), in which one's bodily movements take place, and an "environing space" (*Umwelt*) in which one's actions are oriented with respect to the actions of others. The *Umwelt* is the horizon of "practical structures," the everyday "familiarity" with others and the objective world that surrounds us. Schutz developed Husserl's ideas by focusing on the ways in which people structure the horizons of life world. Schutz sees an artificiality in the concept of "life world" produced by Husserl's method of reduction and as an alternative, he proposes that intersubjectivity is a given of everyday life rather than a category which needs to be derived philosophically. Thus, Schutz's analysis moves at the level of daily life itself, emphasizing the mundane features of everyday life, as well as experiential conditions under which individuals navigate its dimensions of time and space. This suggests that for social phenomenology, the leading question is not simply "what is everyday reality" but "for whom is what everyday reality in which respect"? Habermas drew on Schutz's ideas while developing an interpretation of life world in the context of communicative action. By life world Habermas means the shared common understandings, including values, that develop through face-to-face contacts over time in various social

groups, ranging from families to communities. Habermas emphasizes the constitutive role of language and culture for the life world, asserting that Schutz played down the importance of language, the linguistic mediation of social interaction in particular, since he operated on the premises of the philosophy of consciousness. Thus, according to Habermas, Schutz conceptualized life world in an "abridged and culturalist fashion." Habermas preferred a more dynamic concept of the "sociocultural life world" because communicative actions are not only processes of interpretation in which cultural knowledge (stock of knowledge) is "tested against the world"; they are at the same time processes of social integration and socialization. Researchers inspired by Marxian ideas have adopted an even more critical stand toward Schutz' inherently conservative approach to life world and the practices of everyday life. They claim that Schutz has no real motivation to go beyond a surface description of these practices, so as to grasp the underlying mechanisms of domination, and to provide a moral critique of existing social arrangement with an eye to transforming them. The present study acknowledges the importance of the critical views of these kinds. However, since issues such as social integration, socialization, and emancipation will not be specifically thematized in the present study, the phenomena of life world will be approached from the perspective proposed by Schutz.]

69. Habermas, *The Theory of Communicative Action*, 138.

70. Silverstone, *Television and Everyday Life*, 20.

71. Silverstone, *Television and Everyday Life*, 168.

72. David Chaney, *Cultural Change and Everyday Life* (Houndmills, Hampshire, UK: Palgrave, 2002), 11.

73. Reimer, *The Most Common of Practices*.

74. Rita Felski, "The Invention of Everyday Life," *New Formations* 39 (1999), 18, 22, 26, 31. [Inspired by the ideas of Schutz, Heller, and Lefebvre, among others, Felski emphasizes that three facets are constitutive of everyday life, that is, time, space, and modality. According to her, the temporality of everyday life is that of repetition, what happens "day after day." Thus, the cyclical structure of everyday life is its quintessential feature. Felski speculates that the spatial ordering of the everyday is anchored in a particular "sense of home." Since home is associated with familiarity, and familiarity combines with promise of protection and warmth, home stands for a privileged symbol of everyday life, even though the workplace may be an important location of everyday action as well. Finally, Felski maintains that the characteristic mode of experiencing the everyday is that of habit. The everyday is synonymous with habit, sameness, and routine that may epitomize both the comfort and boredom of the ordinary. Felski emphasizes the pragmatic value of everyday habits drawing on natural attitude, since it is impossible in principle to adopt a critical and self-reflective attitude toward all aspects of everyday life. Thus, habits should not be seen as intrinsically "reactionary." The pragmatic need for repetition, familiarity, and "taken-for-grantedness" in everyday life may be seen as a necessary precondition for human survival. Because habits form the very basis of who we are, it is a delusion to think that habits could be simply abandoned and that people could "embrace an infinitively shifting, self-undermining multiplicity of perspectives."]

75. Reijo Savolainen, "Everyday Life Information Seeking: Approaching Information Seeking in the Context of Way of Life," *Library and Information Science Research* 17, no. 3 (1995); Pierre Bourdieu, *Distinction: A Social Critique of the Judgement of Taste* (London: Routledge, 1984). [In my earlier study, this order was discussed in the context of "way of life" inspired by the theory of habitus developed by Bourdieu. In the most general sense, way of life may be defined as "order of things" which is based on the choices that individuals make in everyday life. "Things" stands for various activities taking place in the daily life world, including not only work-related tasks, but also necessary repetitive tasks such as household care and voluntary activities (hobbies); "order" refers to the preferences given to these activities. Order of things is determined on both objective and subjective grounds. An example of objective grounds is the length of the working day, which determines the amount of daily leisure time available, whereas perceptions of the most pleasant ways to spend leisure time refer to the subjective grounds of order of things. Because in most cases order of things is a relatively well established constellation of work and non-work activities taking place during a day or a week, one easily takes this constellation as the most natural or normal way to organize his or her everyday life. Correspondingly, people have a "cognitive order" indicating their perceptions of how things are when they are "normal." Through their choices, individuals have practically engaged in a certain order of things, and it is in their interest to keep that order as long as they find it meaningful.]

76. Anthony Giddens, *The Constitution of Society: Outline of a Theory of Structuration* (Cambridge, UK: Polity Press, 1984), 21–23.

77. Elfreda A. Chatman, "A Theory of Life in the Round," *Journal of the American Society for Information Science* 50, no. 3 (1999).

78. Chatman, "A Theory of Life in the Round," 211.

79. Pettigrew, Fidel, and Bruce, "Conceptual Frameworks," 55.

80. Paul Solomon, "Information Mosaics: Patterns of Action that Structure," in *Exploring the Contexts of Information Behaviour*, ed. Tom D. Wilson and David K. Allen (London: Taylor Graham, 1999), 170.

81. Alfred Schutz and Thomas Luckmann, *The Structures of the Life-World (Vol. 1)* (Evanston, Ill.: Northwestern University Press, 1973), 21–45.

82. Hektor, *What's the Use? Internet*, 74–76.

83. Hektor, *What's the Use? Internet*, 76.

84. Hartel, "Information Activities."

85. Diane Kelly, "Measuring Online Information Seeking in Context Part 2: Findings and Discussion," *Journal of the American Society for Information Science and Technology* 57, no. 14 (2006).

86. Kelly, "Measuring Online Information," 1863.

87. Giddens, *The Constitution of Society*, 122–26.

88. Sanda Erdelez, "Information Encountering: A Conceptual Framework for Accidental Information Discovery," in *Information Seeking in Context*, ed. Pertti Vakkari, Reijo Savolainen, and Brenda Dervin (London: Taylor Graham, 1997).

89. Schutz and Luckmann, *The Structures of the Life-World (Vol. 1)*, 25–28.

90. Alfred Schutz, *Collected Papers 2: Studies in Social Theory*, ed. Arvid Brodersen (The Hague, The Netherlands: Martinus Nijhoff, 1964), 124.

91. Alfred Schutz, *Reflections on the Problem of Relevance*, ed. Richard M. Zaner (New Haven, Conn.: Yale University Press, 1970); Schutz and Luckmann, *The Structures of the Life-World (Vol. 1)*, 182–241; Ronald R. Cox, *Schutz's Theory of Relevance: A Phenomenological Critique* (The Hague, The Netherlands: Martinus Nijhoff, 1978).

92. Wolfgang Wagner and Nicky Hayes, *Everyday Discourse and Common Sense: The Theory of Representations* (Houndmills, Hampshire, UK: Palgrave, 2005), 24.

93. Schutz and Luckmann, *The Structures of the Life-World (Vol. 2)*, 80.

94. Schutz and Luckmann, *The Structures of the Life-World (Vol. 1)*, 4.

95. Schutz and Luckmann, *The Structures of the Life-World (Vol. 1)*, 139.

96. Schutz, *Collected Papers 2*, 123–27; Schutz and Luckmann, *The Structures of the Life-World (Vol. 1)*, 36–45.

97. Schutz, *Collected Papers 2*, 123–27.

98. Schutz, *Collected Papers 2*, 123–27.

99. Schutz, *Collected Papers 1*, 78.

100. Schutz, *Collected Papers 2*, 123–27; Schutz and Luckmann, *The Structures of the Life-World (Vol. 1)*, 36–45, 50–52; John Heeren, "Alfred Schutz and the Sociology of Common-Sense Knowledge," in *Understanding Everyday Life: Toward the Reconstruction of Sociological Knowledge*, ed. Jack D. Douglas (London: Routledge & Kegan Paul, 1973).

101. Schutz, *Collected Papers 2*, 123–27; Schutz and Luckmann, *The Structures of the Life-World (Vol. 1)*, 36–45; Anthony Giddens, *The Consequences of Modernity* (Cambridge, UK: Polity Press, 1990); Anthony Giddens, *Modernity and Self-Identity: Self and Society in the Late Modern Age* (Cambridge, UK: Polity Press, 1991); Shaun Moores, *Media and Everyday Life in Modern Society* (Edinburgh: Edinburgh University Press, 2000), 36–41. [Schutz characterized the major regions of relevance in his article titled "The Well-Informed Citizen: An Essay on the Social Distribution of Knowledge," originally published in 1946. He returned to the characterizations of the regions (or sectors) of relevance in the late 1950s under the heading "Spatial Arrangement of the Everyday Life-World." Naturally, since that time, the role of information and communication technologies in everyday life has undergone radical changes, particularly due to the popularity of television and the Internet. For example, Giddens asserts that in times of late modernity (or the reflexive modernization referred to in chapter 1), social relationships have increasingly been "lifted out" of situated locales and stretched across often vast geographical distances, resulting in the disembedding of social systems. Thus, relations with others are no longer contained within a bounded locale but is now touched and penetrated to a much greater extent by distant forces such as globalization. The media, printed and electronic, obviously play a central role in this respect, and our daily experiences are increasingly mediated by them as we live in "electronic landscapes," as suggested by Moores. Since Schutz's framework primarily serves the methodological ends of the sociology of everyday knowledge, his ideas have retained their relevance, despite specific sociotechnical developments such as the breakthrough of the Internet.]

102. Schutz and Luckmann, *The Structures of the Life-World (Vol. 1)*, 125.

103. Diane H. Sonnenwald, "Evolving Perspectives of Human Information Behaviour: Contexts, Situations, Social Networks and Information Horizons," in *Exploring the Contexts of Information Behaviour*, ed. Tom D. Wilson and David K. Allen (London: Taylor Graham, 1999); Diane H. Sonnenwald, Barbara M. Wildemuth, and Gary T. Harmon, "A Research Method to Investigate Information Seeking Using the Concept of Information Horizons: An Example from a Study of Lower Socio-Economic Students' Information-Seeking Behaviour," *The New Review of Information Behaviour Research* 2 (2001), 65–86.

104. Sonnenwald, "Evolving Perspectives," 184.

105. Andrew K. Shenton and Pat Dixon, "Issues Arising from Youngsters' Information-Seeking Behavior," *Library and Information Science Research* 26, no. 2 (2004), 1032; Elfreda A. Chatman, *The Information World of Retired Women* (Westport, Conn.: Greenwood Press, 1992); Robert S. Taylor, "Information Use Environments," in *Progress in Communication Sciences*. Vol. 10, ed. Brenda Dervin (Norwood, N.J.: Ablex, 1991); Kirsty Williamson, "Discovered by Chance: The Role of Incidental Information Acquisition in an Ecological Model of Information Use," *Library and Information Science Research* 20, no. 1 (1998); Kirsty Williamson, "Ecological Theory of Human Information Behavior," in *Theories of Information Behavior*, ed. Karen E. Fisher, Sanda Erdelez, and Lynne McKechnie (Medford, N.J.: Information Today, Inc., 2005). [There are related spatial metaphors which describe the ways in which information sources are available to the users. Shenton and Dixon refer to an "information universe" which stands for the circumstances within which an individual requires and pursues information. The concept of an "information universe" seems to be broader than "information horizon" since the former does not merely encompass information sources but also the methods employed for their exploitation. Chatman uses a similar kind of metaphor when talking about the "information world" of retired women. Taylor introduces the concept of "information use environment," it refers to the set of elements that affect the flow and use of information messages into, within and out of any definable entity. Secondly, information use environment determines the criteria by which the value of information messages will be judged. Finally, Williamson proposes an "ecological model" of human information behavior. The model can be called ecological since it sets information seeking and use in the context of the social and cultural factors that may have an influence on the ways of selecting and using information sources. The model makes use of a spatial metaphor (circles within circles) in that most significant information sources are located closest to the user standing in the center of the figure; sources of lesser importance are placed farther on other circles depicting the "ecology of sources." Importantly, Williamson's ecological model sheds light upon the complex setting of factors affecting the ways in which information sources are prioritized and consulted, either purposefully or incidentally.]

106. Sonnenwald, Wildemuth, and Harmon, "A Research Method."

107. Sonnenwald, Wildemuth, and Harmon, "A Research Method," 70.

108. Reijo Savolainen and Jarkko Kari, "Placing the Internet in Information Source Horizons: A Study of Information Seeking by Internet Users in the Context of Self-Development," *Library and Information Science Research* 26, no. 4 (2004).

109. Savolainen and Kari, "Placing the Internet," 418.

110. Savolainen and Kari, "Placing the Internet," 418.

111. J. David Johnson et al., "Fields and Pathways: Contrasting or Complementary Views of Information Seeking," *Information Processing and Management* 42, no. 2 (2006).

112. Wilson, "On User Studies." [Tom Wilson, in fact, presented a closely related concept in the early 1980s. He specified "information-seeking paths" or "search paths" indicating the ways in which people access various kinds of information resources available in the context of one's life world, most notably his or her "world of work," such as, a reference group. On the other hand, the idea of an information-seeking path remains somewhat ambiguous because it is also referred to as a "search strategy," such as, employing a librarian to satisfy a demand for information.]

113. Johnson, *Information Seeking*, 33–43; J. David Johnson, "On Contexts of Information Seeking," *Information Processing and Management* 39, no. 5 (2003).

114. Johnson, "On Contexts of Information Seeking," 748–53.

115. Johnson et al., "Fields and Pathways."

116. Johnson et al., "Fields and Pathways," 572.

Chapter Four

Drawing the Empirical Picture
of Information Practices

The conceptual ideas elaborated previously provide the basis for the empirical study of everyday information practices (see chapters 5–7). In the present chapter, we characterize the material to be used in the empirical investigation. It will draw on the experiences and views of two groups: environmental activists and unemployed people. The intriguing question giving rise to the selection of these groups concerned the similarities and differences of everyday information practices of people belonging to these groups. On the one hand, it was assumed that the groups' activity level might differ significantly with regard to information seeking, use, and sharing. It was hypothesized that the environmental activists would fare better in this respect, while the information practices of the unemployed people might be characterized by passivity and alienation, due to their difficult life situation.[1] It was assumed that there might be individual variation within these groups because people have everyday projects of different kinds and these differences may be reflected in their ways to seek, use, and share information.

The empirical study draws on qualitative research strategies because the main interest of this book lies in the ways in which people construct their everyday information practices as meaningful. Therefore, semi-structured interviews, supported by the critical incident method and the mapping of information source horizons were utilized in order to capture a sufficiently nuanced picture of the construction of the meanings attached to everyday information practices. The preference for a qualitative research approach may also be grounded on the assumption that compared to questionnaire surveys it resonates better with the ideas of social phenomenology. Large-scale surveys can yield a statistically generalized picture of people's source preferences: on the other hand, this picture may remain at a coarse level and be contextually insensitive.

The primary material of the study consists of the interviews conducted with environmental activists and unemployed people during the period between 2005 and 2006 in Tampere, Finland. In addition, studies based on interviews with various groups of people conducted between 1993 and 2000 will be used to provide comparative (secondary) material for the study. The earlier studies are useful in that they make it possible to identify the ways in which everyday information practices have changed since the mid-1990s. Table 4.1 specifies the empirical material used in the present study.

Common to these studies is their focus, that is, everyday-life information-seeking practices. However, this book will also discuss information use and information sharing. All five studies were conducted in Tampere, Finland. The first study, drawing on interviews made in 1993, compared the everyday-life information-seeking practices of industrial workers and teachers.[2] The study was mainly inspired by the ideas of habitus developed by Pierre Bourdieu; an attempt was made to find out how the ways of life characteristic of working class versus middle class directs everyday-life information seeking (ELIS). The next interviews conducted in 1997 concentrated on the ways in which the breakthrough of the Internet had affected ELIS practices. The study drew on a convenience sample of twenty-three active users of the Internet.[3] The third study also centered on the role of networked sources, although the focus was on the use of the World Wide Web in ELIS. For that study, eighteen people interested in self-development projects such as different hobbies were recruited by a convenience sample. In this study, the strategies of web searching were

Table 4.1. The Primary and Secondary Empirical Materials of the Study

Participants	Focus of the Study
18 unemployed persons, fall 2006	Everyday information practices[a]
20 environmental activists, fall 2005	Everyday information practices[a]
18 people interested in self-development, fall 2000–winter 2001	The role of the Web in everyday-life information seeking[b]
23 Internet users, spring 1997	The role of the Internet in everyday-life information seeking[c]
11 industrial workers and 11 teachers, fall 1993	Everyday-life information seeking[d]

Main references of the studies:
[a] The present book.
[b] Reijo Savolainen and Jarkko Kari, "Placing the Internet in Information Source Horizons: A Study of Information Seeking by Internet Users in the Context of Self-Development," *Library and Information Science Research* 26, no. 4 (2004).
[c] Reijo Savolainen, "Seeking and Using Information from the Internet: The Context of Non-Work Use, in *Exploring the Contexts of Information Behaviour*, eds. Tom D. Wilson and David K. Allen (London: Taylor Graham, 1999).
[d] Reijo Savolainen, "Everyday Life Information Seeking: Approaching Information Seeking in the Context of Way of Life," *Library and Information Science Research* 17, no. 3 (1995).

investigated in detail.[4] Since the information source horizons were also explored, this study provides relevant findings for the comparative notions.

As this book draws primarily on the most recent interviews, the empirical data of these studies will be characterized in detail. The data were gathered by semi-structured interviews with twenty environmental activists and eighteen unemployed people, drawing on convenience samples. The environmental activists were mainly recruited by using the electronic mailing list of the local association for environmental protection. In addition, a couple of interviewees were acquired by the snowball method: one person being interviewed asked his or her friends, also active in environmental issues, to participate in the study. In turn, the recruitment of the unemployed people was based on the announcements calling for interviewees distributed to two local service centers for the unemployed. Since it was apparent that a small sum of money would better motivate them to participate, 15 euros were paid to each interviewee. This incentive appeared to be fairly effective and a sufficient number of interviewees was recruited within a period of three weeks.

The interviews were conducted in Tampere, Finland. The environmental activists were interviewed in August–September 2005, and the unemployed people in September–December 2006. In both groups, the interviews lasted one hour on average. I interviewed the environmental activists; in most cases, the interviews were conducted in my office. The research assistant interviewed the unemployed people; most of these interviews were conducted in the premises of the local service centers for the unemployed.

Of the environmental activists, fourteen were females and six were males, while of the unemployed people, fourteen were females and four were males. Thus, in both groups, the sample is biased toward females. Since the study does not cover gender issues, the bias is not a problem here. The ages of the informants ranged from 21–61 years old, averaging 34 years old for the environmental activists and 46 years old for the unemployed people. Of the environmental activists, eight had university degrees, five had completed vocational education, and seven were university undergraduates. Of the unemployed, two had university degrees and sixteen had completed elementary school or high school and had acquired vocational education. Thus, on average, the unemployed people were somewhat older and their educational level was lower.

The environmental activists worked in engineering, guiding, taxi driving, and teaching. Among the unemployed people, several occupations were represented; for example, office worker, cleaner, cook, dressmaker, and computer expert. On the other hand, three unemployed participants had no occupation. Five out of eighteen unemployed people could be classified as long-term unemployed since they had been without work for over three years;

the longest uninterrupted period had lasted eight years. The unemployment periods of other interviewees were shorter, ranging from a few weeks up to three years. It was characteristic of most interviewees (eleven out of eighteen) that periods of employment and unemployment had followed each other. At times, they had worked part-time or participated in practical training. The life situation of the environmental activists differed markedly from that of the un-employed informants in that four had a permanent job and five had temporary employment, whereas three were unemployed and one was on maternity leave. Thus, three unemployed persons were, in fact, in a similar position to those interviewed in the fall of 2006. However, for purposes of comparison, the groups were kept separate in the empirical analysis.

Social phenomenology is usually associated with the use of qualitative research methods such as conceptual analysis, linguistic analysis, and the historical-critical method. However, as Tom D. Wilson suggests, the usual di-vision into qualitative and quantitative methods seems confusing in the con-text of social phenomenology; for example, semi-structured interviews may be analyzed to identify underlying concepts and the occurrence of these con-cepts may be counted.[5] Following this idea, the present study employs both qualitative and quantitative methods. The latter refers to the use of descrip-tive statistics in the analysis of source preferences in chapter 5. However, the major emphasis is on qualitative content analysis constantly comparing the articulations of everyday information practices.[6] The emphasis on the quali-tative research strategy is well founded, because the main interest of the study is on the ways in which people construct their everyday information practices to be meaningful. Construction of this kind may be approached by focusing on the ways in which people make their experiences and choices accountable for themselves (and the researcher) in the context of the interview. The ac-counts may concern, for example, the criteria by which information sources are accessed or avoided.

Since the research questions concerning specific information practices dif-fered to some extent, they will be discussed in greater detail in chapters 5–7. First, the everyday practices of information seeking will be discussed (chap-ter 5), followed by the review of information use (chapter 6), and information sharing (chapter 7).

NOTES

1. Elfreda A. Chatman, "Life in a Small World: Applicability of Gratification The-ory to Information-Seeking Behavior," *Journal of the American Society for Informa-tion Science* 42, no. 6 (1991).

2. Reijo Savolainen, "Everyday Life Information Seeking: Approaching Information Seeking in the Context of Way of Life," *Library and Information Science Research* 17, no. 3 (1995).

3. Reijo Savolainen, "The Role of the Internet in Information seeking: Putting the Networked Services in Context," *Information Processing and Management* 35, no. 6 (1999).

4. Reijo Savolainen and Jarkko Kari, "Placing the Internet in Information Source Horizons: A Study of Information Seeking by Internet Users in the Context of Self-Development," *Library and Information Science Research* 26, no. 4 (2004); Reijo Savolainen and Jarkko Kari, "Facing and Bridging Gaps in Web Searching," *Information Processing and Management* 42, no. 2 (2006).

5. Tom D. Wilson, "Alfred Schutz: Phenomenology and Research Methodology for Information Behaviour Research," *The New Review of Information Behaviour Research* 3 (2002), 77–78.

6. Yvonna S. Lincoln and Egon G. Guba, *Naturalistic Inquiry* (Newbury Park, Calif.: Sage, 1985).

Chapter Five

Practices of Everyday-Life Information Seeking

Information seeking is a major component of everyday information practices. A major distinction used in this chapter concerns the primary purpose of the information being sought. On the one hand, we may differentiate the *seeking of orienting information* that can serve the need of monitoring everyday events; information seeking of this type will be discussed first in the present chapter. Then, the discussion will turn to the *seeking of problem-specific information* that may be used for solving individual problems or performing specific tasks. The distinction between orienting and practical information seeking serves analytic ends; in real acts of information seeking the dimensions of orienting and practical information may be closely intertwined. However, the distinction is useful here, because it makes possible a more specified analysis of everyday-life information seeking (ELIS) practices.

SEEKING ORIENTING INFORMATION

The practice of seeking orienting information may be exemplified by daily media habits such as reading the newspaper before leaving for work, listening to radio news while driving home, and watching television news in a routine, sometimes absentminded way in the evening. Media habits constitutive of one's daily rhythms may also be identified in the utilization of less traditional media, as exemplified by the routine ways of checking e-mail. The monitoring of everyday-life events can be conceived of as a generic longtime project that is focused on the care of everyday matters. People engage in continuous overall monitoring of various events occurring in the life world because the conditions of daily activity might not necessarily remain the same.

At least, it is necessary to ascertain that radical changes affecting internal and external conditions of daily routines have not gone unnoticed.

Patrick Wilson discussed this issue by pointing out that every individual has developed a habitual monitoring system that changes with time.[1] The monitoring system depends on the perception of everyday events and conditions of activity, for example, state of health, weather, and enough food on hand. In the model of information-seeking behavior developed by James Krikelas, the seeking of orienting information is understood as information gathering. More specifically, it may be understood as an attempt to continually construct a cognitive environmental map to facilitate the need to cope with uncertainty.[2] Thus, in a broad sense, information gathering serves the need to keep abreast of developments in everyday contexts.

However, the boundary between seeking orienting and problem-specific information may be vague, and both types of information are often sought at the same time. Some dramatic events may sharpen our attention to the media, particularly if our interests are affected, leading to active monitoring of everyday events. For example, one may be planning a journey to some exotic country but radio news reports of the increased risk of an earthquake in that region may put a stop to these plans. Information received from the radio may lead to consulting other information sources, for example, a travel agency because it may be necessary to give up the long-awaited journey. Cases like this exemplify dynamic aspects of seeking orienting information; suddenly, there is no longer a question of merely registering occasional messages but of systematically hunting information on problematic issues. Likewise, one might think that systematic seeking of orienting information helps to solve specific problems; for example, newspapers may occasionally report on how others have survived similar problem situations.

Setting the Scene: Basic Features of Seeking Orienting Information

In information studies, the issues of seeking orienting information have been discussed since the late 1960s, although so far, the number of studies focusing on this topic has been small. Probably the first study in this field was that conducted in Fresno and San Mateo, California, by Edwin Parker and William J. Paisley in 1966. Their report on *Patterns of Adult Information Seeking* characterized the ways in which adults use mass media and interpersonal providers of information in daily information seeking.[3] Interestingly, this pioneering study showed that people live in an "information environment" with many alternative sources. The authors concluded that level of education could explain how people use formal, institutional, and interpersonal information sources. Unsurprisingly, it appeared that the well educated were more likely than others to seek information from the media and public libraries than others.[4]

In a study conducted in Australia, Kirsty Williamson examined the characteristics of ELIS by devoting specific attention to the role of incidental information seeking among older adults.[5] Although there were variations according to topic, the following sources were used most frequently: family members, newspapers, friends, television, printed information, and radio. It appeared, for example, that most respondents had frequent interaction with family members and friends and that this resulted in an exchange of information that was useful for everyday living. Wider personal networks through clubs and voluntary organizations are also included in this category. Although the respondents usually spent longer periods of time watching television than reading newspapers, the latter were more highly regarded as a source of information. Daily papers were considered very useful, but local papers were seen to give outstanding coverage of particular topics (e.g., environmental issues such as recycling and waste disposal). Information from newspapers was more frequently acquired incidentally than purposefully. However, for some topics, purposeful use was substantial, and was related to the availability of certain newspaper sections. For example, the respondents purposefully sought information from the employment sections and financial pages included in most newspapers.[6]

In a comparative study based on interviews with eleven industrial workers and eleven teachers in Tampere, Finland, Reijo Savolainen found that the use of different media was habitual in both groups.[7] Television viewing and newspaper reading were particularly popular in the seeking of orienting information. Both groups stressed the importance of regularly watching television news and teachers especially valued documentaries. Teachers and workers appeared to use this type of media in multiple ways, seeking both serious programs and entertainment. However, particularly among workers, the role of entertainment tended to be emphasized in listening to the radio and watching television. The teachers took a more critical stand toward the supply of light entertainment from radio, television, newspapers, and magazines. Personal interests alone cannot explain this orientation. The requirements of daily work matter here: the role of a teacher requires a systematic monitoring of current affairs in society. However, the occupational tasks of an industrial worker are not necessarily connected with leisure time activities, but the interest in informational pursuits is better explained on the basis of occasional interest in current affairs, not the requirements of daily work per se.

The comparison of the use of sources providing orienting information revealed that newspapers were not necessarily posited as inferior to electronic media because many interviewees ranked newspapers as equally important to

radio and television. They valued the fact that even though newspaper reading might be as ritualistic as watching the evening news on television, when
reading the newspaper one can concentrate more thoroughly on interesting
topics and ignore others. However, some informants felt that they faced difficulties in trying to get the whole picture of daily events. Because information pours incessantly from various channels, they easily feel saturated with
information, only a small fraction of the media supply will be noteworthy.
Despite these problems, the majority felt that they sufficiently monitored
daily events through the media. It seemed that the typical information environment of both groups was perceived as self-evident, built on common unit-
ing elements. In the course of a day, people tended to read the same newspaper in the morning. The majority of people read the regionally dominating
newspaper called *Aamulehti* (the Finnish word means "Morning Paper") and
watched similar television news.[8]

Similar findings were obtained in Bo Reimer's study focusing on media
use practices in Sweden.[9] The empirical study based on questionnaire surveys
conducted in 1986 and 1992 showed, for example, that for most Swedes,
newspapers[10] have become commonplace in everyday life.[11] Reading the local morning paper or the evening paper is practiced on a regular basis. About
80% of the population may be classified as regular daily newspaper readers,
and 70% read the local newspaper at least six days a week. There are many
reasons behind the widespread reading of daily newspapers. A main reason
often put forward has to do with the feeling of attachment and belonging to
the community. The daily newspapers build upon communities and
strengthen them. The newspaper is a sign of belonging, and in order to see
how the community evolves, it is necessary to read a paper on a regular basis. In addition, the local newspaper delivers information necessary to have in
order to participate in everyday-life conversations.

The issues of seeking orienting information acquired new features after the
advent of the Internet. In a study based on a nationwide questionnaire survey
conducted in Finland in 1996 and semi-structured interviews with twenty-
three people in Tampere, Finland in 1997, Savolainen found that at that time,
seeking orienting information through the Internet was somewhat more frequent than searches for problem-specific information.[12] In most cases, people
looked for orienting information from electronic newspapers but sometimes
merely surfed from one link to another and hoped that something relevant
would be found. The seeking of orienting information manifested itself in the
active monitoring of network sources (e.g., reading electronic newspapers).
On the other hand, mailing lists could also be used for this purpose, in that
readers exposed themselves to messages flowing daily through this channel.

There appeared to be not much variation in the ways in which the informants read printed newspapers. They had kept their central position as sources of orienting information. In general, the printed newspaper was perceived to be superior in its coverage and user friendliness. The electronic versions merely complemented them in some respects. In addition, the routine of reading a printed newspaper was very well established and could not be abandoned easily. Reading a newspaper and drinking a cup of coffee in the morning was one of the rituals frequently mentioned in the interviews. In terms of ergonomics, the electronic versions were still problematic. The competitive position of electronic newspapers was also undermined by the fact that corresponding information could be obtained quite easily from alternative media such as radio and television. Because other media already provide news abundantly, the need for a new channel is insignificant. In contrast, the electronic versions may very well serve the needs of foreign newspapers because their availability is often problematic. The study showed that in the late 1990s, the Internet had not been able to replace other media such as telephone, television, radio, and newspaper in information seeking. On the contrary, the network services complemented them both in job-related and non-work contexts.

Finally, in an empirical study based on theme interviews with eighteen people in Tampere in 2001–2002, Reijo Savolainen and Jarkko Kari explored the role of the World Wide Web in ELIS, more specifically, in issues related to personal self-development.[13] Typically, these issues or projects deal with hobbies that may vary considerably, reflecting the personal interests of people and their preferences to allocate free time among competing alternatives. Individual projects focused on topics such as genealogy, high school courses, and the biography and works of Johann Sebastian Bach. In the interviews, the participants were asked to specify how they monitored everyday events in general, that is, not solely related to issues of self-development. The main goal of the study was to achieve a more detailed picture of how people position the Internet as an information source as compared to informal contacts, television, newspapers, libraries, and other sources of information. More generally, the question of how people prioritize information sources was perceived to be central as there are a growing number of sources and channels competing for attention in the everyday world. In the analysis of source preferences, accessibility and quality were seen as relevant criteria.

The study showed that traditional media occupies a strong position in this context.[14] Television, newspapers, and radio were mentioned most often as sources of orienting information, followed by the Internet, other people, magazines, mailing lists, text TV, and the web. These findings confirmed the conclusions of the earlier study by showing that the Internet does not replace traditional media in the field of seeking orienting information.[15] Soo Young Rieh, in a study focusing on web searching at home also found that the Internet did not play a particularly prominent role in seeking orienting information.[16] These findings seem to agree with An Nguyen and Mark Western, who concluded, based on a national survey conducted in Australia in 2003, that there will be no replacement of traditional media such as newspapers and television: they will continue to complement the Internet in serving human beings' needs for orienting information.[17] This suggests that in seeking orienting information, source preferences change quite slowly. Overall, this supports the view that the practices of seeking orienting information tend to be rather conservative; they are heavily dependent on habits and sometimes even ritualistic activities such as reading a printed newspaper in the morning before going to work.

The Setting of the Empirical Study

The findings of the studies reviewed previously provide a useful background for the empirical study of seeking orienting information. The general starting point of the study is the model of everyday information practices discussed in chapter 3. For that purpose, the following research questions are addressed:

- In which ways do the environmental activists and the unemployed people monitor daily events and seek orienting information to help in their everyday projects?
- How do they construct their information source horizons in the context of seeking orienting information?
- By which criteria do they prefer information sources and channels within these horizons?

In the interviews with environmental activists and the unemployed people, the focus was on the criteria by which the informants prefer or avoid information sources in non-work contexts. During the interview, the participants were asked to map the information source horizon with regard to seeking orienting information. More specifically, they were asked to place the sources of orienting information they typically used in order of importance by drawing on the idea of the information source horizon discussed in chapter 3 (cf. figure 3.2). When drawing the maps, the participants were to specify the reasons for the source preferences, more specifically, the criteria by which diverse sources and channels were preferred or seen as peripheral in seeking orienting information. Figure 5.1 provides an illustrative example of the mappings.

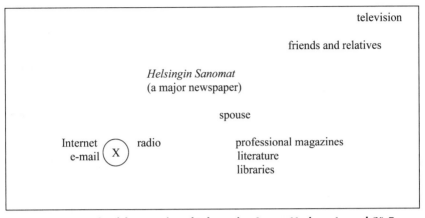

Figure 5.1. Example of the Mapping of Information Source Horizon: Legend (X) Represents the Information Seeker.

Except for one of the unemployed people, all the interviewees were able to draw a map of information source horizons depicting the preferences of orienting information. Although the complexity[18] of the mapping and the articulations of source preferences varied to some extent, most participants were able to explain their source preferences in sufficient detail. In general, the task of plotting information sources on the map was not felt to be particularly difficult although none of the participants had considered these issues before.

The empirical data were analyzed by means of qualitative content analysis by inductively identifying and comparing the articulations of source preferences. The transcribed interview data were compared to the maps of information source horizons in order to check for possible inconsistencies between the articulations and the maps. In addition, the maps were useful in counting the frequency of the information sources and channels mentioned in the interviews.

The maps were also used to identify the zones of the information source horizon. The maps were analyzed by placing the sources identified into concentric zones according to the distance between the information seeker placed at the center of the map and information sources of various types. Since the drawings were fairly well specified and the interview data could be used to support the interpretation, this research task appeared quite unambiguous. For example, in figure 5.1, the Internet, e-mail, and radio were placed in Zone 1, newspaper, spouse, professional magazines, literature, and libraries in Zone 2, and television, friends, and relatives in Zone 3. However, there were a few boundary cases since three informants placed the sources in two groups, that is, significant and peripheral. Some participants located them in four groups, proceeding from the most important sources to the peripheral ones. In the former case, the original grouping was not altered, while in the latter case, the two peripheral groups were combined into one. Thus, in most cases, the analysis of information source horizons is based on the review of information sources visualized in three concentric zones.

The starting point of the empirical analysis is the assumption that objects in the everyday world capture a person's attention through his or her interests (see chapter 3 for details). Because the interest gives a general direction to thinking and provides a horizon for action, the interest also articulates the problems that may be solved by means of thinking and action.[19] Ultimately, interest also implies selection, and thus, preference in the context of seeking orienting information. This means that people are not interested in the whole spectrum of everyday-life events and issues when they monitor them through the media, for example. People tend to direct their major attention to issues concerning "the world within actual reach" or the region of primary interest, as suggested by Alfred Schutz.[20] Less attention is paid to the region of secondary relevance, and the peripheral region of relevance may attract only occasional attention. As suggested, source preferences may be examined in detail in the context of an information source horizon.

The relationships between the two major concepts discussed previously, that is, regions of relevance and information source horizon are illustrated in figure 5.2. (Reprinted with permission from "Information Source Horizons and Source Preferences of Environmental Activists: A Social Phenomenological Approach," *Journal of the American Society for Information Science and Technology*, 2007. Copyright: Wiley Periodicals, Inc.) Since the present study focuses on the ways in which people define their source[21] preferences, a third component, that is, source preference criteria has been added to figure 5.2.

The major idea of the framework illustrated by figure 5.2 is that the information source horizon is constructed by drawing on diverse source preference criteria, and that the definition of these criteria is affected by the regions of relevance of everyday issues. For illustrative purposes, the information source horizon is described in figure 5.2 by referring to three major zones of decreasing importance analogous to the regions of relevance, that is, sources perceived as most significant (Zone 1), somewhat important (Zone 2), and marginal (Zone 3). In the context of information source horizons, references are made to diverse source types such as printed media and networked sources; these types will be discussed in more detail in the context of the empirical study. Finally, figure 5.2 refers to source preference criteria such as content of information that may be used in the construction of information source horizons. The individual source preference criteria mentioned in figure 5.2 originate from the empirical study, and they too will be characterized in detail.

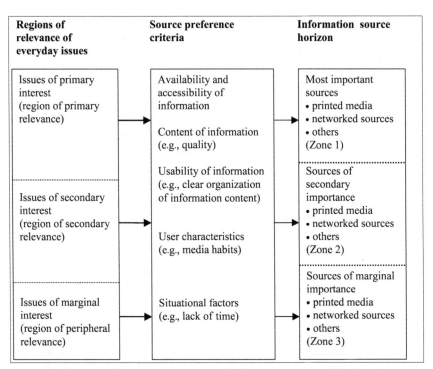

Regions of relevance of everyday issues	Source preference criteria	Information source horizon
Issues of primary interest (region of primary relevance)	Availability and accessibility of information Content of information (e.g., quality)	Most important sources • printed media • networked sources • others (Zone 1)
Issues of secondary interest (region of secondary relevance)	Usability of information (e.g., clear organization of information content) User characteristics (e.g., media habits)	Sources of secondary importance • printed media • networked sources • others (Zone 2)
Issues of marginal interest (region of peripheral relevance)	Situational factors (e.g., lack of time)	Sources of marginal importance • printed media • networked sources • others (Zone 3)

Figure 5.2. Information Source Horizons and Source Preferences in the Context of Seeking Orienting Information.

However, we may analyze this framework further at a general level. As discussed, the regions of relevance indicate the degree to which information about diverse events and issues of the everyday world are perceived as interesting. The region of primary relevance may include issues such as local environmental policy that the person finds most interesting when reading newspapers, for example. There may also be issues of secondary interest like, international politics. Finally, marginally interesting issues may include ice hockey, for example.

The framework suggests that the regions of decreasing relevance provide a general direction for the definition of specific source preference criteria in that these regions motivate information seekers to prefer certain issues or topics to others. Thus, the definition of source preferences is anchored in the regions of relevance at the level of interest, but the regions of relevance in themselves do not directly constitute the information source horizon. It is constructed by drawing on specific source preference criteria that may vary, depending on the intensity of interest. For example, the person interested in environmental protection at the local level, as an everyday project, may prefer newspapers and the Internet, but by different criteria. In the case of the newspaper, he or she may emphasize the criterion of easy availability of a source that broadly discusses issues of local environmental policy, while the preference for a web page may be based on the topicality of the information content. This case exemplifies the way in which two sources may be placed in Zone 1 of the information source horizon.

On the other hand, this person may perceive television news as a source of secondary importance (Zone 2) when seeking information about local environmental policy, because this medium is seldom able to provide a focused view on the recent environmental debate. Finally, he or she may obtain fragmentary information about environmental policy through face-to-face discussion with neighbors, but these sources may be perceived as marginal (Zone 3), due to their superficiality. Issues of secondary and marginal interest such as the directives issued by the European Union or the prospects of the local ice hockey team in the next play-off match may also lead to seeking orienting information. Again, diverse criteria may be used to assess the importance of sources providing information about these issues, and drawing on these criteria; the sources may be placed in the information source horizon.

The previous examples illustrate the diverse ways in which information source horizons may be constructed. Construction could be affected by the interest in an everyday project; or a number of preference criteria may be used when assessing the significance of individual sources to seek information that would help in the pursuit of various projects. The picture is complicated in that these criteria may be emphasized differently with regards to sources of various types.

The framework depicted in figure 5.2 serves as a starting-point in the specification of the empirical research setting. Thus, no attempt will be made to test this framework by systematically exploring the connections between the factors specified in figure 5.2. The main focus will be on the construction of information source horizons, more specifically, the criteria by which diverse information sources and channels are placed in the information source horizon. The issues concerning the regions of relevance are discussed at a general level to provide a background for the questions of source preferences. The regions of relevance are referred to when describing the everyday events and topics most participants were interested in.

To sharpen the focus of the empirical study, a few additional limitations appeared to be necessary. First, no attention was paid to the actual processes of seeking orienting information, for example, the ways in which the participants read or browse newspapers.[22] Thus, the present study draws on the ex post facto accounts of reading newspapers and other everyday information practices given in an interview. Second, the specific strategies of seeking orienting information were not studied. For example, no attention was paid to issues such as to what degree browsing a newspaper or watching TV could be characterized as habitual, opportunistic, goal-oriented, or regular and systematic versus purely random and undirected.[23] Third, the connections between seeking orienting and practical information were not explored (the specific issues of seeking practical information will be discussed later in the present chapter).

Life Situation and Everyday Projects

Most participants characterized their current way of life as relatively well established. They maintained that everyday life tends to go on in a routine way and there are no major problems such as life-threatening illness looming large in the near future. The interviewees found it somewhat difficult to identify everyday projects of particular importance. Among the unemployed people, getting a job was a major and almost self-evident change project. Some of the participants preferred to talk about the opportunities to retire, because their chances of obtaining a permanent job appeared to be slight. Among the environmental activists, the interest in environmental issues such as global warming and climate change was a major pursuit project, although it may also incorporate some elements of change projects. Overall, the interviewees found it easier to talk about concrete projects related to diverse hobbies, such as an interest in bird watching. As noted previously, the issue of monitoring daily events, may be perceived as a generic everyday project because it is shared by most people, regardless of their life situation and the nature of their hobbies. On the other hand, monitoring daily events in the field of environmental protection in particular, may serve as a pursuit project, too.

As expected, the major differentiating factor between the groups was the role of work in everyday life, since almost all the environmental activists had full- or part-time jobs. In addition, a considerable number of activists were full-time students. Among the unemployed people, the alternation of work and leisure did not give rhythm to everyday life. However, the long-term unemployed had adapted themselves to their life situation by changing consumption models and restructuring daily time budgets. Although unemployment continually elicited feelings of frustration and marginalization, and forced them to live frugally, "freedom from work" was seen as positive. There is no need to wake up early in the morning and be stressed by work. On the other hand, the lack of binding daily schedules may cause passivity and undermine the meaning of everyday projects in general.

Predictably, the main hobbies of many environmental activists were related to environmental issues, for example, an interest in bird watching and gardening.

In addition, hobbies such as reading and physical exercise were also mentioned frequently. Seven interviewees may be classified as environmental activists in the literal sense of the word, and these activities formed a major life-project. However, no one sympathized with the militant approach characteristic, for example, of Greenpeace, to put pressure on local decision-making in environmental issues. Seven of the interviewees were very active in the local or regional environmental associations. Others can be characterized as less active members of these associations; sometimes they participated in the meetings or events organized by the associations or read messages distributed through mailing lists. Hobbies such as reading and physical exercise were popular among the unemployed people, too. Hobbies did not differ much among the subgroups. However, the unemployed people appeared to be more interested in handwork such as knitting. Compared to environmental activists, they were less interested in activities such as participating in the activities of various clubs. For some reason, none of the unemployed interviewees indicated an interest in environmental issues.

General Features of Seeking Orienting Information

The interviews revealed that the repertoire of major topics triggering seeking orienting information tends to be fairly constant from year to year. For example, those mainly interested in domestic and local news retain this preference when reading newspapers and watching television news. On the other hand, people who routinely skip sports news rarely become interested in them and change their media habits.

Environmental activists and the unemployed people mentioned a number of different topics they were interested in while reading newspapers and using other sources providing orienting information. Both domestic and international issues were monitored, at least broadly. Predictably, most of the environmental activists were interested in environmental issues and devoted specific attention to them when using the media. Areas of particular interest included, for example, climate change, particularly global warming. Dramatic events like Hurricane Katrina, which caused catastrophic damage in New Orleans in August 2005, were also mentioned in this context. At the local level, issues of town planning were of interest because they are environmentally sensitive. However, some interviewees felt that while environmental issues are significant, many other topics are equally interesting. For example, political debates at local, national, and international level, and questions about women's rights were mentioned in this context.

Many of the unemployed interviewees indicated their interest in news dealing with labor market developments particularly cases when people had been made redundant due to business reorganization. Often, this interest originated from the empathy toward the people who had been laid-off because the interviewees may have encountered similar problems. In both groups, topics related to world politics such as the war in the Middle East elicited interest, although some participants had grown tired with the endless reporting of recurrent conflicts in this region. Again, there was individual variation since some of the interviewees reported skipping the international news sections when reading newspapers. For some reason, many of the interviewees in both groups deliberately avoided sports news when reading newspapers and watching television.

As a whole, the interviewees had not faced insurmountable problems in seeking orienting information. However, many of them had struggled with information overload and faced problems related to the credibility of information; these issues will be discussed in more detail in the context of information use in chapter 6. Some participants also felt that shortage of time tends to constrain information seeking as does tiredness and lack of motivation. The unemployed group included three people who had migrated from Russia. Among them, a major barrier to information seeking appeared to be the lack of access to Russian television channels available through pay television only. These channels often provide information unavailable in Finnish or in other international news programs or documentaries. Among the unemployed in particular, seeking orienting information was hampered by the fact that to save money, many of them did not subscribe to newspapers. Thus, to read the daily newspaper, they would have had to visit the public library. Other problems constraining information seeking and use included the superficiality and political bias of newspaper articles.

Most of the interviewees had established habits of monitoring everyday events through the media. In both groups, newspaper and television were the most popular sources of orienting information. One of the favorite habits appeared to be reading a newspaper at breakfast and watching television news in the evening. However, some preferred to watch television news or access the Internet as a part of their morning ritual to prepare for the day, for example, checking the weather forecast. In this case, the main news was checked on television or on the web and the newspaper was read in the evening. Finally, some of the unemployed people were in the habit of reading the newspaper in the public library or at the local service center for the unemployed.

Media habits tend to be similar from day to day. However, on the weekends, more time tends to be used for newspaper reading in both groups, partly due to the fact that the Sunday issues contain more pages. Some of the environmental activists saw summer vacation, particularly trips abroad, as periods when media habits were changed. These trips provide a morally acceptable opportunity to take a break from everyday media routines, with less worry about what is going on at home. Thus, domestic news may be temporarily relegated to the peripheral region of relevance. Only major international news, such as the reporting of dramatic events may be read during holidays.

Media habits are perceived unquestionably, assuming that they allow the actors to go on as they have done previously and that they "can do it again."[24] The strength of this natural attitude manifested itself when the participants were asked to reflect on the nature of their habits: no one was able to elaborate on them in more detail. As one of the interviewees (E-2)[25] put it: "Perhaps it is a kind of a habit, and if you deviate from it somehow . . . if you don't read the daily newspaper something seems to be lacking and you feel a little bit like standing in the darkness." Another participant (U-2) believed that her way to seek orienting information from the media ". . . may be due to some kind of habit . . . you just read, the rhythm of the day is simply like that."

Except for one participant prone to avoiding information provided by newspapers and television, the interviewees were active and regular users of diverse media when monitoring everyday events. Typically, they spent 1–2 hours per day on these activities. The amount of time ranged from 20 minutes to 5 hours. The exceptionally large amount of 5 hours per day was explained by the fact that the interviewee held a position of trust in the local environmental association and had many duties, including monitoring numerous mailing lists. It appeared that among the participants, reading newspapers took from 20 minutes to 2 hours, and watching TV news and documentaries 1–2 hours. The amount of time spent using the Internet was most difficult to estimate since the same session might include reading e-mail, browsing the web pages of organizations providing news, and seeking problem-specific information.

Most participants felt that the total amount of time used daily for seeking orienting information is reasonable. Thinking of the daily time budget, 2 hours for monitoring everyday events was not seen as something that would distract one's attention from matters of importance.

Information Source Horizons

In the maps of information source horizons, environmental activists mentioned 15 unique sources and the unemployed mentioned 9. Some sources, for example, newspaper and television were referred to several times so that the total number of individual sources mentioned by environmental activists amounted to 104, on average 5 sources per interviewee. Unemployed people mentioned 67 individual sources, that is, on average 3.9 sources per participant. This suggests that the repertoire of sources used in the seeking of orienting information is somewhat broader among the environmental activists. The number of individual sources mentioned by participants varied between 2 and 10. Since some sources such as books, studying, and trade unions were mentioned only 1–2 times, the sources placed in the information horizons were condensed into six major groups, as in an earlier study focusing on the information source horizons of people interested in self-development.[26] In this way, the following source types were identified:

- Human sources[27] (e.g., spouse, friends, and acquaintances)
- Broadcast media (e.g., radio and television)
- Printed media (e.g., newspapers, magazines, newsletters, free newspapers, local leaflets, books, and other printed material)
- Networked sources (e.g., e-mail, mailing lists, World Wide Web)
- Organizational sources (e.g., public libraries and associations)
- Other sources (e.g., courses and the daily living environment)

We can characterize the source preferences in more detail by specifying the ways in which the source types were located in various zones of information source horizons.

Quantitative Overview

To provide background for the qualitative analysis to be discussed, we will first draw an overall quantitative overview of the source preferences. First, we review the preferences of the environmental activists (see table 5.1).

Table 5.1.   Percentage Distribution of Source Types in Zones of Information Source Horizons among Environmental Activists (n = 113)

	Zone 1 (n = 36)	Zone 2 (n = 49)	Zone 3 (n = 28)
Printed media	38.9	35.0	35.7
Networked sources	27.8	17.5	10.7
Broadcast media	19.4	20.0	42.9
Human sources	11.1	17.5	7.1
Organizational sources	0	5.0	0
Other sources	2.8	5.0	3.6
TOTAL	100.0	100.0	100.0

Source: Reijo Savolainen (2007). Reprinted with permission from "Information Source Horizons and Source Preferences of Environmental Activists: A Social Phenomenological Approach," *Journal of the American Society for Information Science and Technology* 58, no. 12 (2007), p. 1715, Copyright: Wiley Periodicals, Inc., 2007.

Printed media occupied a prominent position in all zones. If we count Zone 1 and Zone 2, that is, most important and somewhat important sources, printed media received about 74%, which is the highest share among all sources with regard to Zones 1 and 2. The printed media also included many sources placed in the peripheral zone, for example, free newspapers. The networked sources occupied a fairly prominent position in the information source horizons; they were rarely seen as peripheral. Broadcast media were represented evenly in Zones 1 and 2, but in many cases, these media were located on the periphery. This suggests that television and radio primarily complement printed media and the networked services. In seeking orienting information, human sources were not reported to be particularly important. This is not surprising, since human sources are rarely able to compete with newspapers, television, and the Internet in the dissemination of news. However, human sources may be useful in that they filter and interpret information provided by other sources. Finally, organizational sources such as public libraries appeared to be marginal in seeking orienting information. This is understandable, since these sources are not primarily intended to meet the needs of monitoring everyday events. The source preferences of the unemployed people are summarized in table 5.2.

The unemployed people differed most clearly from the environmental activists in that they strongly preferred broadcast media, in particular, television. If we count Zone 1 and Zone 2, this source type received about 82% of all mentions, while among the environmental activists, the corresponding share of these media was about 38%. On the other hand, the unemployed people often placed broadcast media, particularly radio in the peripheral zone. Printed media were also important for the unemployed people, although the popularity of these media was reduced by the fact that nine out of eighteen interviewees did not subscribe to a newspaper, probably for financial reasons.

Table 5.2. Percentage Distribution of Source Types in Zones of Information Source Horizons among Unemployed People (n = 67)

	Zone 1 (n = 28)	Zone 2 (n = 17)	Zone 3 (n = 22)
Printed media	38.9	35.0	35.7
Broadcast media	46.4	35.3	31.9
Printed media	35.7	35.3	31.9
Networked sources	14.3	5.9	22.7
Human sources	3.6	11.7	4.5
Organizational sources	0	0	4.5
Other sources	0	11.7	4.5
TOTAL	100.0	99.9	100.0

These people read newspapers occasionally, for example, when visiting a friend. Interestingly, the Internet occupied a marginal position in the information source horizons. Like the environmental activists, the unemployed did not favor human sources, organizational sources, or other sources in seeking orienting information.

As a whole, the distribution of source types among environmental activists was similar to that in the earlier study conducted by Savolainen and Kari in that the number of sources mentioned was highest in the intermediate zone, while the participants were more selective about placing sources in Zones 1 and 3.[28] Interestingly, the results of the unemployed informants differed from this in that the number of sources was highest in Zone 1, followed by Zone 3 and Zone 2. This suggests that on average, the unemployed people tend to value the information sources in a more dichotomous way: the sources were perceived as really significant or marginal, while the role of somewhat important sources (Zone 2) was less crucial. This approach is explained by the fact that their repertoire of sources providing orienting information was narrow, on average 3.9 sources. As the range of alternatives is limited, this may easily lead to dichotomous grouping of useful versus marginal sources.

In the following sections, the main findings will be discussed according to the source types identified previously. The environmental activists mentioned 116 individual source preference criteria and the unemployed people mentioned 74 criteria; however, some of them, for example, "habit of use" and "easy availability" were mentioned several times. Based on the qualitative content analysis, the criteria were condensed into five major groups pertaining to:

- Availability and accessibility of information (examples of individual criteria: easily accessible and regularly available)
- Content of information (e.g., reliable, in-depth content, provides superficial information)
- Situational factors of information seeking (e.g., lack of time)
- Usability of information sources and channels (e.g., easy to use, well-organized sections of a newspaper)
- User characteristics (e.g., a long-standing habit: "I'm not used to watching TV").

The preference criteria may be reviewed by zones of information source horizons. The environmental activists will be discussed first (see table 5.3).

The criteria pertaining to the content of information sources were reported to be most important in all zones, followed by criteria dealing with availability and accessibility. The content of information was reported to be particularly important in the intermediate zone. On the other hand, if information

Table 5.3. Source Preference Criteria by Zones of Information Source Horizons among Environmental Activists (n = 118)

	Zone 1 (n = 48)	Zone 2 (n = 38)	Zone 3 (n = 32)
Content of information	39.6	76.3	56.3
Availability and accessibility	27.1	10.5	12.5
User characteristics	16.7	5.3	18.8
Usability of information	16.7	7.9	3.1
Situational factors	0	0	9.3
TOTAL	100.1	100.0	100.0

Source: Reijo Savolainen (2007). Reprinted with permission from "Information Source Horizons and Source Preferences of Environmental Activists: A Social Phenomenological Approach," *Journal of the American Society for Information Science and Technology* 58, no. 12 (2007), p. 1716, Copyright: Wiley Periodicals, Inc., 2007.

sources were judged as peripheral, the problematic content of information was the most central criterion. Availability and accessibility were considered particularly important criteria in Zone 1. The criteria pertaining to usability and user characteristics appeared to be of some significance in Zone 1, while situational factors were mentioned only in the context of the peripheral sources.

We may compare these findings by reviewing the preference criteria identified by the unemployed participants (see table 5.4).

As a whole, the differences between the groups remained fairly insignificant. Among the unemployed people, content of information was also the most important criterion of source preference, but user characteristics such as habit of use were emphasized more strongly than among the environmental activists. Availability and accessibility of information and usability of information had some significance, while situational factors such as the chance to read a newspaper when visiting a friend did not much affect the source preferences.

Table 5.4. Source Preference Criteria by Zones of Information Source Horizons among Unemployed People (n= 78)

	Zone 1 (n = 43)	Zone 2 (n = 19)	Zone 3 (n = 16)
Content of information	37.2	57.9	62.5
User characteristics	25.6	15.8	6.3
Availability and accessibility	20.9	10.5	6.3
Usability of information	16.3	10.5	6.3
Situational factors	0	5.3	18.6
TOTAL	100.0	100.0	100.0

Table 5.5. Source Preference Criteria by Source Type among Environmental Activists
(n = 118)

	Printed (n = 39)	Broadcast (n = 27)	Networked (n = 31)	Human (n = 16)	Organiz. (n = 2)	Other (n = 3)
Content of information	61.5	33.3	48.4	87.5	100.0	66.7
Availability and accessibility	10.3	22.2	32.3	6.3	0	33.3
User characteristics	10.3	33.3	3.2	0	0	0
Usability of information	15.4	3.7	16.1	6.3	0	0
Situational factors	2.5	7.4	0	0	0	0
TOTAL	100.0	99.9	100.0	100.1	100.0	100.0

Source: Reijo Savolainen (2008). Reprinted with permission from "Information Source Horizons and Source Preferences of Environmental Activists: A Social Phenomenological Approach," *Journal of the American Society for Information Science and Technology* 58, no. 12 (2007), p. 1716. Copyright: Wiley Periodicals, Inc., 2007.

Finally, the distribution of the preference criteria by information source types among the environmental activists is presented in table 5.5. Since the findings of the qualitative study will be reported by source type, table 5.5 (as well as table 5.6) provides essential background to the following section of the book.

Preference criteria pertaining to the content of information were mentioned most frequently. This criterion was reported to be particularly important when printed, networked, and human sources were preferred. Criteria pertaining to availability and accessibility were especially valued in the selection of networked sources. Usability of information sources and channels as well as user characteristics were less significant as preference criteria. Somewhat surprisingly, situational factors were referred to very seldom as preference criteria.

Finally, we may compare the same setting among the unemployed interviewees (see table 5.6).

Again, the preferences were similar. Content of information was the most important criterion, independent of source type. It was particularly important in the case of broadcast media because this group favored it in seeking orienting information. Compared to the environmental activists, the unemployed people valued the criteria pertaining to user characteristics somewhat more. The role of availability and accessibility was equally important in both groups. Among the unemployed, usability of information, for example, easy use of a source seemed to be somewhat more important. Ease of use was the criterion for choosing television. Finally, situational factors figured only in the selection of printed media, mainly newspapers.

Table 5.6.   Source Preference Criteria by Source Type among Unemployed People
(n = 78)

	Printed (n = 25)	Broadcast (n = 34)	Networked (n = 13)	Human (n = 1)	Organiz. (n = 2)	Other (n = 3)
Content of information	40.0	44.1	46.1	100.0	100.0	100.0
User characteristics	20.0	20.6	23.1	0	0	0
Availability and accessibility	16.0	14.7	23.1	0	0	0
Usability of information	8.0	20.6	7.7	0	0	0
Situational factors	16.0	0	0	0	0	0
TOTAL	100.0	100.0	100.0	100.0	100.0	100.0

Qualitative Picture

Due to the small sample, the descriptive statistical analysis discussed primarily provides background data for the qualitative analysis. We may enhance the quantitative picture by discussing in more detail how the participants explained their source preference criteria. The following section is based on the qualitative content analysis of the interviews. The findings will be discussed by source type, beginning with printed media, which were reported to be the most important sources overall, and ending with human sources, which were reported to be somewhat marginal in the context of seeking orienting information. Due to the insignificant role given to organizational sources and other sources, they will not be discussed in the qualitative analysis.

Printed Media

In general, the environmental activists felt that newspapers were the most important sources for monitoring everyday events; also, the unemployed people used this media quite extensively. Similar to the findings of earlier studies,[29] the local newspaper *Aamulehti* was the most popular printed medium. Many participants habitually read it in the morning while having breakfast. This habit appeared to be deeply ingrained and sometimes even ritualistic in both groups.

Since the electronic versions of most Finnish newspapers are no longer available free of charge, their use seems to have decreased since the early 2000s. Instead, electronic news is read on the free web sites provided by Finnish television companies. These sources may be checked several times during the day, both at home and at the workplace. One of the participants interested in the political developments in Armenia used the portals of international news services providing hyperlinks to news published in English by local journals. He also used the electronic version of the *New York Times* because in the Finnish media the developments in Armenia were seldom discussed. Since the newspapers provide only a limited amount of news on environmental topics, newsletters, bulletins, and magazines published by environmental associations were regularly used.

As discussed, the criteria pertaining to the content of information were mentioned most frequently when the interviewees expressed a preference for printed media. On the other hand, the interviewees were unable to reflect on the meaning of this preference criterion in more detail. In most cases, the participants were satisfied with overall characterizations such as "provides a broad range of news," "provides news about local events in particular," and "in-depth source." The local newspaper was also preferred because it is widely read in the region of Tampere. Hence, in everyday chatting people may consider it a common source of information: "today, there was a news story about it in *Aamulehti*, did you read it?" In general, these strengths were emphasized in the characterization of newspapers when they were located in Zone 1 of the information source horizons.

Other newspapers also were valued highly if they were able to provide complementary information and offer an alternative viewpoint to the main local newspaper. One of the unemployed informants valued a politically oriented newspaper highly even though it was published only once a week.

> In my view, it is relevant. It focuses on social issues, not entertainment. Even though it is a small paper and seldom discusses local matters, I tend to read it thoroughly. *Aamulehti* and television news do not necessarily provide such a focused view, they tend to ramble around. But this newspaper offers background information and provides arguments to support issues, even though it is done from an alternative perspective and in a slightly different way. (U-7)

One of the criteria for preferring newspapers appeared to be easy availability; this is not surprising, since the newspapers that people subscribed to are delivered early in the morning. The printed newspaper is a medium that can be consulted many times almost anywhere and anytime without opening a network connection.

Long-term reading habits and the ways in which the news is structured into familiar sections were seen as one of the major strengths of newspapers. Many of the interviewees indicated their great dependence on the habit of reading the local newspaper in the morning. An interviewee (U-10) emphasized the importance of this morning ritual; he felt that on the occasions when the newspaper was not delivered to the mailbox "tend to ruin my morning." Another interviewee (E-4) explained her habitual preference by emphasizing the model acquired from family members. More generally, her experiences support the view that one's stock of knowledge is shaped by the recipe-like assumptions of the ways in which information about daily events may be accessed:

> Well, perhaps this is because of some kinds of tradition. In fact, I learned already as a child that a newspaper will appear every day and that they will report what has happened in the world. It is so easy to take the newspaper and read it when needed, and things are discussed there in a routine way. Specific things are located in certain places there and if you want to read an article about a specific topic, it is easy to open the newspaper to find it. There is a kind of visuality there so that you can easily skim the paper and search for the information you are most interested in. (E-4)

In cases when printed media was placed in Zone 2 in the information source horizons, the comments mainly focused on magazines, free circulars, or local newspapers that have been subscribed to in order to complement the news provided by *Aamulehti*. The secondary role given to these media was largely based on the view that there is not enough time to scrutinize the supplementary sources in more detail. One of the interviewees (E-8) lived in a remote rural village where the major newspaper was not delivered before noon. Due to this temporal mismatch, she preferred to read the morning news on the web. Naturally, the newspaper may be browsed in the evening but it would have commanded more attention if it had been available in the morning. Among the unemployed people, one of the major reasons for locating newspapers in the intermediate category was their situational availability. In themselves, newspapers were valued as sources of information, but they were read only if they happened to be freely available in public places, for example, in cafeterias.

Quite often the printed media were only given a peripheral role, corresponding to Zone 3. In particular, afternoon papers were not particularly valued as sources of reliable information. Similarly, free circulars and advertising leaflets were located in the peripheral zone. However, these sources were not always thrown away; they were browsed, at least superficially. One of the participants (E-19) tended "to browse all papers that have been pushed into our mailbox." Among the environmental activists, one of the major reasons for the infrequent use of printed media was lack of time. For example, focused and regular reading of magazines published by environmental associations may be useful, but this would consume a considerable amount of free time. Hence, these media were used occasionally, depending on whether the issues discussed in the articles happened to coincide with current areas of interest.

On the other hand, major newspapers such as *Aamulehti* may also be read selectively; it could also be perceived to be peripheral in the information source horizon. One of the interviewees (E-3) boycotted *Aamulehti* since in her opinion the newspaper is politically biased in sensitive issues of environmental protection. However, she read this newspaper occasionally; her friends used to inform her by calling or e-mailing on days when *Aamulehti* had reported something particularly interesting on environmental issues.

Broadcast Media

Television occupied a significant place in the information source horizons among the unemployed in particular. Again, there appeared to be ritualistic elements in watching TV news at a specific time in the evening. Similar to the findings of an earlier study,[30] radio was not perceived as a medium that primarily meets the needs of orienting information. Listening to the radio may be a secondary activity, and radio news may only be listened to, for example, when driving home or puttering around in the kitchen.

> The radio is on all the time close to me. Radio is good when you monitor events in an intensive way, if you happen to have such needs. If needed, you may prick up your ears when something interesting is broadcast. (E-8)

There were three major criteria in evaluating the strengths of broadcast media: the provision of selected and relatively reliable information, ingrained habits of use, and easy access.

> Perhaps it is simply because it (television) is so easy to put on. In addition, I find it a reliable source, at least compared to net material, even though there may be electronic newspapers available in the net. However, television does not provide just any stuff similar to the net, for example, all kinds of wild speculations about the domestic conspiracy explaining the planes crashing into the *World Trade Center*. Television provides better information because there are people who edit it. (U-12)

> Well, it (television) is so easy to access and understand. I'm used to watching television a lot in the evenings. I tend to be television-bound and no one should disturb me at that time. (U-11)

Even though the dependence on the fixed times of television news broadcasting may constrain information seeking, such time slots also structure it in a positive way because information is provided regularly and the format of news programs tends to be similar. Thus, information seekers may predict what kind of information is usually available and in how much detail the topics will be discussed.

On the other hand, broadcast media were often placed in the intermediate zone, particularly if listening to the radio or watching TV news tends to occur periodically, or if these activities take place simultaneously with another activity, such as, reading a newspaper. Broadcast media were also seen as peripheral sources located in Zone 3. The interviewees may not habitually use this media and consult it only occasionally, for example, TV news may be watched when visiting a friend and the television happens to be on at that time.

Particularly among the environmental activists, television was often seen as a peripheral source, due to problems of information content. The problem was that television news was able to provide only glimpses of complicated events. If the television news program lasts 20 minutes, only a few seconds or minutes may be allocated to discussing a specific event. The reports may therefore remain superficial and there is no time to elaborate on the issue. Documentaries may meet these requirements better but there may be difficulties in identifying these programs; in addition, the time when documentaries are available may be inconvenient for the potential viewer. The marginal importance of television was also explained by referring to its role as a provider of entertaining programs. Overall, among the environmental activists, television was perceived as a less "serious" source of orienting information compared to newspapers, while the unemployed people valued television more due to its easy availability and their ingrained habits of use.

Networked Sources

The significance of the Internet as a channel for orienting information varied to some extent. In general, the environmental activists valued it more strongly than the unemployed people did. Some participants preferred the web to check news in the morning and they also used portals or other networked services to access more detailed information unavailable in the Finnish media. In addition, some participants regularly checked mailing lists to monitor the developments of environmentally sensitive issues, for example, logging that threatens the ecological balance. Information on such issues may be used to mobilize civic action, for example, demonstrations protesting against the logging projects of Finnish forest industry companies. Web pages of organizations such as *Birdlife Finland* (http://www.birdlife.fi/english/index.shtml) were seen as providers of useful information for birdwatchers.

Somewhat unsurprisingly, the major criteria for preferring the Internet concerned the content of information as well as its availability and accessibility. The Internet was preferred due to its exhaustive range of information sources, the option to update information sources at frequent intervals, rapid access to information sources, and the opportunity to obtain more detailed information about current topics. These criteria were common when articulating reasons for placing the networked sources in Zone 1. Interestingly, in both groups, the criteria by which the networked sources were placed in Zone 2 did not essentially differ from those by which sources of this type were located in Zone 1. This suggests that people tend to evaluate the usefulness of the networked sources in dichotomous ways; they are seen as central or peripheral, but seldom as something in-between.

Easy access to the networked sources when working with the computer was one of the preference criteria. One of the unemployed (U-5) did not subscribe to a newspaper, and an integral element of his morning routine appeared to be the checking of news on the web. Another interviewee (E-1) pointed out that seeking orienting information may be incidental, and having a look at the news sites provides an opportunity to take a short break from work.

> The Internet is there at home . . . it tends to be used when working with the computer, if you happen to sit in front of the screen. So, at times you may interrupt your work and your thoughts and look at what's new on the website of the Finnish Broadcasting Corporation or elsewhere. There may be an interesting issue and you just go on and read it. (E-1)

E-mail and mailing lists may be equally important since they provide focused information unavailable from other sources.

> Well, the use of mailing lists is related to issues of environmental protection and environment because there are discussions going on all the time and news that concern my daily work and my activities in associations. So these things are related to my views . . . they (mailing lists) are important because they provide a selection of the most essential issues that I'm monitoring. When in the net you may be present there all the time and look at what is happening, that's why I will draw on it. Primarily, I will search information in the net because I will get the information that I want, so I will not ferret it out from books, for example, in order to read a longer text. In fact, I have noticed that I'm apt to get impatient, to get information quickly. (E-8)

Some informants felt it was difficult to articulate preference criteria when talking about the role of the Internet. Interestingly, when drawing her information source horizons, one of the interviewees (E-17) characterized the Internet as if it were "a kind of an amorphous amoeba" whose importance is difficult to evaluate in more detail. Some websites are quite well known and regularly used, while others are vague. In this context, the participants referred, for example, to pages providing information about local weather conditions when planning a drive in winter.

Only in a few cases were the networked sources placed on the periphery. The low preference was explained by three major reasons. First, the networked sources were seen to be less important, due to an emotionally loaded view of information and communication technology. One of the interviewees (E-7) pointed out that "being advanced in years I tend to dislike technology even though sometimes I have to accept and use it." Another participant (U-7) complained about the ergonomic problems caused by poor quality interfaces. Second, the quality of web material may arouse suspicion, for example, due to web pages that have not been updated for years. Third, the networked sources may be able to provide complementary information only compared to other media such as newspapers and television.

> If it is not possible for me read the newspaper in detail or watch television news and I know some big things have taken place, something of particular interest to me, I will access the net pages of international media. Some of my acquaintances live abroad and I may check what is happening there. For example, these bomb attacks in London . . . one of my acquaintances lives there. So I checked the events taking place there in great detail. (U-1)

Human Sources

Primarily, the human sources were seen to be significant in that they complement information received from newspapers, television, and the Internet. One of the interviewees (U-11) had immigrated to Finland from Russia and unlike her friends, she had no access to the Russian channels available only through pay TV. Therefore, she often called her friends and asked for further information about recent events taking place in her former home country. The personal sources were used occasionally, for example, when running across a friend who was interested in the broadcasts describing how Hurricane Katrina might strike New Orleans. However, in these cases, the personal sources primarily provided opinions about the matter, not brand new information unavailable in the media. Of the informants, personal sources appeared to be most important to the environmental activists. One of them (E-3) characterized herself as a "major node" of the local and regional contact network. She had been active in environmental issues for over fifteen years and was widely known in the Tampere region through interviews in the local media. In cases when there is a risk that "something catastrophic will take place," for example, in town planning, people worried about these matters tend to call her and ask "what to do next?"

More generally, people active in the environmental associations were also seen as useful sources because they may have background information about topical issues that are being brought up for official decision-making. Human sources are also important in that they can provide different opinions. In this context, the participants mentioned, for example, university teachers and other students that may bring fresh arguments to environmental debates in lectures or informal discussions. This dialogue may greatly help to put things into a broader context:

> So, it is important when thinking what's happening in the world in general. My close friends provide an opportunity to ponder these things, to talk about them, and somehow relate them to other issues, to think about where is the world going? My circle of acquaintances includes very different people. For example, my parents live in the countryside, and I try to think how these issues are related to their circumstances there. (E-18)

Naturally, information seeking of this kind presupposes that those sharing information trust each other (cf. chapter 7). On the other hand, the significance of trust for the maintenance of contact networks may be reflected in the fact that some networks are closed and that information will be shared among a chosen few. This viewpoint was exemplified by an interviewee (E-13) describing a case about the protection of a nesting white-backed woodpecker — a rare and timid bird that would be disturbed if a lot of curious people were to rush in to observe it after having read a report in the local newspaper.

In monitoring everyday events, human sources were rarely seen to be that important, and they were often placed in the intermediate zone. Similar to the networked sources, the criteria by which human sources were posited as most significant or second most important did not differ much. The human sources were particularly valued when there was a need to ask for advice or a personal opinion about a current issue.

> Sometimes it happens that I have not read my newspaper in detail or watched television news, and something important may go unnoticed. It may concern the unemployed, for example, forthcoming courses of practical training. In these cases, my acquaintances may bridge such gaps. I think nowadays people have to be terribly alert because there is a constant change going on in society. So you have to be aware of current issues. (U-13)

Similarly, human sources are seen as central when planning a project, for example, drafting a petition to promote environmental protection. People participating in these activities are seen as reliable and it is felt they can be trusted if there is a need to ask and pass on confidential information.

In some cases, the human sources were seen to be rather peripheral. This was explained by the fact they are able to deliver "a kind of occasional information" (E-15) and that information received from them may be "unspecific and dependent on memory" (E-20).

Reflection on Source Preferences

The interviewees were also asked to deliberate the extent to which they perceived their source preferences as self-evident and stable or subject to change. Like the reflection on media habits, this question was considered difficult because the interviewees had not previously contemplated their source preferences in more detail. In the terms of Anthony Giddens, issues such as these tend to belong to the realm of practical consciousness.[31] It consists of all the things which actors know tacitly about how to go on in mundane contexts without being able to give them direct expression.

Many interviewees gave reasons for their preferences by referring to daily routines that are difficult to elaborate on because they "come naturally" or because they form a constitutive part of an established way of living.

> I guess so far I have not had much thought about issues such as why to monitor a specific information source better or in greater detail than before. It is just a fairly instinctive thing for me. (U-1)

> In fact, I have not thought about this matter, things just go that way. It is not a question of making choices, for example, thinking that today I want to read a newspaper and tomorrow I will watch TV news or . . . these things just come in various situations. You just don't think about it. It is a kind of activity to "fill" your life, you just do it, like washing dishes. (E-4)

However, some interviewees were able to deliberate on this question in more detail. Some of them referred to their deeply ingrained habits of media use as a major reason. One of the participants (U-5) believed that source preferences originate from "a learned habit; it refers to the inherent curiosity of human beings who want to know what is happening around them." Interestingly, he pointed out that the source preferences need not necessarily be static. For example, highly dramatic events such as the terrorist attacks in New York on September 11, 2001, may change people's source preferences at least temporarily. We may think, for example, that that information is reported on more quickly by web pages reporting the details of a catastrophe.

The interviewees favoring human sources considered that this preference is natural since the human contact network is felt to be generally more important in everyday activities.

> Well, because I'm a social being. I think we do these things together and that people participating in these issues have been selected through this process. I'm not a lone wolf. In my view, we share the world and we also share responsibility for it. They are great people with moral fiber. (E-3)

Another participant (E-17) thought that the current preference order is largely determined by the tasks and duties originating from being in a key position in an environmental association. Without these duties, her source preferences might be different because the time currently used for scrutinizing newspapers and monitoring mailing lists could be reallocated to reading magazines, for example. This suggests that the source preferences may be altered, even though the changes may be gradual and slow, due to the inherent conservatism characteristic of everyday media habits.

Discussion

The social phenomenological approach provides novel ideas to understanding the practices of seeking orienting information and the construction of information source horizons. The major idea is the interests that structure everyday knowledge into regions of decreasing relevance and that this structuring is also reflected in the ways in which actors assess the importance of these sources. The framework outlined in the study suggests that seeking orienting information is most active in cases where people consult sources providing information about issues that are of primary interest to them. In contrast, information seeking tends to be fragmentary and passive in cases where the sources provide information about marginally interesting issues.

The concept of information source horizons appeared to be a useful methodological construct to specify source preferences. Information source horizons were defined as imaginary fields that indicate the ways in which actors prefer sources that are believed to provide information about everyday issues. On average, printed media (newspapers) and broadcast media (particularly television) were most preferred, followed by networked sources and human sources. Interestingly, there appeared to be differences between the environmental activists and unemployed people in that the former favored printed media and networked sources while the latter preferred broadcast and printed media. In addition, there was individual variation between both groups with regard to preferred sources. Due to the small sample, no statistical evidence can be provided to explain these differences. However, it seems that level of education and levels of income are major factors here, as already found by Edwin Parker and William Paisley.[32] Overall, the environmental activists were better off in this regard. They had better economic resources to subscribe to newspapers and to acquire network connections to the home, while the unemployed could primarily afford television and radio.

The results support the findings of Savolainen[33] and Williamson[34] emphasizing the significance of printed media in seeking orienting information. On the other hand, the order of preference suggests that media habits significantly affect source preferences since the most popular sources, that is, newspapers and television, tend to be used daily, sometimes even in a ritualistic way. Recently, the habitual use of the Internet has increased and it has assumed an established position in people's information source horizons. Overall, the significance of habitualization suggests that seeking orienting information is a spatiotemporally sensitive practice.

The content of information appeared to be the most central criterion of source preference. This finding supports the assumption that topicality is also a crucially important relevance criterion in the context of ELIS. In cases of most important sources (Zone 1) and somewhat important sources (Zone 2), the content of information was emphasized as the primary criterion. The wide range of information provided by various media was valued highly, likewise currency of information. Availability and easy accessibility of information were also seen as important criteria of source preference among the unemployed in particular. On the other hand, usability of information such as clear organization of information content seems to be a less important criterion. Although the criteria pertaining to user characteristics such as ingrained media habits were not particularly referred to as explicit preference criteria, probably due to their self-evident nature, these habits are important in orienting the selection of sources. Situational factors such as lack of time were seldom used as a major criterion in the selection of sources and channels. This suggests that the seeking of orienting information is a relatively well-established practice largely drawing on the regular use of familiar sources.

SEEKING PROBLEM-SPECIFIC INFORMATION

Solving problems or making sense of problematic situations forms a major context for ELIS. This part of the chapter concentrates on the practices of seeking problem-specific information, more specifically, the criteria by which people prefer information sources when solving everyday problems. In the context of the life world, these problems often stem from the pursuit of change or pursuit projects.

Patrick Wilson developed one of the earliest models of ELIS.[35] He proposed a tripartite conception of interest, concern, and caring in order to render comprehensible the intensity and focus of ELIS in various phases of solving everyday problems. In general, the model is based on the assumption that people want to have some control or influence over things that happen in their world.

In Wilson's model, the category of *interest*[36] refers to a general level of orientation toward some issue. Interest may manifest itself as simply as wanting to know how things are going in some areas. What is characteristic of interest is that it does not necessarily imply one's readiness to engage in action to change or control the objects of interest. Interest may be passive or active. In the former case, information is received if it happens to become available. If an interest is active, a person is inclined to find out more about a topic. For example, the topic of diabetes can be approached on the level of an interest. The person may be interested in this topic and occasionally he or she may read a newspaper article discussing the growing number of diabetics among obese people and the ways in which diabetes may be prevented by changing one's eating habits. Because this problem is not seen to be of personal concern, the person, however, may or may not make further attempts to seek out more information about diabetes.

However, if it happens that this same person develops typical symptoms of diabetes, his or her interest turns into *concern*. Concern implies one's readiness to act, to exert control, or influence. Similar to an interest, a concern may be passive, or as Wilson says, "closed," not necessarily causing a person to seek information.[37] In the case of active concern, a person tries to find out more information to make sense of the situation or solve a problem. For example, the person starts to seek information more systematically in order to learn more about the long-term risks of this chronic disease and he or she may consider contacting the doctor. If, in fact, he or she is diagnosed with diabetes, then concern turns to *caring*. The person engages in action in order to change or control the situation. He or she tries to acquire information systematically about the required diet and other issues relevant to coping with diabetes. The process may also go in a reverse direction. With the help of proper medication, the health problems may no longer seem as life threatening, and caring may gradually turn into concern or interest. At the same time, the role of seeking orienting information occupies a more central position compared to acquiring problem-specific information.

According to Wilson, information seeking often results in relative satisfaction rather than absolute satisfaction.[38] Information seekers try to obtain enough information to serve as a basis for decisions and action in areas of concern and enough to satisfy their appetites for information bearing on their interests. If concern is closed and interest passive, people tend to be satisfied with the information they already have and feel no need for a flow of new information at all. If concern is open and an interest active, they will want a satisfactory rather than absolute flow of new information.

Wilson's model provides a rare example of the ways in which the questions of seeking problem-specific information may be approached from the perspective of everyday projects. On the other hand, the number of ELIS studies focusing on issues such as source preference criteria used in seeking problem-specific information has remained low.[39] The present study of context-sensitive source preferences provides a novel viewpoint to understand how people perceive their daily information environments and how they evaluate the usefulness of alternative sources in these contexts.

Compared to seeking orienting information, seeking problem-specific information may be episodic in nature. The processes may have a relatively clear starting-point, for example, finding a fact, and it may also be possible to tell when the problem has reached a solution. However, information seeking of this type may last a fairly long time, depending on the characteristics of the problem or task at hand constitutive of an everyday project, for example, getting a new job. In the case of long-term unemployment, there may be a number of individual problem situations that require seeking information. As noted previously, the boundary between the seeking of orienting and practical information is not necessarily clear. Seeking of problem-specific information may also serve the purposes of monitoring everyday events, for example, the development of job markets in a specific field. Interestingly, the category of "active scanning"[40] proposed by Pamela McKenzie is descriptive in this case since it refers to semi-directed browsing or scanning in likely locations, focusing on specific themes (see chapter 3). Likewise, one might think that the systematic seeking of orienting information helps to solve specific problems because newspapers, for example, may occasionally report how others have survived similar problem situations.

Setting the Scene: Major Findings of Earlier Studies

ELIS studies provide a broad array of empirical findings concerning peoples problem-specific information needs and the ways in which these needs are met by using diverse information sources. In fact, many of the basic issues of ELIS were already identified in the 1970s when extensive surveys were conducted to chart citizen information needs and seeking. Based on a survey conducted in Baltimore, Edward Warner and his colleagues identified almost

9,000 questions or problems faced by residents in everyday contexts. These problems were condensed into broader problem areas indicating daily information needs.[41] The major problem areas included issues pertaining to consumption, health, education, employment, transportation, recreation, financial, and legal matters.

Later ELIS studies of problem-specific information needs have confirmed the heterogeneous nature of everyday information needs.[42] These studies indicate that the major problem areas of everyday life identified by Warner and his colleagues are still valid. This also suggests that the major areas of everyday problems are fairly universal and they tend to change slowly.

The Baltimore study[43] was also pioneering in that it revealed the broad variety of information sources used in ELIS. It appeared, for example, that interpersonal sources such as friends and colleagues were conceived of as the most accessible types of sources. Later surveys have indicated the importance of other sources such as doctors, lawyers, newspapers, magazines, books, companies, and business organizations.[44] Most recent studies have shown the growing importance of the Internet as a source of problem-specific information.[45]

We may return here to my earlier study comparing the information seeking practices of industrial workers and teachers.[46] It appeared that teachers were more active in seeking problem-specific information. The differences became most clearly visible in the review of the information sources used in problem solving. Both workers and teachers preferred informal sources, primarily personal communication, whereas the utilization of organizational sources such as libraries remained surprisingly low. The teachers differed from the workers most markedly regarding the utilization of contact networks. Among their friends, there were people, for example, lawyers and physicians who could be contacted in problematic cases. It also seemed as if the teachers were more determined to contact experts or decision-makers who were not easily available.

In general, the workers were more dependent on information sources that were easily available. The factor of "immediate availability" was quite significant in directing the way they sought out orienting information. This practice is, of course, problematic because the information sources most easily available and accessible may not necessarily be the most optimal in problem solving. The most useful sources, for example, articles focusing on the problem at hand may be "hiding" somewhere in libraries. Seeking and using them requires additional effort, possibly a sufficient command of a foreign language which workers do not necessarily have.[47]

Prior ELIS studies have also demonstrated that despite the growing popularity of the Internet, information seekers have not rejected traditional sources such as doctors or lawyers, but use them both in a complementary way. My empirical study conducted in the mid-1990s revealed that the Internet was used to some extent as a source of problem-specific information.[48] At that time, however, most searches were limited to individual facts or to relatively well defined problem areas, for example, timetables of airlines and prices of various products and services. In addition, networked sources were consulted to obtain health-related information. For example, "net clinics" providing information about pharmaceuticals were consulted. In general, well-established practices of information seeking employing informal contacts and printed sources were preferred over the Internet.[49] If, however, there were positive experiences in using the networked sources, they might be utilized, in particular when there was an urgent task to perform and the traditional ways of information seeking were seen as less functional.

In another study, Savolainen explored the ways in which people make use of an Internet discussion group when seeking information for consumer problems.[50] The study focused on a Finnish newsgroup *sfnet.kuluttajat* (the Finnish word "*kuluttajat*" means "consumers"; henceforth, the newsgroup will be referred to as the Consumer Group). A sample of 100 consecutive threads containing 894 messages posted from November 1999–January 2000 was downloaded for empirical analysis. The messages were analyzed by devoting attention to the ways in which the participants searched for information or responded to questions presented by others. It appeared that a considerable part of the messages sent to the Consumer Group dealt with information needs and information seeking. Altogether, 55% of threads incorporated more or less explicit issues of information seeking. About 10% of the messages contained explicit requests indicating specific information needs. The share is fairly high and compares well with the findings of Yitzhak Berman's study focusing on job-related information seeking.[51] Overall, the information needs articulated in the Consumer Group varied quite a lot, ranging from the penalties for deceptive advertisements to questions on how to compare kilograms and ounces. Consumer rights occupied a central position in information needs: what are the fair practices in marketing and selling products and services and what to do if these rights have been infringed upon?

It is characteristic of newsgroups particularly in non-work contexts that the advice provided by helpers is not always compatible. In particular, the information seeker may be baffled because the expertise of local advisors was challenged. Typical of many discussions on the Internet, the debate remained fragmentary and inconclusive: there was no authoritative "judge" giving "the last word." In the worst case, the information seeker may abandon further attempts to seek information. Alternatively, he or she may go on to consult alternative sources. Thus, conflicting advice may not stop a persistent information seeker but the required information will be sought off the Internet. Problems of information seeking were also encountered in cases where the questions elicited no answers or where they remained incomplete. The topics of discussions varied a lot, thus reflecting the wide spectrum of consumer problems. On the one hand, there were well-focused threads yielding useful advice to information seekers. On the other hand, there was unfocused chatting which rambled from one subtopic to another, with no intentions of information seeking.[52]

These findings suggest that source preferences do not depend solely on the availability of alternative sources—printed or electronic—because the preferences vary according to the specific requirements of the problem. For example, homeless people tend to prefer organizational sources such as social service agency staff to meet information needs related, for example, to childcare.[53] Individuals struggling with problems related to maintaining normal weight may favor sources such as doctors, health magazines, and Internet clinics.[54]

Mostly, the major features of ELIS discussed previously may be condensed into the principles of information seeking proposed by Roma Harris and Patricia Dewdney.[55] Most importantly, these principles suggest that the needs for problem-specific information arise from the situations in which seekers find themselves; any need for help or information is situationally based and dependent on a particular context. People also tend to look for the information that is most accessible, sometimes referred to as the principle of least effort. On the other hand, studies drawing on the ideas of the framework of information use environments proposed by Robert S. Taylor[56] may be used to identify the major starting points of work-related, as well as non-work information seeking. Chun Wei Choo has aptly encapsulated these assumptions by pointing out that:

> the ways in which people view their problems and what they anticipate as resolution constitute a built-in though unconscious means of controlling the amount of information used. Thus, people's perceptions and anticipations indirectly control the breadth and depth of their information search—including the time and effort to spend on searching, where to search, how information encountered is to be filtered, and how much and what kinds of information are required.[57]

Characterizations such as these provide a useful overall picture of the factors triggering the seeking of problem-specific information. However, from the viewpoint of this study, these characterizations are wanting, in that they do not discuss in detail the criteria by which people prefer information sources in these contexts. For example, Ching-chih Chen and Peter Hernon approached the preference criteria in a general way and found that information seekers tend to favor information sources by drawing on criteria such as the accuracy and understandability of information.[58] Overall, Chen and Hernon's findings indicated that in ELIS, people tend to favor familiar sources that have functioned reliably in the past. Savolainen found that in problem-specific information seeking, teachers and industrial workers mainly drew on preference criteria such as availability and accessibility of the information source, as well as the ease of use.[59]

In a recent study, Heidi Julien and David Michels identified two major criteria of source selection in ELIS contexts, that is, ease and speed of use, and value of information.[60] Karen Fisher and her associates drew similar conclusions in a study on information grounds; the participants were asked to explain the reasons for the source or information seeking habit. They identified preference criteria such as "gives reliable information/trustworthy," "quick to contact/access/convenient," "inexpensive," "easy to use or communicate with," and "knows me and understands my needs."[61] However, due to the generality of these research approaches, the source preference criteria of seeking problem-specific information were not discussed in sufficient detail.

The Setting of the Empirical Study

The findings discussed previously provide a useful background for the review of the practices of problem-specific information seeking. They will be elaborated on by devoting attention to source preference criteria, similar to the previous discussion of seeking orienting information. In the study of seeking problem-specific information, the concept of information source horizon is central. In addition, the concept of information pathways will be utilized to specify the picture obtained from the mappings of information source horizons.

The empirical study drew on the model of everyday information practices described in chapter 3. However, in order to address the specific issues characteristic of problem-specific information seeking, the conceptual framework was refined further, as illustrated in figure 5.3. (Reprinted with permission from "Source Preferences in the Context of Seeking Problem-Specific Information," *Information Processing and Management.* Copyright: Elsevier, 2008.)

Figure 5.3 suggests that making sense of the problem or problematic situations triggers the process of information seeking. The specific everyday project driving information seeking is not depicted here. Based on the information requirements of the problem, the information seeker considers the opportunities to access potentially useful information sources in the perceived

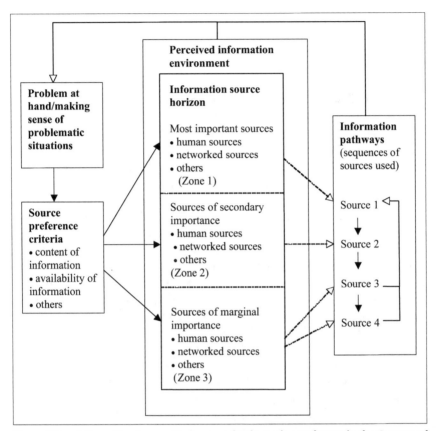

Figure 5.3.   Information Source Horizons and Information Pathways in the Context of Seeking Problem-Specific Information.

information environment. Then, based on diverse source preference criteria, for example, content of information or easy access to an information source, the information seeker places the sources, of which he or she is aware, in order of preference within the information source horizon.

To simplify figure 5.3, only three major preference areas or zones of information source horizon are identified, that is, sources perceived as most significant (Zone 1), somewhat important (Zone 2), and marginal (Zone 3). Naturally, in individual information seeking situations, people may use more than three zones and in some cases, all the information sources could be located in just two zones. In addition, an individual may have no stated preference between two sources, for example, Internet and magazines, and they could equally be accessed within a zone.[62] Both source preference criteria and sources placed in the various zones of the information source horizon will be characterized in more detail in the empirical study following. For the sake of illustration, only two source types (human sources and networked sources), and two preference criteria (content of information and availability of information) are included in figure 5.3.

Finally, figure 5.3 refers to information pathways that stand for the sequences of sources used during the information-seeking process. Again, to simplify, only four sources and four steps constituting the information pathway are included. More specifically, a step denotes here the consultation of an individual source within the pathway, for example, a friend who is asked for help in solving a problem.[63] Thus, a step does not refer to the act required to move from one source to another, for example, walking to the nearest computer terminal to access the Internet after having received a potentially useful URL from a friend. On the other hand, figure 5.3 provides a simplified picture because in real information seeking situations, the number of information sources consulted and thus, the steps constituting the information pathways may vary. However, figure 5.3 suggests that the information seeker consult the sources by following the order of importance depicted on the information source horizon. To begin with, he or she consults Source 1 first, deemed most important and thus located in Zone 1. Then, he or she continues by using Source 2 perceived to be of some importance (placed in Zone 2). Finally, peripheral Sources 3 and 4 placed in Zone 3 may be consulted to obtain additional information.

The dashed lines on the right side of the source sequence suggest that if necessary, the information seeker may return to Source 1, for example, to check some facts from the Internet in more detail. Experiences obtained from the use of these sources may also affect the perception of the problem, and lead to its redefinition, for example, the lowering of an overly ambitious level of problem solving. Specifications such as these may affect the source preference criteria and result in (partial) reconstitution of the information source horizon.

The previous examples illustrate the diverse ways in which information source horizons may be constructed. Figure 5.3 provides a simplified picture since a considerable number of preference criteria may be used when assessing the significance of individual sources. The picture is also simplified because in reality these criteria may be emphasized differently with regards to sources of various types. Thus, the framework depicted in figure 5.3 primarily serves the needs of the specification of the empirical research setting. This means that no attempt will be made to test this framework by systematically exploring the connections between the factors specified in figure 5.3. The main focus will be on the construction of information source horizons, more specifically, the identification of criteria by which diverse information sources are placed on the information source horizon. The information pathways will be discussed on a more general level to complement the analysis of source preferences. In this part of the study, attention will be paid to the order in which the information seekers consult the preferred sources during the problem-solving process.

By drawing on the framework presented in figure 5.3, the following research questions are addressed:

- What kinds of information sources do the environmental activists and the unemployed people include in their information source horizons in the context of seeking problem-specific information?
- According to what criteria do they prefer information sources when constructing their information source horizons in this context?
- What kind of information pathways, that is, sequences of sources do they use when seeking problem-specific information?

Again, to sharpen the focus of the empirical study, a few limitations appeared to be necessary. First, no attention was paid to the actual processes of seeking problem-specific information, for example, the ways in which the participants actually checked specific web pages as the problem-solving process evolved. Thus, the present study draws on ex post facto accounts of the ways in which information sources were selected for seeking problem-specific information. Second, the specific strategies of seeking problem-specific information were not studied. For example, no attention was paid to issues such as the selection of search terms used in web searches. Third, the question of how the use of the preferred sources actually affected source preferences during the problem-solving process was excluded. Closely related to this specification, in the study of information pathways, the sequences of sources were identified at a general level only. Therefore, there was no attempt, for example, to scrutinize the extent to which information sources were revisited as the journey along the information pathway continued.

In the interviews, the participants were encouraged to describe their ways of seeking problem-specific information and to reflect on their source preferences. Again, they were asked to draw the information source horizon, but this time it was combined with the critical incident interview technique developed by John Flanagan.[64] The empirical study conducted by Diane Sonnenwald and her colleagues provided useful ideas on the ways in which this technique may be used in the context of the semi-structured interview.[65]

In the interviews, the participants were encouraged to recall a critical incident, that is, a past situation that had necessitated seeking problem-specific information. The interviewees were free to choose the topics[66] of these incidents.

This strategy was due to the exploratory nature of the present study; its major aim is to draw an overall picture of the source preference criteria used in various situations of everyday problem solving. Two unemployed persons failed to identify a personal topic of critical incident but they discussed a fictitious case of everyday-life problem solving dealing with moving to another city. Unfortunately, two interviewees in both groups failed to discuss any critical incident, real or fictitious. These people were excluded from the analysis, and thus, the present section will draw on the data obtained from eighteen environmental activists and sixteen unemployed persons.

All the interviewees were able to draw the information source horizons. Unfortunately, one of the environmental activists failed to recall the exact order in which he had consulted the information sources, although he specified the source preference criteria. Thus, the analysis of information pathways discussed will draw on the reports of seventeen environmental activists and sixteen unemployed persons. While interviews tend to have shortcomings in that the interviewees are not able to recall all details, it is apparent that the articulations of critical incidents provide reasonably valid data. In the analysis, the transcribed interview data were compared to the maps of information source horizons in order to check for possible discrepancies between the articulations and the maps. In addition, the maps were useful in counting the frequencies of the information sources mentioned in the interviews.

Most interviewees experienced difficulties in recalling an individual problem or tasks related to an everyday project that had specifically required information seeking. However, later, when a problem suitable for the discussion of a critical incident was found, the participants were able to identify the major information sources used in problem solving. They were also able to specify the main criteria of source preferences, as well as the order in which the preferred sources were actually used. In addition, the informants described in detail the context and origin of their problem, as well as the phases of the problem-solving process, and the development of their approach to the problem. At the end of these stories they were asked to specify how well they had succeeded in problem solving so far, or whether the process was still going on.

Thematically, the critical incidents ranged over a broad area, and they primarily dealt with change projects. The incidents concerned the purchase of a computer or computer software (five cases); preparation for a medical operation (three cases); moving (three cases); renovation (three cases); finding new accommodation (two cases); and retirement issues (two cases). Other reports (one case each) concerned such diverse topics as retiring; the acquisition of a medical certificate; childcare (in particular, breast-feeding); finding a support person for a friend; health insurance; organizing a trip, purchase of a digital camera; applying for housing subsidy; looking for a job; seeking a study grant application; and applying for unemployment benefits. Similar to the findings of earlier ELIS studies, the problem areas seem to be fairly heterogeneous; however, consumer issues and health problems were mentioned more frequently than others.[67]

Most of the critical incidents were fairly recent; they had occurred within the last year. Of these cases, five problems were still in the process of being solved at the time of the interviews, while twenty-nine had been solved in some way. Typically, problem solving took 1–2 weeks. This time range was common, particularly in cases dealing with purchasing consumer goods such as computers. On the other hand, problem-solving processes related for example, to health issues tended to last longer, in some cases up to 3–4 years.

Perceptions of the Availability of Useful Information

In order to obtain a picture of the perceived information environment, the interviewees were encouraged to describe the information sources that they would most probably use to solve everyday problems. In general, the answers to this question revealed that the interviewees were aware of a number of alternative potentially useful sources. Overall, they felt that nowadays there is a sufficient variety of information sources available for these problem-solving needs. A number of information sources were mentioned in this context.

> I may consult a doctor in health issues and if I need to purchase something specific, I will go to the town. If I need information about special offers, I check *Aamulehti* and other newspapers. In addition, there are telephone books that I can use. (U-2)

However, most interviewees would first try the Internet to look for problem-specific information. Particularly in cases in which the information is needed quickly, the Internet appeared to be a natural first choice.

> Well, in such situations, the Internet is certainly number one. You may search it by using key words or consulting the web pages of a public authority or a department that functions in the specific field in question. (E-2)

> It is the Internet. Books are pretty good but they tend to provide information that is a little bit out of date. So, usually I get it (information) through the net because somehow I'm dependent on this machine. (U-18)

Another popular way to start information seeking appeared to be calling experts or discussing it with friends or family members.

> The telephone book is important. I have well established contacts, for example, with the health services. So there is no need to ponder it any longer because I know the people to call first. (E-3)

> I have good friends, I can discuss with them and ask for their advice. In addition, I may turn to my son. He is an adult and in my view, he is a smart guy. I seldom use the Internet but my son uses it a lot. It may be because of this that he is a good source of information. (U-15)

Naturally, the strengths of these sources may be combined. The Internet together with telephone book and the Yellow Pages may provide a good start for problem solvers.

> Usually, I start by checking the web pages of the relevant authority or organization. There may be clear information available, at least the telephone numbers of contact persons. If they are unable to provide any information, they can forward my question to another person. Often, public organizations also have paper brochures that provide detailed information but naturally there are exceptions and you have to call them. (U-1)

A few interviewees' also valued public libraries as useful channels providing access to information sources. Often, the library becomes relevant when there is a need for more detailed information that can be relied on in decision-making.

> Well, in addition to the net there are friends, acquaintances, and my family. The library is also an important source for me, particularly if I'm unable to find information in the net. You may find conflicting information there and it is difficult to say which piece of information is reliable. In these cases I tend to go to the library to find a book or two discussing the problematic topic. In that way, the range of conflicting interpretations may be narrowed. (E-4)

Overall, the participants were optimistic about their chances of finding problem-specific information quite easily, thanks to the rich variety of information sources available. They believed that the active seeking of information would result in finding information, eventually. Except for particularly complex issues such as legal problems, information may be obtained with reasonable effort.

> Of course, there may be considerable variation in this respect, depending on the problem at hand. Some topics are fairly easy, for example, health and economic issues, household, and so on. On the other hand, it may be really difficult to find relevant information if you are going to purchase a computer because the ways

in which computer magazines discuss these things tend to differ from the needs of ordinary users or home users. (U-2)

Although it may be quite easy to identify potentially useful sources, finding relevant information may require a lot of effort. For example, finding useful information to support the decision to purchase a computer may be difficult due to the lack of objective information about the qualities of alternative products. Many interviewees emphasized that the selection of information sources is dependent on the nature of the specific issue, for example, the scope or urgency of the problem. Hence, there are no source preferences in a general or abstract sense.

> It (source selection) depends on the problem. The Internet may be a sufficient source in many cases, but if you need more specific information about local issues, you may use sources such as our local net-TV and *Hervannan Sanomat* (a newspaper). You may also ask your friends and acquaintances and so on. (U-17)

Information Source Horizons

The information source horizon maps of the environmental activists included altogether twenty-nine unique sources while the unemployed interviewees mentioned twenty sources. However, since some sources, for example the Internet and friends were referred to several times, the total number of individual sources mentioned by environmental activists amounted to sixty-four, and those mentioned by the unemployed people totaled forty-three. On average, the interviewees in both groups used three sources per individual critical incident. The number of individual sources mentioned by participants varied between one and six.

To compare the empirical findings, the sources placed on the information source horizons were classified into five major groups, as in the study of seeking orienting information discussed previously. However, the original classification of source types was modified slightly in that, broadcast media (radio and television) were omitted because they were not referred to as sources of problem-specific information. The information source horizons may be characterized in more detail by specifying the ways in which the source types were preferred by the environmental activists (see table 5.7).

With regard to the sources placed in Zones 1 and 2, human sources were preferred most strongly, followed by networked sources, printed media, and organizational sources. Networked sources were also perceived as significant, and interestingly, they were never placed in the peripheral zone. Organizational and printed media were not rated as particularly significant: the role of sources of miscellaneous type likewise remained marginal in Zones 1 and 2.

Table 5.7.   Percentage Distribution of Source Types in Zones of Information Source Horizons among Environmental Activists (n = 64)

	Zone 1 (n = 37)	Zone 2 (n = 18)	Zone 3 (n = 9)
Human sources	32.4	27.8	55.6
Networked sources	27.0	22.2	0
Organizational sources	16.2	16.7	11.1
Printed media	10.8	27.8	33.3
Other sources	13.5	5.6	0
TOTAL	99.9	100.1	100.0

Source: Reijo Savolainen (2008). Reprinted with permission from "Source Preferences in the Context of Seeking Problem-Specific Information," *Information Processing and Management* 44, no. 1 (2008), p. 283. Copyright: Elsevier, 2008.

In comparison, we may review the source preferences of the unemployed participants (see table 5.8).

Like the environmental activists, the unemployed informants focused on a few sources that were primarily located in Zone 1. The most striking difference is the strong emphasis placed on the organizational sources among the unemployed people; sources such as the employment agency, the social services office, and the Social Insurance Institution of Finland dominated both Zone 1 and Zone 2. Compared to the environmental activists, human sources such as friends and acquaintances were rated as less central, while networked sources were favored almost equally in both groups. Again, the role of printed sources, as well as sources of miscellaneous kinds appeared to be marginal.

Interestingly, the source preferences differ markedly from those related to seeking of orienting information as discussed previously. In that context, the same participants strongly preferred printed media and broadcast media. Networked sources were also perceived as relatively important in the context of seeking orienting information, but human sources and organizational sources

Table 5.8.   Percentage Distribution of Source Types in Zones of Information Source Horizons among Unemployed People (n = 43)

	Zone 1 (n = 28)	Zone 2 (n = 13)	Zone 3 (n = 2)
Organizational sources	39.3	69.2	0
Networked sources	28.6	7.7	0
Human sources	21.4	7.7	50.0
Printed media	10.7	7.7	50.0
Other sources	0	7.7	0
TOTAL	100.0	100.0	100.0

were deemed marginal. In general, the differing preferences seem to boil down to the expectations concerning the varying capacity of diverse information sources to meet the needs of monitoring everyday events or finding information focused on a specific problem at hand. For example, newspaper articles highly useful in the monitoring of everyday events may only occasionally be able to provide focused information about a specific health problem.

The findings presented in tables 5.7 and 5.8 also differ from the results of an earlier study focusing on the role of the web in ELIS among people interested in personal self-development.[68] In that study, the number of sources mentioned was highest in the intermediate zone, while the participants were more selective in placing sources in Zones 1 and 3. People seeking orienting information seem to have similar preferences. This suggests that people seeking problem-specific information are more focused; they favor relatively few sources that are expected to meet their information needs. Therefore, the number of sources of secondary or marginal importance tends to remain low.

In the following, the main findings will be discussed according to source types as identified previously. First, a quantitative overview of the preference criteria will be provided. Then, the findings will be elaborated on by qualitative content analysis focusing on source types. Because other sources were seldom mentioned, this source type will be excluded from the qualitative analysis.

The environmental activists mentioned sixty-eight individual source preference criteria and the unemployed mentioned fifty-one criteria; however, some of them, "provides reliable information," for example, were mentioned several times. In order to see the forest for the trees, the numerous criteria[69] were collapsed into a four major groups: content of information, availability and accessibility of information, usability of information, and user characteristics. The classification is similar to the grouping used in the analysis of source preferences for orienting information; however, situational factors were excluded because the interviewees did not mention them.

This source preference criteria may be reviewed by zones of information source horizons. We may review first the preference criteria identified by the environmental activists (see table 5.9).

As expected, the interviewees were most motivated to specify the preference criteria of the most important and somewhat important sources (Zones 1 and 2). In contrast, the motivation to consider the preference criteria of marginal sources (Zone 3) appeared to be low. The criteria pertaining to the content of information sources were reported to be most important in all zones, followed by criteria dealing with availability and accessibility. The criteria pertaining to user characteristics and usability of information were referred to

Table 5.9.   Source Preference Criteria by Zones of Information Source Horizons among Environmental Activists (n = 68)

	Zone 1 (n = 39)	Zone 2 (n = 22)	Zone 3 (n = 7)
Content of information	72.0	91.0	85.7
Availability and accessibility	20.5	4.5	14.3
User characteristics	5.1	0	0
Usability of information	2.5	4.5	0
TOTAL	100.1	100.0	100.0

Source: Reijo Savolainen (2008). Reprinted with permission from "Source Preferences in the Context of Seeking Problem-Specific Information," *Information Processing and Management* 44, no. 1 (2008), p. 285. Copyright: Elsevier, 2008.

very seldom. In comparison, we may look at the preference criteria identified by the unemployed participants (see table 5.10).

Since the great majority of sources were placed in Zone 1, it is natural that most preference criteria concerned these. The unemployed people emphasized content of information even more strongly than the environmental activists did. The role of other criteria remained very marginal. Interestingly, in contrast to the environmental activists, the unemployed participants did not refer to criteria pertaining to the usability of information.

To compare the findings presented in tables 5.9 and 5.10 we may note that in the context of seeking orienting information, content of information was clearly the most important preference criterion, although in a less dominant way. Interestingly, the criteria pertaining to availability and accessibility of information and user characteristics such as media habits were emphasized more in the context of seeking orienting information. In this comparative light it becomes even more evident that the selection of sources serving the needs of problem-specific information is primarily driven by expectations and beliefs concerning the information content provided by information sources. Compared to this criterion, other factors seem to be fairly insignificant. These

Table 5.10.   Source Preference Criteria by Zones of Information Source Horizons among Unemployed People (n = 51)

	Zone 1 (n = 37)	Zone 2 (n = 12)	Zone 3 (n = 2)
Content of Information	86.5	75.0	100.0
Availability and Accessibility	10.8	0	0
User Characteristics	2.7	25.0	0
TOTAL	100.0	100.0	100.0

Table 5.11.   Source Preference Criteria by Source Type among Environmental
Activists (n = 68)

	Human *(n = 18)*	*Networked* *(n = 22)*	*Printed* *(n = 11)*	*Organiz.* *(n = 8)*	*Other* *(n = 9)*
Content of					
information	94.4	63.6	90.9	87.5	77.8
Availability and					
accessibility	5.6	27.3	9.1	12.5	0
User					
characteristics	0	4.5	0	0	11.1
Usability of					
information	0	4.5	0	0	11.1
TOTAL	100.0	99.9	100.0	100.0	100.0

Source: Reijo Savolainen (2008). Reprinted with permission from "Source Preferences in the Context of Seeking Problem-Specific Information," *Information Processing and Management* 44, no. 1 (2008), p. 285. Copyright: Elsevier, 2008.

assumptions will be discussed in more detail in the context of the qualitative analysis.

Finally, the distributions of the preference criteria by information source types is presented in tables 5.11 and 5.12. Since the findings of the qualitative study will be reported by source type, these tables provide essential background for the next section.

Again, the criteria pertaining to the content of information were predominant in the selection of sources of all types. Availability and accessibility of information were of some importance in the selection of networked sources, but otherwise criteria other than content of information remained marginal. Overall, table 5.11 suggests that people strongly prefer human and networked sources while seeking problem-specific information and that in the selection of sources of these types, the main focus will be on the potential usefulness of the information content, as well as the availability of networked sources.

The empirical study showed that the preference criteria used by the unemployed interviewees were distributed as shown in table 5.12.

Information sources of various types were predominantly preferred due to criteria pertaining to content of information. Similar to the environmental activists, availability and accessibility of information influenced the selection of human and networked sources among the unemployed people. Interestingly, the preference for organizational sources may also be affected by user habit. Again, due to the small sample, the distribution of source preferences is at best indicative, but it provides useful background for the qualitative analysis to be discussed.

Table 5.12. Source Preference Criteria by Source Type among the Unemployed People (n = 51)

	Human (n = 13)	Networked (n = 15)	Printed (n = 5)	Organiz. (n = 17)	Other (n = 1)
Content of information	84.6	80.0	100.0	82.4	10
Availability and accessibility	15.4	13.3	0	0	0
User characteristics	0	6.7	0	17.6	0
TOTAL	100.0	100.0	100.0	100.0	100.0

Information Pathways

The quantitative picture may be specified further by providing a quantitative overview of the information pathways. Their analysis was based on the mapping of the information source horizons and the specifying comments articulated by the participants in the interviews. As noted above, seventeen out of eighteen environmental activists and sixteen out of eighteen unemployed people were able to specify the order in which they consulted the information sources for the needs of the problem-solving process. Thus, the following analysis will be based on the mappings of information source horizons drawn by thirty-five interviewees.

The sequences of sources were analyzed by devoting attention to the number of steps constituting the information pathway, the order of the use of the preferred sources, and the distribution of these source types with regard to the steps. As specified, a step denotes the consultation of an individual source within the pathway. The "lengths" of the pathways varied between one and five steps. However, only in three cases did the pathway consist of one single step. Similarly, there were only three pathways consisting of five steps (see table 5.13).

Table 5.13. Length of Information Pathways Indicated by the Number of Steps

	Environmental Activists	Unemployed People
1 step	1	2
2 steps	3	5
3 steps	6	3
4 steps	6	4
5 steps	1	2

On average, the pathways used by the unemployed people were somewhat shorter ($1 \times 2 + 2 \times 5 + 3 \times 3 + 4 \times 4 + 5 \times 2/16 = 2.9$ steps), as compared to 3.2 steps by the environmental activists. Thus, an average pathway was comprised of three steps, for example, friend to Internet to magazine. The environmental activists identified fifty-four individual sources and the unemployed identified forty-seven sources that were used in the construction of the pathways. As noted in tables 5.7 and 5.8, most of the sources were those placed in Zone 1 in both groups. Except for only two cases, sources placed in Zone 1 were consulted first, that is, the information pathway was started by drawing on sources deemed most important, while the last steps were taken by consulting sources of lesser importance (Zones 2 and 3). We may also review how the source types were used with regard to various steps. Table 5.14 specifies these findings.

In general, the first step taken in the information pathway tended to draw on the use of the Internet or human sources. Organizational sources such as health centers and employment agencies also figured fairly well in the starting phase. The same applies to the second step: the unemployed in particular relied heavily on organizational sources at this stage. Usually, the first two sources were able to meet the primary information need, and characteristic of the third and fourth steps were that they provided additional or complementary information. In particular, printed sources such as magazines or books served this end. It also seems that if more than three steps are needed to solve a problem, human sources tended to be consulted to obtain feedback about the ways in which the information seeker intends to solve the problem (fourth and fifth steps).

Naturally, due to the small sample of this study, these findings are only indicative, and further research is needed to explore the characteristics of information pathways in more detail. However, the quantitative findings concerning information source horizons and information pathways support each

Table 5.14. Distribution of Steps by Source Types, with Numbers Indicating the Mentions of Various Types of Sources (E = Environmental Activists, U = Unemployed People)

	Human	Networked	Printed	Organizational	Other	TOTAL
Step	E/U	E/U	E/U	E/U	E/U	E/U
1	6/6	8/6	1/2	5/2	1/0	21/16
2	5/2	4/3	1/1	5/10	1/0	16/16
3	2/1	1/3	4/1	4/3	2/1	13/9
4	4/0	1/1	1/1	1/3	0/0	7/5
5	1/2	0/0	0/0	0/0	0/0	1/2

other in that both demonstrate the significant role of human sources, organizational sources, and the Internet in problem-specific information seeking.

Qualitative Picture of Source Preferences

We may enhance the quantitative review by discussing in more detail how the participants explained their source preference criteria. The following review is based on the qualitative content analysis of the interviews. The findings will be discussed by source type, beginning with human sources and ending with organizational sources.

Human Sources

The quantitative review indicated that the environmental activists favored human sources most strongly when seeking problem-specific information. These sources were significant for the unemployed, too. In both groups, human sources were predominantly placed in Zone 1 or 2, and almost without exception, the human sources were preferred by referring to criteria pertaining to the content of information.

In cases where human sources were preferred most strongly, they were praised for their capacity to provide filtered and experience-based information about the problem. Thus, people that have solved similar problems before are particularly useful sources of information.

> I got information from my pals, based on their experiences. They were able to put the promises given by computer magazines on a reasonable scale. At least I felt that hardware that was ranked high in computer magazines was two times more expensive than hardware that my pals found equally as good. Computer magazines tend to glamorize information technology, but from the perspective of the experiences of my pals and my experiences, too, this glorification is not necessarily well founded. (E-2)

Human sources were also favored since they may provide easy and quick access to information and clarify complicated issues in an interactive way since they may provide immediate feedback.

> It is important that someone recently retired can share truthful information about everyday issues related to it. Then you can discuss with people that are going to retire soon. You can compare experiences and the problems they have faced. I may consult these people because of my laziness. When you try to seek information elsewhere, it demands patience. (E-7)

Other people, for example colleagues, were also valued as sources of ideas. One of the interviewees had pondered the opportunities to take a leave of absence from work, at least for a while, and try an alternative way of life. In her case, a human source appeared to be very central in supporting the final decision.

> I had worked there several years and it (work) grew worse and worse all the time. One of my work mates said that "hey, have you ever followed the recent debate on the legislative reform related to unemployment issues? You seem to belong to the last age group that may benefit from the current law." Then I went on to check the law and thought what if? Well, it was her idea, it stemmed from that. She had heard about it from the media. I would never have been able to find that by myself . . . you may leave work. It was a good decision. She just gave me a hint about this opportunity. (E-16)

In some cases, problem-specific information was sought collaboratively from human sources; McKenzie refers to this mode of ELIS as "information seeking by proxy."[70] Other people aware of the information need of a person may help him or her, for example, by monitoring newspapers and other media, and letting the person in question know if something relevant has been found. A university student who lived in a neighboring city at the time she was looking for accommodation reported this practice. In this case, information seeking by proxy greatly helped her problem solving.

> My friends living in Tampere checked, for example, the University bulletin board because sometimes there are announcements about flats to rent. (E-6)

Although human sources occupy the central position in seeking problem-specific information, they may provide opinions or interpretations that are not necessarily useful. An interviewee asking for his friends' opinion before making the final decision to purchase a laptop computer exemplified this problem.

> In a way, it was natural for me to ask about their experiences in these matters. Anyway, it came as a surprise to me how strongly some guys commented on the technical details, for example, saying directly "don't be taken in" or "don't believe that." I felt that was rather frightening. (E-2)

In a few cases, the human sources were placed in the peripheral zone of the information source horizons. This was because the most important information for decision-making was obtained from other sources, for example, the Internet or special magazines. Therefore, human sources were used to support a decision that was already made. This approach was particularly characteristic of purchase decisions. One of the participants reported on his way of deciding on purchasing a computer.

> Then, I finally had two or three candidates (computers) there. One day, once again I talked with my acquaintances about it and said, well, I have considered these three, what would you say? (E-1)

The opinions provided by other people may affect the final decision, in particular if their arguments are based on actual experiences of using computers of similar kinds. However, human sources seem to be preferred more markedly in cases where they provide a strong idea to launch a major project, for example, to abandon work. If the decision has already been made, for example, to purchase the most powerful computer available in a local shop, despite its high price, critical information obtained from human sources was valued less because other people's opinions may provide only complementary information that will not change the decision.

Networked Sources

The Internet, though mentioned less frequently as a source of problem-specific information, occupied a significant position on the information source horizons. Similar to human sources, the participants tended to place the Internet in Zones 1 or 2; interestingly, no one located this source in the peripheral zone.

In the case of the networked sources, too, content of information, as well as its availability and accessibility were emphasized as preference criteria. In an almost self-evident manner, the Internet was conceived of as an enormous and easily accessible repository of facts and opinions, that enabled rapid information seeking. Although in recent years, the Internet has become a mundane source of information and it has lost much of its novel charm, some participants still were enthusiastic about the potential of the networked sources.[71]

> The Internet comes first because it is the easiest (source) and because it contains most of all information. When you get a major idea at home and you have to find out something more about it, there you have the Internet. It is just how to hit the right search words in there . . . then it (information) will come from there. (E-4)

> My daughter said to me "Hey mum, why have you not checked the Internet! Have a look at it, you will find that information there." At that time I realized how useful the net can be. It is clear that you will get the most reliable information there, unambiguous facts and rapidly. Had I instead asked my friends to

make a guess about this issue, I'm afraid I would have got not much because they may provide conflicting opinions. (U-8)

The Internet was also preferred due to positive use experiences, particularly in cases in which the information need was well defined and a few facts would meet it rapidly. An interviewee described his way of identifying a favorite restaurant to a visitor.

In fact, I already knew how to do it because I had solved a prior problem in a similar way. I just took Google and put "Tampere restaurants" there and found fairly soon the *Huviopas.net* [Entertainment Guide.net]. I knew this way and it worked very well. (U-12)

In the construction of source preference for the Internet, references were not only made to the actual strengths of the networked sources such as extensive and rapidly updated information content, but these strengths were further emphasized by discussing the weakness of "static" traditional sources such as printed newspapers. The following quote illustrates the comparative approach. The lengthy excerpt is taken from a critical incident dealing with the search for a student apartment.

Naturally, I started with the Internet, because there is information about organizations providing student housing, their websites and information about the rented flats provided by the town. At that time I lived in Jyväskylä. There I checked the various announcements related to "looking for accommodation." People insert announcements on the net, and you have to check them every day. If there is an announcement, and someone gets interested in it, it may take only an hour or two, and that flat has gone to someone. So, you have to be quick. In addition, there may be more announcements about flats for rent than in newspapers. The problem with the newspaper announcements is that they tend to the useful only if you live in the locality where you are looking for housing. In addition, these announcements may contain no floor plans and so you may never be sure whether the flat will be OK. (E-6)

Another major reason for the preference of networked sources is the opportunity to make comparisons across information sources and conduct specifying searches as the problem-solving process evolves. These strengths of the Internet may become evident, for example, when planning a move to another city.

It (the Internet) was terrific in information seeking. I even managed to find out the price differences between companies providing moving services. I also found information that may be used to calculate whether it is more economical to move our current pieces of furniture or to purchase new ones in the new location. (U-18)

The Internet was also valued because it may provide an interactive forum to support decision-making. For example, an individual comparing the quality/ price relationships may benefit from the feedback provided by people who have recently purchased computers. The Internet was also preferred as a source providing access to alternative viewpoints. One of the participants (E-19) had consulted a discussion group focused on childcare in order to support her arguments when debating with health professionals about whether breast-feeding would be harmful to a baby's teeth. She believed that breast-feeding mothers sharing their recent experiences in web forums might be more credible sources than the health professionals working in child health clinics. Thus, the Internet can be used as a supplementary source of information that helps to challenge the authoritative interpretations offered by professionals.

However, the networked sources were also criticized in cases where they were located in the group of information sources of some importance (Zone 2). In these cases, the seeking of information had required considerable effort. The varying level of quality of information available in electronic discussion groups was sometimes perceived as frustrating.

Organizational Sources

Organizational sources were preferred more markedly among the unemployed people than the environmental activists. This preference reflects more generally their specific life situation of being unemployed: they were more dependent on the services of unemployment agencies and social welfare offices, for example. On the other hand, many of these people were fairly critical when they assessed the usefulness of organizational sources of these kinds; we discuss this issue in more detail later on.

Almost without exception, the information content was the primary preference criterion in both groups. In contrast to other source types, organizational sources were mainly chosen because in practice there were no alternatives to them. For example, solving certain health problems is often difficult without consulting professionals such as doctors or dentists. Similarly, an unemployed person has no choice but to contact an unemployment agency in order to obtain information concerning his or her unemployment benefits. Interestingly, the interviewees were not willing to explain their preferences for organizational sources such as these, probably because the source preferences are "forced."

One of the interviewees (E-5) preparing himself for a major dental operation, first contacted the student health care service by pointing out that this source was "a kind of automatic choice." Another participant planning a trip to Mexico needed a vaccination, and her choice also appeared to be obvious.

> Well, because I'm studying at this university, it came first to my mind to contact the Student Health Care Service. (E-17)

Organizational sources were also preferred due to their expertise. For example, computer shops may provide useful information that helps in the decision-making.

> Well, it was a shop with expertise in this field. I just went there and described the properties of the new computer I needed. I also specified the price level and asked them to recommend some alternatives. (U-13)

One of the interviewees preparing herself for medical treatment was interested in learning more about the forthcoming operation. She had first consulted the Internet, but noticed that more specific information was needed. In this phase of information seeking, an organizational source, that is, the public library appeared to be particularly useful.

> In fact, I was not able to see these things exactly. So, I thought that the library might even provide Finnish literature on this topic. I knew that there are experts in this field in Finland and that they have written books in Finnish. Then I walked to the library, and the book was there. In fact, I soon realized that I have to go to the library because the Internet appeared to be insufficient. This was because I had to consider what kind of knowledge I could trust. In a way, the Internet searches conditioned me to seek additional information from the library, because I thought I might find more specific information there. On the other hand, my knowledge appeared to be insufficient and I was no longer able to filter the essential information found in the Internet. (E-4)

As this example suggests, organizational sources may occupy a significant position in the information source horizon although they are not necessarily consulted first. Particularly in cases where the problems are complicated, the Internet may be able to provide "first aid" only. Organizational sources such as health centers tend to be associated with cognitive authority, and libraries are also believed to give access to filtered high quality information. On the other hand, the cognitive authority of organizational sources like child health centers may also be challenged by drawing on networked sources, as exemplified by the case of breast-feeding discussed previously. This suggests that ultimately information sources are not perceived as useful per se, but their usefulness is judged from the perspective of the requirements of the problem in question.

Printed Media

It was characteristic of the role of printed media that they were almost equally placed in various zones of information source horizons. This suggests that printed sources such as books and magazines can also be used to supplement information received from other human or networked sources. The content of information was also perceived as a primary preference criterion.

Printed media were mainly favored because they provide facts for example, about new products and services available on the market. One of the interviewees (E-10) had obtained a major idea from a newspaper advertisement when considering the purchase of a laptop computer. Another interviewee (E-1) praised the usefulness of computer magazines since they may provide an overview of the products available.

> I favored the computer magazines. One reason for this is that our employee subscribes to them. So, I browsed them at the workplace, not systematically, but anyway. I just looked whether there were comparisons of various computers. In that way, I succeeded in getting "onto the scene" to know what is available, what kind of computers, what kind of prices, and so on. The process started that way and I began to think what kind of features I would need in my computer. In fact, I had kept my eyes open even before. For example, when visiting my friends, I used to have a look at computer magazines if they happened to be available there. (E-1)

This example suggests that the seeking of job-related information at the workplace may also serve the seeking of non-work information. Similarly, seeking orienting and problem-specific information may intertwine. Further, information may be found by chance. Naturally, this may be the case when using human and networked sources, too.

Printed media, particularly newspapers and magazines were also valued as sources of supplementary information when the problem solving continued. As the review of the information pathways indicated, information seeking often began by consulting human and networked sources, and the printed media was used to obtain additional information. As discussed previously, the Internet may be the most effective source, for example, for students looking for rooms to rent, since information can be sought and shared rapidly in an interactive way. However, not all websites serving these needs are necessarily available free of charge, and in this case, the information seeker may prefer printed newspapers freely accessible in public libraries. One of the participants (E-15) preferred newspapers since they occasionally provided useful information about renovations—a fairly expensive and longtime project for her family. In this case, too, seeking orienting information on renovation projects more generally, and seeking problem-specific information about the availability of, for example, building materials intertwined. Another interviewee planning to buy a television set had browsed magazines to find additional information.

> They were supporting media only. I read them in the public library, primarily *Tekniikan Maailma* [a Finnish magazine called *World of Technology*]. I don't subscribe to them, I cannot afford such magazines. However, because I had time to visit the library, I sometimes browsed them. (U-10)

Printed media were also placed in the peripheral zone of information source horizons because these media were primarily perceived as entertaining and only marginally useful. One of the interviewees (E-5) mentioned a magazine reporting on a major dental operation—similar to what he was preparing for at the time. Though interesting in itself, the article was not able to provide any new facts that compared to information received from other sources. However, such articles may be valued since they provide emotional support and thus motivate problem solving.

Barriers to Seeking Problem-Specific Information: The Case of Organizational Sources

Information overload was seen as less of a barrier to seeking problem-specific information than in seeking orienting information (the issues of information overload will be discussed in chapter 6). As in seeking orienting information, there were problems related to the credibility of the information; these issues will also be looked at in chapter 6. Here we focus on the barriers characteristic of seeking problem-specific information from organizational sources in particular because the interviewees perceived these barriers to be the most stressful.

One of the major problems identified by both groups was identifying and accessing relevant human sources in public sector organizations such as employment agencies, hospitals, and the Social Insurance Institution of Finland. These organizations have informative websites but information seekers unfamiliar with the bureaucracy may easily get lost when trying to find the relevant person capable of providing an answer to a specific question. Often, information seeking was hampered by the fact that public officials tend to focus on their own narrow specialty. Thus, they do not necessarily know who can provide the answer needed for the issue at hand. We may exemplify this bureaucratic problem by a rare case related to seeking unemployment benefits for one single day.

In itself, the website of the unemployment fund provides unambiguous guidelines but anyway, I had to call the fund and ask for further information. As a whole, I think I had to consult too many people to find out how to proceed. I then called the employment agency and of course, they said "please, call the unemployment fund." People there in turn told me that "you have to contact the employment agency." So, I had to ask the same questions in different places and go back and forth. Finally, it appeared that none of them knew who was in charge of this specific issue. Of course, when filling in bureaucratic forms you have to read them several times and scrutinize the questions presented there. (U-1)

Similar problems caused by narrow specialties may be encountered in hospitals, too. One of the interviewees preparing himself for a dental operation had asked the doctor and nurses whether there would be any negative side effects arising from acupuncture treatments before the operation. To his surprise, the medical experts were unable to provide any clear answer. To be on the safe side, he also consulted an acupuncture clinic, and finally they recommended that in order to avoid potential side effects, no treatment should be taken before the dental operation.

Another major problem related to seeking information from organizational sources was the slowness of bureaucratic processes. For example, in some cases, it may take several weeks for the social welfare office to make a decision concerning an individual's application for social benefits. Again, information seeking may be complicated if one has to consult other public service organizations to find answers to his or her specific problem.

Well, I think there is no lack of information sources, but the difficult question is how these sources are able to respond to people's problems, I mean an individual problem and its solution? There are different viewpoints conflicting here. On the one hand, there is the official problem-solving machinery, mechanism, bureaucracy, whatever you may call it. Even though the problem-solvers are professional helpers, this question remains. (E-18)

Finally, information seeking from organizational sources may also be hampered by extra financial costs originating from waiting on the telephone.

For example, when contacting the Social Insurance Institution of Finland, hospitals, and dentists, you have to wait on the telephone and it is really expensive. It is like a meter ticking all the time. In some places, the office hours for telephone consultation are limited, for example, 30 minutes twice a week to call the doctor who may have several hundred patients. (U-5)

As these examples suggest, seeking information from organizational sources may be hampered by the narrow specialties characteristic of bureaucracy.

These problems may stem from insufficient cooperation between organizations and a lack of human resources. These problems are often emphasized by the fact that there are no real alternatives to the organizational information sources, particularly if they are authorized by law.

Discussion

The mapping of information source horizons and information pathways, combined with the critical incident technique provides a useful way to identify source preferences in the context of seeking problem-specific information. In ELIS studies so far, the source preferences have not been discussed in detail in this context.

The study revealed that characteristic of the practice of seeking problem-specific information is the high preference given to human, networked, and organizational sources. Printed media also figure in the information source horizons, but less importantly. The content of information appeared to be the main criterion of source preference in the case of all source types. Availability and accessibility of information are of some importance, while selecting sources was deemed most important. The role of other preference criteria, that is, usability of information and user characteristics remained marginal. Somewhat surprisingly, situational factors such as lack of time were not referred to as criteria used in source selection. This may be due in part to the limitations of the critical incident technique: the interviewees were no longer able to recall the situational details of the information-seeking process, even though it had occurred quite recently.

The analysis of the information pathways complemented the review of the information source horizons. The findings suggest that in most cases people use three or four information sources when seeking problem-specific information and that they tend to start the information-seeking process by consulting networked and human sources. If more sources are needed, information seekers are likely to next try printed sources such as magazines or to contact organizational sources by telephone or visiting. The nature of the problem, for example, its urgency, may significantly direct the first choice in individual cases. This may be the case particularly when the individual faces health problems. In less acute cases, however, the most obvious organizational sources such as doctors are not necessarily consulted first, but preliminary information may be sought from the Internet.[72] Earlier use experiences are also important here, because people tend to use sources that have proved useful while solving similar problems. However, several factors may hamper the seeking of problem-specific information. In addition to information overload, problems related to the credibility of information sources, bureaucracy, and lack of competent human resources in public service organizations may complicate or slow down information seeking.

Overall, the findings confirm the results of earlier studies suggesting that health and consumption related issues tend to trigger most processes of problem-specific information seeking in everyday contexts.[73] On the other hand, the varying topics of the critical incidents reported in the interviews support the view that everyday-life information needs are heterogeneous.[74] Further, the study confirmed the findings about the growing importance of networked sources in ELIS.[75] The findings also support the view that even though human and networked sources are preferred most strongly in problem-specific information seeking, information sources tend to be used in a complementary way.[76]

The findings also specify the picture of source preference criteria yielded by earlier studies. Similar to the studies conducted by Julien and Michels,[77] and Fisher and her colleagues[78] the findings emphasize the significance of the content of information, as well as availability and accessibility of information. The findings of the present study emphasize more strongly the significance of the content of information, as compared to availability and accessibility. This difference becomes even more clear if we review the major principles of information seeking proposed by Harris and Dewdney. They suggested, among others, that "people tend to seek information that is most accessible," thus echoing the significance of the principle of least effort.[79] Currently, these factors seem to be less important, due to the availability and accessibility of networked sources at the workplace, as well as at home. In many cases, easy availability and accessibility may be taken as self-evident, and when considering preference criteria, the focus lies on the content of information. Interestingly, these notions are in line with the findings of studies showing that topicality is the most important relevance criterion in information seeking.[80]

NOTES

1. Patrick Wilson, *Public Knowledge, Private Ignorance: Toward a Library and Information Policy* (Westport, Conn.: Greenwood Press, 1977), 36–37.

2. James Krikelas, "Information-Seeking Behavior: Patterns and Concepts," *Drexel Library Quarterly* 19, no. 6 (1983), 9.

3. Edwin B. Parker and William J. Paisley, *Patterns of Adult Information Seeking* (Stanford, Calif.: Stanford University, Institute for Communication Research, 1966).

4. Parker and Paisley, *Patterns of Adult Information Seeking*.

5. Kirsty Williamson, "Discovered by Chance: The Role of Incidental Information Acquisition in an Ecological Model of Information Use," *Library and Information Science Research* 20, no. 1 (1998).

6. Williamson, "Discovered by Chance," 29–33.

7. Reijo Savolainen, "Everyday Life Information Seeking: Approaching Information Seeking in the Context of Way of Life," *Library and Information Science Research* 17, no. 3 (1995).

8. Savolainen, "Everyday Life Information Seeking."

9. Bo Reimer, *The Most Common of Practices: On Mass Media Use in Late Modernity* (Stockholm: Almqvist & Wiksell International, 1994).

10. Erkki Hujanen, *Lukijakunnan rajamailla: Sanomalehden muuttuvat merkitykset arjessa* [On the Fringes of Readership: The Changing Meanings of Newspaper in Everyday Life] (Jyväskylä, Finland: University of Jyväskylä, 2007), 25, 125. http://julkaisut.jyu.fi/?id=978-951-39-2730-1 (10 May 2007). [The regular subscription to newspapers is particularly characteristic of Finnish, Norwegian, and Swedish people. In the region of the European Union (EU) in 2005, the circulation of newspapers published 4–7 times a week was highest in Finland, that is, 522 items per 1,000 inhabitants. Sweden occupied second place (489 items). Other EU countries lagged behind, the United Kingdom (331), Germany (313), and the Netherlands (302), to mention a few. In the Scandinavian countries, about 70% of all newspapers are delivered to the home, while in Southern Europe the share is only 10%. On average, however, the circulation of printed newspapers began dropping in Finland in the early 1990s. This trend may be explained by such factors as people's changing ways of life (e.g., the hectic pace); growing interest in the entertainment media, particularly television; easy access to free news material available on the Internet; and the availability of free papers in public places such as subway stations. This suggests that although newspapers still occupy a central place in the daily information world, it is possible that subscribed newspapers no longer play an obvious part in people's lives and daily routines as it did in the early 1990s, for example.]

11. Reimer, *The Most Common of Practices*, 133–34.

12. Reijo Savolainen, "The Role of the Internet in Information Seeking: Putting the Networked Services in Context," *Information Processing and Management* 35, no. 6 (1999); Reijo Savolainen, "Seeking and Using Information from the Internet: The Context of Non-Work Use," in *Exploring the Contexts of Information Behaviour*, eds. Tom D. Wilson and David K. Allen (London: Taylor Graham, 1999).

13. Reijo Savolainen and Jarkko Kari, "Placing the Internet in Information Source Horizons: A Study of Information Seeking by Internet Users in the Context of Self-Development," *Library and Information Science Research* 26, no. 4 (2004).

14. Savolainen and Kari, "Placing the Internet."

15. Savolainen, "The Role of the Internet."

16. Soo Young Rieh, "On the Web at Home: Information Seeking and Web Searching in the Home Environment," *Journal of the American Society for Information Science and Technology* 55, no. 8 (2004), 747–49.

17. An Nguyen and Mark Western, "The Complementary Relationship between the Internet and Traditional Mass Media: The Case of Online News and Information," *Information Research* 11, no. 3 (2006). http://InformationR.net/ir/11-3/paper259.html (10 May 2007).

18. Alfred Schutz, *Reflections on the Problem of Relevance*, ed. Richard M. Zaner (New Haven, Conn.: Yale University Press, 1970), 45–52; Kwong Bor Ng, "Towards a Theoretical Framework for Understanding the Relationship between Situated Action and Planned Action Models of Behavior in Information Retrieval Contexts: Contributions from Phenomenology," *Information Processing and Management* 38, no. 5 (2002), 617. [The validity of the information source mappings depends on how exactly the participants were able to describe their typical preferred information sources. Schutz distinguishes two kinds of motives by which people can make their action understandable. First, the "because" motive is reconstructed retrospectively after the action. The actor may explain his or her source preference by stating, for example, that he or she preferred the newspaper because he or she believed it would provide the easiest access to information about daily events. Second, the "in-order-to" motive is in the actor's mind when he or she actually performs an action, for example, seeks information to monitor everyday events. As Kwong Bor Ng points out, the because motive reconstructed retrospectively may not necessarily be the same as the in-order-to motive experienced by the actor when he or she actually starts information seeking in a specific context. In the present study, the mappings of information source horizons drew on the articulations of because motives, since it was not possible to observe the ways in which the interviewees selected and accessed information sources in real-time contexts.]

19. Alfred Schutz, *Collected Papers 2: Studies in Social Theory*, ed. Arvid Brodersen (The Hague, The Netherlands: Martinus Nijhoff, 1964), 123–27.

20. Schutz, *Collected Papers 2*.

21. In the empirical analysis of the source preferences, no distinction is made between information sources and information seeking channels; henceforth, both will be referred to as information sources. This is because the present study focuses on the preference criteria, not the ways in which sources and channels per se may be differentiated from each other in the context of seeking orienting or problem-specific information.

22. Elaine G. Toms, "What Motivates the Browser?" in *Exploring the Contexts of Information Behaviour*, eds. Tom D. Wilson and David K. Allen (London: Taylor Graham, 1999).

23. Anders Hektor, *What's the Use? Internet and Information Behavior in Everyday Life* (Linköping, Sweden: Linköping University, 2001), 233–34; Ronald E. Rice, Maureen McCreadie, and Shan-Ju Chang, *Accessing and Browsing Information and Communication* (Cambridge: MIT Press. 2001), 179.

24. Alfred Schutz, *Collected Papers 1: The Problem of Social Reality*, ed. Maurice Natanson (The Hague, The Netherlands: Martinus Nijhoff, 1962), 224.

25. In the codes to be used henceforth, E stands for "environmental activist," U for "unemployed people" and the number identifies the individual participant.

26. Savolainen and Kari, "Placing the Internet," 422–23.

27. The category of "human sources" is ambiguous in that in the final analysis other source types discussed in the study, that is, broadcast media, printed media, networked sources, and organizational sources may also be classified as "human" because they originate from the cognitive activities of human beings. However, to draw

a more nuanced picture, "human sources" are discussed as an individual category. This refers to sources that provide information through the spoken word, more specifically, by face-to-face contacts, by telephone, or by private e-mail messages. Actors typically providing information of this kind include friends, acquaintances, and family members. Human sources differ from organizational sources in that the latter refer to actors who, as providers of information, draw on their professional role such as physician, librarian, teacher, or civil servant. Collectively, organizational sources also refers to organizations providing information, for example, libraries and health centers. In the present study, however, the organizational sources available on the Internet such as the websites of public libraries were classified as networked sources. This is mainly due to the interest in exploring, in more detail, how the networked sources have established their position in people's information source horizons.

28. Savolainen and Kari, "Placing the Internet."

29. Savolainen, "Everyday Life Information Seeking"; Savolainen, "Seeking and Using Information."

30. Savolainen, "Everyday Life Information Seeking."

31. Anthony Giddens, *The Constitution of Society: Outline of a Theory of Structuration* (Cambridge, UK: Polity Press, 1984).

32. Parker and Paisley, *Patterns of Adult Information Seeking*.

33. Savolainen, "Everyday Life Information Seeking."

34. Williamson, "Discovered by Chance."

35. Wilson, *Public Knowledge, Private Ignorance*, 41–45.

36. Schutz, *Collected Papers 2*, 124; Wilson, *Public Knowledge, Private Ignorance*. [Compared to Schutz's approach to the category of interest, Wilson defined this concept in a more specific manner. Wilson primarily discussed interest as a trigger of information seeking while Schutz conceptualized interest more broadly as a prime mover that motivates all our thinking, projecting, and acting. Schutz also emphasized that interests determine the relevance of objects selected for closer consideration. Therefore, the individual's interest determines the direction of the judgments as to what elements from the ontological structure of the available world—as represented in the individual's stock of knowledge—are seen to be relevant with regard to the definition of a situation and possible action.]

37. Wilson, *Public Knowledge, Private Ignorance*, 44.

38. Wilson, *Public Knowledge, Private Ignorance*, 56–57.

39. Ching-chih Chen and Peter Hernon, *Information Seeking: Assessing and Anticipating User Need* (New York: Neal-Schuman, 1982); Karen E. Fisher et al., "Something Old, Something New: Preliminary Findings from an Exploratory Study about People's Information Habits and Information Grounds," *Information Research* 10, no. 2 (2005). http://InformationR.net/ir/10-2/paper223.html (10 May 2007).

40. Pamela J. McKenzie, "A Model of Information Practices in Accounts of Everyday Life Information Seeking," *Journal of Documentation* 59, no. 1 (2003).

41. Edward Warner, Ann D. Murray, and Vernon E. Palmour, *Information Needs of Urban Citizens: Final Report* (Washington, D.C.: U.S. Department of Health, Education and Welfare, Office of Education, Bureau of Libraries and Learning Resources, 1973), 96.

42. Denise E. Agosto and Sandra Hughes-Hassell, "Toward a Model of the Everyday Life Information Needs of Urban Teenagers, Part 1: Theoretical Model," *Journal of the American Society for Information Science and Technology* 57, no. 10 (2006); Denise E. Agosto and Sandra Hughes-Hassell, "Toward a Model of the Everyday Life Information Needs of Urban Teenagers, Part 2: Empirical Model," *Journal of the American Society for Information Science and Technology* 57, no. 11 (2006); Chen and Hernon, *Information Seeking*; Julie Hersberger, "Everyday Information Needs and Information Sources of Homeless Parents," *The New Review of Information Behaviour Research* 2 (2001); Rita Marcella and Graeme Baxter, "The Information Needs and the Information-Seeking Behaviour of a National Sample of the Population in the United Kingdom, with Special Reference to Needs Related to Citizenship," *Journal of Documentation* 55, no. 2 (1999).

43. Warner, Murray, and Palmour, *Information Needs.*

44. Chen and Hernon, *Information Seeking*; Marcella and Baxter, "The Information Needs."

45. Rieh, "On the Web at Home"; Savolainen, "Seeking and Using Information."

46. Savolainen, "Everyday Life Information Seeking."

47. Savolainen, "Everyday Life Information Seeking."

48. Savolainen, "The Role of the Internet."

49. Savolainen, "Seeking and Using Information."

50. Reijo Savolainen, "'Living Encyclopedia' or Idle Talk? Seeking and Providing Consumer Information in an Internet Newsgroup," *Library and Information Science Research* 23, no. 1 (2001).

51. Yitzhak Berman, "Discussion Groups on the Internet as Sources of Information: The Case of Social Work," *Aslib Proceedings* 48, no. 2 (1999).

52. Savolainen, "Living Encyclopedia."

53. Hersberger, "Everyday Information Needs."

54. Judit Bar-Ilan et al., "The Role of Information in a Lifetime Process: A Model of Weight Maintenance by Women over Long Time Periods," *Information Research* 11, no. 4 (2006). http://InformationR.net/ir/11-4/paper263.html (10 May 2007).

55. Roma M. Harris and Patricia Dewdney*, Barriers to Information: How Formal Help Systems Fail Battered Women* (Westport, Conn.: Greenwood Press, 1994), 20–27; Nadine C. Wathen and Roma M. Harris, "An Examination of the Health Information Seeking Experiences of Women in Rural Ontario, Canada," *Information Research* 11, no. 4 (2006). http://InformationR.net/ir/11-4/paper267.html (10 May 2007).

56. Robert S. Taylor, "Information Use Environments," in *Progress in Communication Sciences*. Vol. 10, ed. Brenda Dervin (Norwood, N.J.: Ablex, 1991).

57. Chun Wei Choo, *The Knowing Organization: How Organizations Use Information to Construct Meaning, Create Knowledge and Make Decisions*, 2nd edition (New York: Oxford University Press, 2006), 55.

58. Chen and Hernon, *Information Seeking.*

59. Savolainen, "Everyday Life Information Seeking."

60. Heidi E. Julien and David Michels, "Intra-Individual Information Behaviour in Daily Life," *Information Processing and Management* 40, no. 3 (2004).

61. Fisher et al., "Something Old, Something New"; Karen E. Fisher and Charles M. Naumer, "Information Grounds: Theoretical Basis and Empirical Findings on Information Flow in Social Settings," in *New Directions in Human Information Behavior*, eds. Amanda Spink and Charles Cole (Dordrecht, The Netherlands: Springer, 2006).

62. Diane H. Sonnenwald, Barbara M. Wildemuth, and Gary T. Harmon, "A Research Method to Investigate Information Seeking Using the Concept of Information Horizons: An Example from a Study of Lower Socio-Economic Student's Information Seeking Behaviour," *The New Review of Information Behaviour Research* 2 (2001), 72.

63. J. David Johnson et al., "Fields and Pathways: Contrasting or Complementary Views of Information Seeking," *Information Processing and Management* 42, no. 2 (2006), 576–77.

64. John C. Flanagan, "The Critical Incident Technique," *Psychological Bulletin* 51, no. 4 (1954).

65. Sonnenwald, Wildemuth, and Harmon, "A Research Method," 69–70.

66. The original intention was to elicit critical incidents related to their roles as environmental activists or unemployed people. Unfortunately, this proved impossible since it appeared from the very beginning that the participants were not willing to discuss critical incidents related to this topic. In fact, only one of the environmental activists preferred a topic related to her role as an activist, that is, organizing a trip, while two of the unemployed people chose to report their experiences related to looking for a job and applying for unemployment benefits. Other participants claimed that they found it difficult to recall individual problems worth reporting as far as their current roles were concerned. They felt that recent problems such as how to organize the separate collection of recycling in the home or to contact a potential employer by telephone would not be particularly interesting from the viewpoint of information seeking. Thus, the data gathering strategy had to be modified; those not willing to discuss critical incidents related to their activist roles or surviving unemployment were encouraged to choose another topic related to non-work problem solving. This strategy appeared successful in eliciting critical incidents. On the other hand, the strict definition of the topic of the critical incident would have served to obtain a homogenous sample of information seeking situations. Since this goal was not achieved, the sample reported only problems that could be relevant to any individual.

67. Chen and Hernon, *Information Seeking*, 48; Debbie Ellen, "Telecentres and the Provision of Community-Based Access to Electronic Information in Everyday Life in the UK," *Information Research* 8, no. 2 (2003). http://InformationR.net/ir/8-2/paper146.html (10 May 2007); Savolainen, "Everyday Life Information Seeking."

68. Savolainen and Kari, "Placing the Internet."

69. Carol L. Barry and Linda Schamber, "User's Criteria for Relevance Evaluation: A Cross-situational Comparison," *Information Processing and Management* 34, nos. 2–3 (1998). [The criteria used may be compared with the "finite list" of relevance criteria identified by Barry and Schamber. According to them, ten major relevance criteria (other than the inherent topicality) include the following: depth/scope/specificity, accuracy/validity, clarity, currency, tangibility, quality of

sources, accessibility, availability of information/sources of information, verification, and effectiveness. Overall, the criterion of content of information corresponds to topicality, which is excluded from Barry and Schamber's list. Availability and accessibility also figure as relevance criteria as suggested by Barry and Schamber. In contrast, it is more difficult to find how usability of information and user characteristics are related to the list of relevance criteria. However, for example, clarity and usability of information seem to denote similar qualities, while user characteristics may refer to "effectiveness," among others. Overall, the fact that the classifications of source preference criteria and relevance criteria differ to some extent stems not only from a variation in the empirical data (the topics discussed in the interviews) but also the ways in which generic concepts such "validity" and "specificity" are interpreted. In the present study, these qualities were not approached as separate preference criteria since they were understood as the qualifiers of the content of information, that is, the depth, specificity, and quality of information provided by a source.]

70. McKenzie, "A Model of Information Practices."

71. Reijo Savolainen, "Enthusiastic, Realistic and Critical: Discourses of Internet Use in the Context of Everyday Life Information Seeking," *Information Research* 10, no. 1 (2004). http://InformationR.net/ir/10-1/paper198.html (10 May 2007).

72. Johnson et al., "Fields and Pathways," 574.

73. Warner, Murray, and Palmour, *Information Needs*; Ellen, "Telecentres and the Provision."

74. Chen and Hernon, *Information Seeking*; Marcella and Baxter, "The Information Needs."

75. Johnson et al., "Fields and Pathways"; Rieh, "On the Web at Home."

76. Nguyen and Western, "The Complementary Relationship."

77. Julien and Michels, "Intra-Individual Information."

78. Fisher et al., "Something Old, Something New"; Fisher and Naumer, "Information Grounds."

79. Harris and Dewdney, *Barriers to Information,* 21–24.

80. Soo Young Rieh, "Judgment of Information Quality and Cognitive Authority in the Web," *Journal of the American Society for Information Science and Technology* 53, no. 2 (2002); Anastasios Tombros, Ian Ruthven, and Joemon M. Jose, "How Users Assess Web Pages for Information Seeking," *Journal of the American Society for Information Science and Technology* 56, no. 4 (2005).

Chapter Six

Information Use in Everyday Contexts

As noted in chapter 1, there is no consensus in information studies about the definition of the concept of information use. The phenomena of information use may be explored at varying levels of generality. Micro-level studies often draw on experimental (or quasi-experimental) research designs and aim at identifying the changes that absorbed information causes to an individual's cognitive structures.[1] In contrast, macro-level studies concentrate on the ways in which people interpret the value of information sources more generally and how they wield information to orient their action, for example, the furtherance of everyday projects.

This chapter approaches information use at the macro level. This approach is preferable, since it makes it possible to thematize information use as a practice that can be articulated in interviews, like the information seeking discussed previously. In this chapter, two major issues of information use practices will be discussed. First, media credibility and cognitive authority will be investigated in the context of using orienting information. Second, in the same context, the strategies that people use to cope with information overload will be explored. These themes are important since they clarify the strategies by which people filter information available in diverse sources.

MEDIA CREDIBILITY AND COGNITIVE AUTHORITY:
THE CASE OF USING ORIENTING INFORMATION

The perceptions of the reliability and trustworthiness of information may significantly affect the selection and use of information sources. In particular, the significance of these criteria is emphasized when information seekers encounter conflicting information. In these situations, they have to assess the credibility and cognitive authority of alternative sources. Unfortunately, these questions have not been researched in the context of everyday information practices. However, the topic is significant, given the fact that an increasing number of alternative sources are competing for people's attention in the daily information environment.

Factors of Media Credibility and Cognitive Authority

The everyday-life information seeking (ELIS) studies have identified a number of criteria by which people select information sources in non-work contexts. For example, Ching-chih Chen and Peter Hernon showed that in the selection of information sources people frequently draw on criteria such as past experience gained from the use of a source, easy accessibility, and usability.[2] Elfreda A. Chatman,[3] drawing largely on Patrick Wilson's[4] ideas of cognitive authority found that low-skilled workers placed greater faith in human sources available in their immediate social milieu. Information originating outside of this "small world" was not of great interest to them and was not perceived to be as sufficiently authoritative or credible. Hence, they favored "first-level information" originating from first-hand experience or hearsay from someone living in the same small world. By contrast, the value of "second-level information" received from outsiders was mistrusted and often ignored because this type information was not compatible with the commonsense reality of their own small world.

Empirical studies such as these have not reviewed media credibility and cognitive authority as factors that determine the use of information sources. Media credibility and cognitive authority denote closely related concepts that are difficult to define unambiguously. This is partly because they overlap with concepts like quality of information, believability of media, and the reliability and trustworthiness of information.[5] The conceptual setting is further complicated by the fact that information scientists and communication researchers use different terminology to refer to these issues. Information scientists tend to favor the concept of cognitive authority, while communication researchers prefer concepts such as source credibility, message credibility, medium credibility, and media credibility.[6]

The preference for the concept of cognitive authority among information scientists seems to be mainly due to Patrick Wilson's influential book *Second-Hand Knowledge: An Inquiry into Cognitive Authority*.[7] Wilson characterized cognitive authority by departing from the assumption that people know the world in two major ways: either based on their firsthand experiences of the everyday world or on what they have learned secondhand from others. However, only those who are deemed to be individuals who "know something we do not know" and who "know what they are talking about" are recognized somewhat as cognitive authorities.[8] This is because they are thought to be intrinsically plausible, convincing, persuasive, and thus credible and worthy of belief; they are also perceived to be potentially able to influence one's thinking in a specific sphere of interest. Therefore, cognitive authority is related to credibility. According to Wilson, cognitive authority has two major components, namely competence and trustworthiness.[9] As Wilson points out, cognitive authorities are valued not just for their stock of knowledge (answers to closed questions) but their opinions (answers to open questions).[10] However, the intrinsic plausibility of the answers thus given is not enough; they may be rejected if they are not compatible with the important values and aspirations of the information seeker.[11]

Cognitive authority is not confined to individuals; this authority can also be recognized in institutions like university libraries and information sources such as quality newspapers. Depending on the significance of the questions needing answers, the attitudes to cognitive authority, for example, established newspaper columnists, may vary. In general, the more serious and the more involved a person is in monitoring everyday events through the media, the more important is the authority of his or her information sources.[12] However, monitoring daily events through the media does not necessarily mean blind faith in these sources because they may be biased and more or less intentionally misleading. Thus, ideally, the reflective information seeker should constantly question the ultimate cognitive authority of such sources.

By drawing on Wilson's ideas, Pamela McKenzie explored from a constructionist perspective how a specific group of information seekers, that is, pregnant women with twins identify the context-specific discursive techniques they used in enhancing or undermining the authority of peer and professional sources.[13] For the study, nineteen women were interviewed. The descriptions of cognitive authority arose in response to general questions about concerns and information needs, and also specific questions dealing with instances of receiving advice or information that they did not want; that was untrue or wrong; that was not right for them; that conflicted with something they knew previously; or that disagreed with information from another source. The study revealed that the pregnant women used several forms of personal positioning to validate or contest the authority of information sources. Sometimes they relied on themselves as cognitive authorities, using their own reasoning, bodies, or experience as evidence against which to test the authority of medical professionals, for example, ultrasound technicians.[14] Overall, the specific varieties of broadly accepted authoritative knowledge, such as biomedical and experiential forms, were not necessarily sufficient to constitute an ascription of "cognitive authority," as it was developed, presented, challenged, and accepted in a conversational interaction.

Soo Young Rieh used Wilson's ideas of cognitive authority to discuss the relation to the factors of information quality in the specific context of web searching.[15] Information quality was defined as "a user criterion, which has to do with excellence or in some cases truthfulness in labeling." In turn, cognitive authority was understood as something "that a user would recognize as proper because the information therein is thought to be credible and worthy of belief."[16] Cognitive authority was characterized as "the extent to which users think they can trust the information."[17] These definitions suggest that cognitive authority and the credibility of information sources are closely related. Overall, cognitive authority was characterized as having six facets; trustworthiness, reliability, scholarly, credibility, official, and authoritative, of these, trustworthiness was perceived as the primary facet.[18] The concept of information quality—defined by facets such as good, accurate, current, useful, and important—is closely related to cognitive authority in that the users often make judgments on information quality based on authority of sources.[19] The authority of sources provides the potential pool in which users can make judgments of information quality.

These findings suggest that despite terminological differences, the issues of cognitive authority overlap with those of credibility of information sources. This is exemplified by Johan Olaisen's study discussing credibility in electronic media.[20] Interestingly, he equates cognitive authority with influence and influence with credibility. Olaisen proposed that when people process information they give credit and authority to certain persons and sources depending on their social position.[21] Thus, one's social position "will greatly influence quality factors like credibility (i.e., reliability), relevance, and perceived value of information."[22]

In a major literature review, C. Nadine Wathen and Jacquelyn Burkell clarified the entangled issues of the concept of credibility. In their view, credibility may be understood by equating it with "believability."[23] Similar to cognitive authority, credibility is always a perceived quality: it does not per se reside in an object, a person, or piece of information but can be assigned to them as a result of a judgment made by a subject.[24] In general, credible information sources may be described as trustworthy and having expertise similar to the assumptions presented by Rieh[25] and Wilson.[26]

Most studies focusing on media or source credibility originate from communication research. These empirical studies date back to the early 1950s; experimental investigations were made to find out how modifications in source characteristics influence people's willingness to alter their attitudes to certain topics.[27] This approach directs attention to the qualities of the sender of the message, as well as its content. These studies revealed, for example, that the trustworthiness of a source significantly affects acceptance of the message and changes in opinions.

In turn, it is characteristic of studies on media credibility that they focus on the channel through which the content is delivered.[28] Typically, these studies have explored the criteria by which diverse media such as newspapers, radio, and television are perceived as believable sources of information. As early as the 1950s, regular surveys of media credibility were conducted in the United States by asking respondents to indicate which medium they would believe if they got conflicting reports of the same news story from radio, television, magazines, and newspapers.[29]

The advent of the Internet aroused new interest in the issues of media credibility.[30] An empirical survey conducted in the late 1990s in Germany revealed that the credibility of the web was fairly high among the general public, although printed newspapers were rated ahead of it.[31] Compared to the web, newspapers were perceived as more clear, serious, thorough, detailed, critical, generally credible, balanced, competent, and professional. The differences between television and the web were less significant in regards to these qualities. The web was conceived of as more up-to-date than newspaper and television. Newspapers were considered more biased than television and the web. This is because although most newspapers call themselves neutral they nevertheless may have a political bias. The greater bias of newspapers may be seen as positive since they articulate alternative positions in public discourse. Interestingly, when asked which medium they would prefer in the case of contradictory news on the same issue, the respondents would mainly place their trust in traditional media.[32] It appeared that in these cases, 77% of web users would rather trust newspapers than the web and 72% of web users indicated a preference for television. The findings suggest that in terms of media credibility, people's preferences change slowly and that in cases of doubt, people tend to favor traditional media.

These results were supported by the survey conducted by Andrew Flanagin and Miriam Metzger in the United States.[33] Newspapers were clearly rated the most credible medium. In comparison, the Internet, the World Wide Web, television, magazines, and radio were perceived as less credible; however, the differences between these media appeared to be marginal. Of the information types provided by these media, news, reference (facts), and entertainment information were perceived to be more credible than commercial information.[34] This finding was to be expected, since commercial information is usually associated with manipulative intent and this has a negative impact on its trustworthiness.

Interestingly, the participants indicated that information obtained from the Internet is usually not verified by using comparative data obtained from other sources.[35] Information was verified only when this was easy to do, for example, by drawing on one's opinion about the credibility of the data. By contrast, there was low motivation for additional efforts to verify the qualifications of the author, for example. Factual information was verified more rigorously than either commercial or entertainment information and news information was also verified more stringently. These findings suggest that people are more motivated to verify information whose accuracy is personally important for the information seeker, while misinformation encountered in reading entertainment material is verified least rigorously.

More generally, it seems that evaluation of media credibility rarely takes place in a systematic and rigorous way. In practice, lack of time renders the attainment of this ideal difficult. Thus, credibility judgments tend to remain at a general level. Nicholas Burbules has identified two paradoxes related to these limitations.[36] Particularly in web contexts, selection of sources is absolutely necessary, but the selectivity that is required to make credibility judgments conflicts with the comprehensiveness that is required as a condition for other credibility judgments. On the other hand, too much comprehensiveness can itself be counterproductive to judgments of credibility. Therefore, the information seekers have to find middle ground between high selectivity and comprehensiveness. They have to draw on tacit preliminary judgments of the truthfulness of information sources of various types, and based on these assessments, an information source may be found interesting, relevant, or useful.[37]

While judging the credibility of information sources, people may draw on their knowledge of the genre of the media and interpret the information accordingly.[38] Distinctions may be made between quality newspapers and tabloids, for example. Sometimes credibility judgments may be based on collaborative efforts: like-minded people sharing a common interest or concern may collectively evaluate the truthfulness and believability of information sources. Burbules aptly refers to such activity as "distributed credibility."[39]

These reviewed studies reveal the complex and multidimensional nature of the concepts of media credibility and cognitive authority. Although these concepts overlap, both of them discuss the issues of believability of information, with different emphasis. This is also reflected in the study approaches. Studies on media credibility operate on a general level by exploring the criteria by which people rate the believability of diverse media in relation to each other. In turn, studies on cognitive authority tend to focus on more specific questions concerning the ways in which individual sources of information are taken seriously and thus perceived to be capable of influencing people's thinking and decision-making. Thus, ultimately, the issues of cognitive authority have much in common with the questions of source credibility discussed by communication researchers.

Empirical Study

In the empirical study, two major questions were addressed as follows:

- In which ways do the environmental activists and the unemployed people perceive media credibility and cognitive authority in the context of seeking and use of orienting information?
- Are there any differences in the ways in which they judge the credibility and cognitive authority of information sources of various types?

It was hypothesized that since many issues of environmental protection tend to be ideologically sensitive, the environmental activists in particular may often encounter contradictory information available in diverse sources, and that such encounters lead them to consider the credibility or cognitive authority of information sources. Similarly, it was assumed that the unemployed people might encounter conflicting information, for example, concerning the growth in the number of new workplaces, and that they have to make sense of such contradictory information.

In the interviews, the participants were encouraged to characterize the experiences they obtained in the encounter with conflicting information and the ways they resolved such discrepancies. More specifically, the following questions were addressed in the interview:

- What do you do if you happen to encounter contradictory information while monitoring everyday events through the media or using other sources of information? In general, are you motivated to solve problems caused by conflicting information, for example, by comparing alternative sources?
- In situations such as these, which information sources or media do you find most credible? Why?

The first question was asked to elicit answers about the ways in which the participants approached encounters with contradictory information in general. Answers given to this question provided background for the second question that probed media credibility and cognitive authority. Because it was assumed that most respondents would be unfamiliar with the concept of "cognitive authority," this term was not used in the interview; instead, the credibility of an information source (in Finnish: *tiedonlähteen uskottavuus*) was referred to since it is often used in everyday contexts, too.

Since the issues of media credibility and cognitive authority overlap, it was sometimes difficult to specify them in the empirical analysis. However, in the analysis of the answers given to the second interview question, those primarily dealing with the believability of diverse sources in relation to each other across situations were coded as issues of media credibility. The answers specifying the believability of individual sources in specific situations were explored as issues of cognitive authority. Thus, for example, the answers mainly dealing with the believability of printed newspapers in relation to networked sources were approached in terms of media credibility. In turn, the answers considering the believability of individual sources such as newspaper columnists commenting on a specific environmental debate were analyzed in terms of cognitive authority.

Overall Credibility of Information Sources

As discussed in chapter 5, printed media (newspapers), broadcast media (television), and the Internet were preferred in seeking orienting information. The most frequently mentioned source preferences were content of information, and availability and accessibility, while usability, user characteristics such as media habits, and situational factors were mentioned less frequently as preference criteria.

Sixteen interviewees out of thirty-eight felt it difficult to identify the most credible media or information sources used to monitor everyday events. They were not able to give any definite answer to questions such as whether; for example, a newspaper was more credible than the Internet in cases of contradictory information. The frequent answer was, "it depends." Media credibility was perceived to be situationally sensitive and closely related to the topic of interest when monitoring events through media or personal sources. For example, eight participants rated newspapers as the most credible medium, although four of them felt that television is equally credible. Seven interviewees believed that television is the most credible medium; however, three participants rated television and newspapers equally credible. Interestingly, the unemployed informants valued television more highly in this respect, as might be expected based on their source preferences (see chapter 5). Finally, four interviewees (all of them environmental activists) relied most heavily on networked sources such as focused information distributed by the environmental associations through newsletters or mailing lists, while three participants rated individuals personally known to them as most credible sources.

Encountering Conflicting Information

The interviewees identified a number of situations in which they had encountered contradictory information. In most cases, this occurred when reading newspapers or using the networked sources; human sources such as members of environmental associations were mentioned rarely in this context. In most cases, the encounter with conflicting information concerned the disparate ways of interpreting the significance of individual events, for example, appeals to protect forests issued by environmental associations or the war in the Middle East.

Interestingly, in both groups, the interviewees did not recognize any absolute cognitive authorities with which they would consult in order to make sense of conflicting information. Instead, the significance of one's own reflection was emphasized.

> You cannot rely on any source 100%, because there is always some kind of opinion behind the messages. In my view, we should be able to rely on the news sections of newspapers, for example. However, the question always remains, whose viewpoints do they advocate? (U-3)

> I may rely most on the Internet but not always. Most of all, I rely on my own experience and my abilities to consider and filter things. I also draw on my university studies, that is, my professional background. (E-4)

In itself, the provision of conflicting views through the media was not seen as a bad thing. The existence of alternative viewpoints is welcome since they suggest that ultimately most issues discussed in the media are complex. Therefore, it is very difficult to make sense of them by drawing on a single explanation.

> In fact, it is good if there is conflicting information available. That's why I monitor the Arabian *Al-Jazeera* news, too, if there happen to be big events. But in itself, I do not rely on any medium. I may obtain conflicting or consistent information about the same issue. Then, I will just try to take my view of it. I have my own philosophy and according to it I cannot say that this or that view is absolutely right or wrong because things are not as simple as they generally look. (E-1)

Sometimes, the encounter with conflicting information may motivate the information seeker to reflect on the ways in which the events are reported in the media. As one of the interviewees (E-4) put it, "I may wonder whatever the writer means by this, what is his or her specialty and did he or she really know this issue?" Naturally, such reflections do not necessarily lead to further efforts to challenge the competence of the reporter by calling him or her, or writing a critical letter to the editor.[40] Only one of the interviewees (E-3) had been very active in this respect in most cases, however, the local newspaper had refused to publish her comments. On the other hand, readers of morning newspapers when encountering conflicting information may not necessarily have the time or the interest to reflect on the issues of media credibility. The significance of the issue at hand is decisive in this respect.

> If two completely conflicting comments are offered, I may make an attempt to think over the issue and seek additional information, provided, however, that the issue is sufficiently important for me. In this case, I may try to find out whether these two media have interpreted the issue differently or whether the reporter has misunderstood something. (U-1)

Conflicting information was most easily identified when the media reported on issues that are politically sensitive. Short news stories providing essential facts of an event, for example, the number of environmental activists having delivered a speech in a demonstration tend to be ideologically neutral. By contrast, newspaper articles speculating on the vested interests behind such a demonstration may no longer be ideologically innocent. These articles may become a source of conflicting information and elicit questions concerning its credibility. We will be discussing issues of these kinds in greater detail.

JUDGING MEDIA CREDIBILITY AND
COGNITIVE AUTHORITY

The previous picture may be specified by a more detailed discussion of the ways in which media credibility and cognitive authority were assessed in the context of two major media used in seeking orienting information, that is, newspapers, and the Internet.

Other media such as television and radio will not be discussed here, mainly because the interviewees were unable to provide detailed explanations for the pros and cons of these media. The major strengths of television were characterized by referring to the overall reliability of the news supply and the strict criteria by which the reporters select news material. One of the interviewees (U-10) pointed out that television and radio news necessarily "draws on selection . . . they have to be based on facts of some kind." Television documentaries were believed to provide "information, not only opinions" (U-16). Finally, television news stories were perceived as most credible because the reported events can be observed firsthand: "Well, I rely on it (news) more if

I can see it with my own eyes on television" (U-6). Another interviewee (U-2) also valued the strength of the immediate visual evidence provided by television news: "People can watch television all over the country and that's why it (television news) cannot normally tell lies."

Newspapers

In general, newspapers were perceived as somewhat more credible information sources than television and radio. However, the interviewees were not able to specify this general preference in great detail. One of the participants (E-2) believed that "basically, the printed word is more reliable than the spoken word or words presented in electronic form." Another interviewee drew on the long tradition of newspaper journalism.

> In the end, however, newspapers are impressive, even though the net sites of newspapers are fairly reliable too. Anyway, this (preference) stems from habits of some kind; it may be a cultural issue. Simply, the printed word is the most awe-inspiring. (U-12)

However, not everything that is printed in newspapers is necessarily beyond all doubt. In particular, the material provided by afternoon papers was deemed of doubtful quality by many interviewees. In addition, the printed newspapers may provide outdated information due to their dependence on fixed printing deadlines.

> Printed newspapers have to put information on their pages quite early, and an event that has been reported there may have changed by the time the newspaper is available. Newspapers may therefore not be exactly up-to-date. Television is a little bit better in this respect, but anyway, I don't believe 100% in all the stuff that is provided through it. (E-14)

However, in most cases, the credibility of newspapers was challenged based on ideological reasons. One of the interviewees (E-3) indicated that she occasionally boycotts *Aamulehti*, the dominant local newspaper because of its political bias. Even though quality newspapers such as *Aamulehti* sometimes provide information that influences one's thinking, characteristic of a cognitive authority, a fairly skeptical stance on news emanating from this medium was apparent among many interviewees.

> Well, sometimes there are visiting columnists that provide alternative viewpoints. But usually the newspaper favors ideas that substantially contradict my thoughts. (E-20)

In judging the credibility of information provided by the newspapers, the type of news is important. For example, short news reports providing individual facts about the damage caused by Hurricane Katrina in New Orleans in August 2005 may be perceived as highly credible. On the other hand, full-length articles or columns speculating on the ways in which the damage could have been avoided may not deal only with technical details, for example, the construction of the dam that burst in New Orleans. Political issues may also be speculated on, for example, by asking why the Bush administration did not take measures to strengthen the dam in time. Obviously, a major factor, for the interviewees, affecting the credibility of newspapers is the way in which the journalists are able to give reasons for their interpretations of environmental issues that are politically sensitive.

> This is not an easy question. Naturally, a competent and ambitious journalist may take a strong stand on an issue. So, his or her explanation model may become accepted more widely than alternative viewpoints, for example, when discussing climate change. However, if another viewpoint draws on the mainstream of the scientific discourse, this view may be presented as an alternative, at least in some way. (E-2)

In order to enhance the credibility of an article, a journalist may interview experts such as academic researchers when drafting the text, but often he or she has to simplify things in the final version and highlight some issues at the expense of others. This suggests that in most cases, the ideal of a newspaper article based on multiperspective and impartial evidence may remain unattainable, and the arguments presented in the article may be biased. Some interviewees felt that such biases seem to be particularly characteristic of articles reporting on economically sensitive topics such the protection of forests. Those taking a critical stance on the local newspaper *Aamulehti* claimed that its articles discussing environmental topics tend to place too much emphasis on the economic aspects, while insufficient attention is devoted to issues of environmental protection. Articles biased in this way may provoke counterreactions among individual readers or groups of like-minded people.

> It is well known that the writing of newspaper articles is a politicized activity and thus conflicting information necessarily results. As to these issues, I will primarily look out for how they report on my activities or the activities of our association. Of course, about some issues, remarkably discrepant information will be published. Thinking of environmental protection, I find it very annoying, because this information is reported in such a purpose-related way. (E-8)

> Nowadays I'm too tired to write as many rejoinders to the newspapers as before, but I have done it a lot, by calling journalists. However, they don't change what

they have written. But we frequently come across with such issues and process them because they intentionally write about environmental and nature protection in an untruthful way. (E-3)

Interestingly, in this case, the environmental activists drew on the "distributed credibility" referred to by Burbules.[41] The major issue is how to interpret the viewpoint provided by the newspaper because it is obvious that the way in which environmental issues are interpreted conflicts with the values adopted by the environmental activists. In such cases, they discussed the issue by telephone or by e-mail and formed their picture of the debatable question. Drawing on the network of like-minded people, the arguments presented in the newspaper article were critically evaluated and an alternative viewpoint developed. Depending on the significance of the case, the alternative view was communicated to other people active in environmental issues by using the mailing list, for example.

In a similar vein, the judgments presented by people familiar with local environmental issues were found more credible than newspaper articles. Since journalists do not necessarily know the local details, they may report the events too generally or dramatize the significance of individual events. This was exemplified by the case speculating on the number of wolves running wild close to the city of Tampere.

They (journalists of *Aamulehti*) speculated that there were no less than ten wolves, but in fact there were only one or two at most. *Aamulehti* reported on the large number of wolves, while *Helsingin Sanomat* (the biggest newspaper in Finland) did not do so. But I know local people who have seen only two wolves there. *Helsingin Sanomat* published an objective article and they drew on the views of researchers maintaining that there are no more than three wolves in that region. But anyway, I rely more on experts, for example, local hunters than the opinions of the man in the street. The same applies to the issue of the flying squirrel. I guess only a few people have ever seen one. (E-11)

This quote suggests that the credibility judgments of newspapers may develop over time, as the same issue is debated and comparative information is available from supplementary sources. In this way, these judgments become constitutive elements of the actual process of information use. On the other hand, the credibility judgments may also affect the ways in which the newspapers will be preferred in future situations, compared to human sources, for example.

The Internet

Unsurprisingly, most interviewees in both groups were well aware of the general credibility problems plaguing the Internet, for example, the fact that it may be difficult to identify high-quality information amidst the vast amount of lower quality, unfiltered material. Despite these problems, the Internet was perceived as a relatively credible source of information that may supplement newspapers and other media. In particular, factual information was perceived to be equally credible on the Internet and in the printed newspaper.

> I tend to use the easiest way, the net, once again. This is because I can get in-formation most easily and most frequently. However, if there happens to be some really conflicting information, the discrepancy should be cleared up some-how. However, the issue should be important, something that I want to know. For example, if it is a question of a scandalous article in an afternoon paper, I'm not going to scrutinize it even though diverse media would discuss it differently. (U-18)

However, the degree to which networked sources of various kinds were per-ceived as credible varied among the interviewees. Discussion groups open to all those interested in environmental issues were approached critically be-cause "anyone may write anything there" (E-6). However, information dis-tributed through the mailing lists accessible only to members of environmen-tal associations was found credible, particularly if the sender of the message was personally known. This finding is in accordance with the assumption that objects or persons that the actor is familiar with seem to increase their liking and thus influence credibility judgments.[42]

Overall, information such as announcements about forthcoming events dis-tributed by environmental associations was perceived as reliable. Compared to newspaper articles, the material distributed by the associations was found more credible.

> Comparing *Aamulehti* and the bulletins issued by (environmental) associations, the events in the Greenpeace camp in the north last spring were approached dif-ferently. In addition, there were differences in reporting between *Aamulehti* and television news programs. However, I know that in fact, things there (in the camp) were not like they were presented in the media. (E-20)

> I would rely more on information issued by *Amnesty* because it has specialized in questions dealing with human rights. (E-10)

On the other hand, the material, for example, electronic newsletters circulated by the environmental associations may also provide "propagandistic ele-ments." Similarly, messages sent through mailing lists may contain opinions that are "colored" or "emotional," as two of the participants (E-14 and E-17) put it. The interviewees felt, however, that in principle all opinions including those presented by the "insiders" should be subjected to critical consideration. In particular, if information thus obtained is used to write a newsletter, the credibility of the source will be checked more carefully than usual. This is because the ways in which people interpret things tend to vary. Some people are broadminded and less interested in technical details, while others draw on facts and are less interested in ideologically colored conclusions.

> Naturally, when we talk about issues of these kinds in our association, I do rely on us! On the other hand, there is seldom a need to deliberate the reliability of "our own people" because at least 97% of our internal communication is based on sharing information: news obtained from electronic newspapers, newsletters issued by our interest groups, tips on research studies and links to them, progress reports of various projects, and announcements of forthcoming events. It is relatively easy to communicate information like this. However, everyone should then select information and assess how well it will serve one's own needs. (E-8)

Low hierarchies characteristic of networked communication forums seems to make it difficult to identify contributors who may be recognized as cognitive authorities or opinion leaders. The interviewees felt that the major factor influencing the credibility of human sources is the degree to which they are able to provide useful and reliable information. Although there may be longtime activists, these people may not be able to provide the final word. This is characteristic of the environmental debates going on in other networked forums, too.

> For example, there is highly conflicting information available about the global warming of the climate and the melting of glaciers, as well as the stopping of the Gulf Stream. Because of the discrepant views, it may be very difficult for the individual to form a conception of these issues. The experts are fighting with each other by asserting that "I'm right in this and he is wrong," while others argue the other way around. (E-6)

Naturally, similar debates may be found in television documentaries, popular science magazines, and in newspaper articles. However, it is apparent that the networked forums in particular have eroded belief in the existence of absolute cognitive authorities of environmental issues. More generally, these developments imply strengthened skepticism about the possibility of finding conclusive answers to complex issues and increasing difficulties to judge the credibility of alternative information sources.

Discussion

Perceived media credibility and cognitive authority significantly and often implicitly, orient the selection and use of information sources. The previous concepts supplement each other in that media credibility deals with the criteria by which diverse media are generally perceived as believable in relation to each other. The questions of cognitive authority concentrate on the ways in which individual sources are recognized as competent and trustworthy enough to be taken seriously and thus capable of influencing the individual's thinking and decision-making.

The empirical case study showed that most people find it difficult to assess questions of cognitive authority and media credibility in a general sense, for example, by comparing the overall credibility of newspapers and the Internet. Thus, these assessments tend to be situationally sensitive. Newspapers, television, and the Internet were frequently used as sources of orienting information, but their credibility varied depending on the actual topic. Overall, the unemployed people rated television and newspapers as the most credible media. The environmental activists were more skeptical in this regard and they relied most heavily on thematically focused sources provided by organizations such as environmental associations. In a way, these associations and their subgroups formed by like-minded people may be characterized as "small worlds"[43] because they tend to put more faith in "firsthand knowledge" produced within this world than in "secondhand knowledge" provided by outsiders. However, in contrast to the low-skilled workers reviewed by Chatman, the environmental activists did not reject the secondhand knowledge outright as alien to their world but subjected it to critical analysis.

In the judgment of conflicting information available in alternative sources, the role of one's own critical reflection was emphasized as the final instance in both groups. Interestingly, this finding supports the results obtained in McKenzie's[44] study showing that in many cases people rely on themselves as cognitive authorities, using their own reasoning, and not accepting without question the authority of biomedical information, for example. Although established columnists of major newspapers and experienced environmental activists may influence one's thinking in specific cases, they were not explicitly accorded the status of a cognitive authority.

Overall, the participants in both groups took a critical attitude to the role of ultimate cognitive authorities, be they individuals, such as experts debating on global warming, or organizational sources, such as newspapers reporting on the issues of forest protection or the war in the Middle East. As noted, the same critical attitude applies to media credibility: no sources are absolutely credible, but the judgments of believability are situationally sensitive. In particular, the Internet seems to have eroded the belief in the authority of established sources like dominant local newspapers. The networked information sources and news services provide new opportunities for the development of "distributed credibility," that is, the critical comparison of information sources among like-minded people. On the other hand, there is no blind faith in the opinions provided by the old-time environmental activists because their view may be biased in some way. Hence, there is a constant need for the critical reflection of the viewpoints provided by the insiders, too.

This conclusion is in line with the characterizations of reflexive modernization suggesting that everyday life is affected by growing individualization and a heightened sense of insecurity. To master their destinies in these conditions, individuals have to take a critical stand on diverse information sources. Ultimately, all information is subject to reinterpretation and only a minor part of the information provided by the media may have a lasting value.

COPING WITH INFORMATION OVERLOAD

With the arrival of the Internet, issues related to information overload have become even more topical. As to information use, these issues are directly relevant because the experiences of information overload affect the ways in which information sources are selected or rejected. The following study sheds additional light upon the macro-level issues of information use practices.

The issues of information overload are controversial; there is no consensus among researchers about the definition of information overload and the significance of this problem. For example, Tonya Tidline maintains that because the existence and description of information overload have not been documented through rigorous investigation within library and information science, information overload is a myth of modern culture, in particular, the information society.[45] On the other hand, empirical studies conducted, for example, in management science suggest that information overload is a real problem that significantly affects task performance and job satisfaction.[46] The studies on information literacy also recognize information overload as an important issue.[47] These studies suggest that a major characteristic of an information literate person is the ability to identify and select the needed information from an overabundant supply.

In general, information overload may be understood as a subjective experience of the insufficiency of time needed to make effective use of information resources available in specific situations. Thus, the encounter with information overload seems to be characterized by the experience of "being overwhelmed."[48] So far, issues of information overload have predominantly been explored in work-related contexts, particularly management and decision-making,[49] while studies focusing on these phenomena in non-work contexts are fairly rare.

Interestingly, many problems of information overload plaguing people's everyday-lives were already characterized in detail in the 1980s. Richard Wurman described the phenomena of "information anxiety" and proposed concrete ways like a "low fat information diet" to combat this problem.[50] Wurman and his associates pointed out that "information anxiety is produced by the ever-widening gap between what we understand and what we think we should understand. Information anxiety is the black hole between data and knowledge."[51] Popular writings such as these are thought-provoking, and may provide useful tips for the needs of personal information management. However, seen from the perspective of information science, popular approaches to information overload are wanting in that they mainly draw on fragmentary or anecdotal evidence. Furthermore, they often portray a dramatized picture of the ways in which information overload plagues people's information practices in everyday contexts.

One of the purposes of the present study is to investigate the significance of information overload by going beyond anecdotal evidence. Therefore, the study is based on actual experiences of people seeking and using information, more specifically, monitoring everyday events through the media. In this way, the study aims at a realistic picture of information overload and the strategies people actually employ to cope with the problems it ultimately causes. The study also provides a comparative view of earlier findings discussing the significance of information overload in work-related contexts.

To explore the issues of information overload, the following research questions were addressed in the empirical study:

- In which ways, if any, do the environmental activists and the unemployed people experience information overload in the context of monitoring everyday events through the media?
- What kind of strategies do they employ to cope with information overload in this context?

In the context of discussing the practices of seeking and use of orienting information, the interviewees were asked to describe the major problems they typically face when monitoring everyday events through the media. In particular, they were asked to characterize their perceptions and experiences of information overload and its impact on information seeking and use. Further, they were encouraged to describe their ways of coping with information overload.

Information Overload: Myth or Real Nuisance?

The problems of information overload have been addressed in several disciplines such as, communication studies, information science, management science, psychology, and sociology, among others. The sociological discussion of the problems of information overload dates back to 1903. Georg Simmel — German sociologist and philosopher — addressed these issues in terms of the metropolitan type of individuality. According to him, it is based on the intensification of nervous stimulation resulting from the swift and uninterrupted change of outer and inner stimuli characterized by the metropolis.[52]

However, probably the first study specifically focusing on the phenomena of information overload is George Miller's article on "Information Input Overload."[53] In his earlier study, Miller had shown that short-term memory has a limited capacity; on average, the limit is seven items, give or take two.[54] Given the limitations of the memory span (seven plus or minus two), individuals processing information try to cope with the eventual overload by drawing on adjustment strategies such as queuing (delaying during peak load periods hoping to catch up later) or filtering (leaving some types of information unprocessed, according to some scheme of priorities).[55] Wilson elaborated the queuing strategy and identified four categories to deal with large quantities of incoming information: (1) to be dealt with immediately; (2) to be followed up when time permits; (3) to be noted and filed for possible future reference; and (4) to be discarded or ignored.[56]

Empirical surveys have revealed concrete embodiments of information overload, for example, the growing piles of documents on the desk of the manager and long lists of unread e-mail messages.[57] These studies suggest that the Internet, particularly e-mail has exacerbated information overload. For example, a survey conducted by Reuters in 1998 revealed that 42% of managers believed the information overload would substantially decrease job satisfaction.[58] Researchers have not only diagnosed the problem: since the late 1990s, there has been a growing interest in developing tools for the needs of personal information management[59] in order to filter e-mail messages, for example. In this context, the findings of research projects such as "How to Keep Found Things Found"[60] have led us to think about how information resources could be managed more effectively by identifying "hits," that is, the most useful information sources and avoiding the storage of useless information.

Similar issues may be faced in non-work contexts, too. Media, like newspapers and the Internet, provide an enormous amount of information about daily events. The supply of this information is increased by the fact that diverse media regurgitate the same news or slightly updated versions of it. However, compared to work-related contexts, the information seekers may take a less demanding approach to personal information management by simply ignoring a major part of the information supply. This is because in non-work contexts there are fewer firm expectations concerning systematic information seeking and use; usually, other people are not going to blame the individual if he or she has not thoroughly read his or her morning newspaper. On the other hand, many people may feel morally obliged to keep abreast of things by monitoring everyday events through the media, newspapers in particular. Ultimately, the motives for regularly reading daily newspapers may be explained by the individual's unreflected feelings of attachment and belonging in the community.[61]

Although the phenomena of information overload have rarely been explored in non-work contexts, there are a few examples available. Particularly in the 1970s and 1980s, these issues were investigated within the field of consumer research.[62] Questions such as whether the large number of brands and their attributes influence consumers' product choices exemplify this field of study. Sociologists have approached issues of overload at a general level by classifying information overload as a major factor affecting the quality of life in the information society. For example, Orrin Klapp maintains that a large amount of information acts like noise when it reaches overload. It tends to cause anxiety, boredom, bad redundancy (repeated receipt of useless information), and distraction.[63]

Similar worries about information anxiety have been voiced by Wurman.[64] He describes frustrating situations giving rise to information anxiety, for example, situations in which the individual does not understand information or feels overwhelmed by the amount of information to be understood. Obviously, the advent of the Internet has exacerbated these problems, making it necessary to find effective ways to combat the "data smog."[65]

Information overload does not seem to exist for many people since they tend to ignore what they do not need or that which is seen as irrelevant.[66] Thus, people may cope with information overload by simply avoiding or ignoring the excessive supply of information. Alternatively, when accessing information sources, they may adopt a highly selective approach and seek information that supports their customary decision choices and practices. Empirical studies conducted in work-related contexts suggest that information seekers are "satisficers"[67] and that they draw on diverse criteria to judge when they have obtained information "good enough" for the needs of task performance or decision-making.[68] These criteria may originate from personal preferences (e.g., lack of interest in specific topics such as sports or the insufficient credibility of a newspaper due to its political bias), cognitive constraints (e.g., textual overload faced on a poorly designed website), and contextual constraints (e.g., time stress). Importantly, people may also draw on similar kinds of "stopping rules of satiation" to cope with information overload in non-work contexts. People tend to be satisficers: they stop information seeking after finding information that is good enough, given the time constraints in specific situations.

Experiences of Information Overload

The findings of these earlier studies provide the background for the empirical analysis of the conceptions provided by the interviewees. As discussed in chapter 5, most of them had developed well established habits of monitoring everyday events through the media. Unsurprisingly, one of the favorite habits appeared to be reading a newspaper at breakfast. However, some preferred to access the Internet as a part of their morning rituals to prepare them for the day, for example, by checking the weather forecast. In this case, the main news was checked on the web and the newspaper was read later in the day.

Overall, the interviewees were active and fairly regular users of diverse media when monitoring everyday events. Typically, they spent 1–2 hours per day on these activities. The amount of time ranged from 20 minutes to 5 hours. Among the participants, reading newspapers took from 20 minutes to 2 hours, and watching TV news and documentaries 1–2 hours. The amount of time spent on using the Internet was most difficult to estimate since the same session might include reading e-mail, browsing the web pages of organizations providing news, and seeking problem-specific information. Most participants felt that the total amount of time used daily for seeking and using orienting information was reasonable. The interviewees in both groups identified a number of problems affecting their ways of monitoring everyday events through the media, but none of these problems was felt to be particularly serious. Interestingly, only one interviewee spontaneously referred to information overload as a major barrier in information seeking and use.

The most frequently mentioned problems affecting the seeking of orienting information were the unavailability of sufficiently specific information provided by the media (six participants out of thirty-eight) and lack of time (five participants). The former problem is caused by the fact that the daily supply of news available tends to provide too general a picture of events on topics that are felt to be personally interesting. For example, Finnish newspapers rarely report the political developments in Armenia in detail, and thus, extra effort is required to consult additional sources on the web. Lack of time was also seen as a factor that inhibits information seeking. This problem was most frequent in the morning when one has to quickly get to work without having sufficient time to read the morning newspaper. Naturally, this problem is not relevant for the unemployed people. One of them (U-2) pointed out "I have plenty of time for myself. So I can decide whether to use fifteen minutes or one hour for newspaper reading." Other factors hampering information seeking were explained by a lack of energy or motivation to monitor everyday events, difficulties in locating individual electronic newspapers, and the fact that many of these newspapers are only accessible for a fee.

All participants appeared to be familiar with the concept of information overload, probably because it is often a topic in the media. The perceptions of information overload were divided equally in both groups: altogether nineteen participants out of thirty-eight had experienced it as a real problem rendering information seeking difficult, at least to some extent. Seventeen interviewees felt that information overload is a minor issue not worth complaining about. Two participants had no opinion on this question.

The study groups differed in that among the environmental activists, the Internet, particularly e-mail, was specified as the major source of information overload, while the unemployed maintained that the major problems originate from the excessive supply of news available in newspapers and on television. On the other hand, the problems caused by e-mail were primarily encountered in work-related contexts.

Experiences of the flood of e-mail messages were also obtained in nonwork contexts. In addition to newspapers, radio, and television, many environmental activists used e-mail and mailing lists to monitor daily events of interest from the viewpoint of environmental issues.

> Well, I often get 50 e-mails a day. So I have no time to read them all, not to mention checking every link. I have to weed them out quite strongly. Sometimes I feel, however, that I should plough through them but in reasonable terms, it is not possible. On the other hand, I will not stress myself on these things. (E-6)

Another interviewee (E-17) elected to a position of trust in the local association for environmental issues was very active in the use of both traditional and new media. She shared similar concerns about how to select essential information and to allocate time to things that she really would like to read. On the other hand, positions of trust are associated with a moral obligation to regularly monitor everyday events, since it is expected that people occupying such positions should seek information for the members of the association, too.

> It is a kind of balancing between things. I may ignore some issues if I'm feeling that way. On the other hand, I think I have a duty to monitor events, and so my time will be spent for that purpose. In fact, I cannot abandon that task. (E-17)

In a few cases, the experiences of information overload were articulated in more ambiguous ways. Sometimes information overload was broadly associated with feelings of boredom caused by the impression that radio and television programs can be repetitive.[69] Hence, the abundant supply of news may make people passive and impervious, and they may lose their sensitivity to react to individual problems requiring immediate measures to be solved.

> Often, not only in the case of afternoon papers, I have wondered about the ways in which the media prioritize issues and how all kinds of rubbish is given broadcasting time and column space, while the most essential issues remain in the shadow. (U-1)

On the other hand, the experience of the information overload may be situation-bound. The problem is tolerated due to its temporary nature.

> I have not experienced it in the long run . . . only momentarily if I have a busy day and many things have to be done. I may take the newspaper and have a quick look at the major events. At that time, I may think that "oh no, I don't have capacity enough today, let's put the paper aside, I will read it tomorrow." However, I don't think I ought to monitor events if I'm feeling that way. (E-4)

Interestingly, as in the case of interviewee E-17, a reference is made to the moral obligation to seek information even on busy days when a number of other things are competing for attention. However, in this case, the problem may be felt to be less urgent since the information seeker only has to answer to herself as to why it was necessary to deviate from her daily habit of reading the newspaper.

As noted previously, seventeen interviewees out of twenty felt that information overload is not a real barrier to seeking orienting information. They maintained that people tend to exaggerate the significance of information overload in non-work contexts because there is no formal obligation to keep up-to-date by reading newspapers or watching television news.

> In my view, it is a quasi-problem of some kind. Of course, it may be a problem for children if the television is always on and they have to face things they cannot understand. However, adult people can control the ways they receive things. You can watch the telly or switch it off if you are going to feel that your head is becoming overheated! (U-8)

The abundance of information was not necessarily perceived as a bad thing because it provides information seekers with more alternatives. Some interviewees believed that the ways in which information overload is experienced tend to vary by generation. Young people have better information seeking skills since they have learned to use the Internet and other information resources in school. By contrast, older people may encounter difficulties with the Internet because they are used to consulting printed sources.

One of the interviewees took a more radical viewpoint and asserted that the debate revolving around the impacts of information overload tends to deal with quasi problems only.

The debate about information overload may originate from the fact that there are experts who believe they know these issues better than the general public, suggesting that those poor people are somehow collectively stupid because first they take all the information that is available and then suffer because they have fallen under that information. (E-5)

This view supports the assumption that ultimately, information overload could be a myth of our time.[70] On the other hand, we may ask whether this myth primarily concerns older people since they are believed to be more easily overwhelmed by too much information.

Strategies for Coping with Information Overload

The empirical analysis revealed two major strategies for coping with information overload. First, the *filtering strategy* based on systematic attempts to weed out useless information from chosen sources. Second, the *withdrawal strategy* that aims at keeping the number of daily information sources at a minimum in order to shelter oneself from the excessive bombardment of information. The basic difference between these two strategies is that the filtering approach focuses on information content available in sources that have been sought or received for use, while the withdrawal strategy operates on a more general level and primarily directs attention to information sources that should be avoided.

The Filtering Strategy

The filtering approach may be used differently, depending on the source type. In the context of networked sources, this approach is often necessary.

Particularly in the net where so much is available, you have to look at the very beginning whether an article is worth reading to the end. So, the selective approach will be taken there almost automatically. (E-5)

Those facing problems with e-mail overload had developed fairly effective coping strategies by immediately deleting spam messages that can be identified on the basis of the sender or the subject field of the message. Overall, filtering skills were perceived as extremely important in combating the problems of information overload. The filtering approach was also used when reading newspapers or magazines.

The amount of the supply of printed stuff is horrible and so far I have not been able to resolve this problem in the best way. Perhaps I should take a course on speed reading. I try to go on by browsing material before I throw it away. However, you never can be sure whether there is an important piece of information that has gone unnoticed. It may be a piece that could help me to go on in my current life situation. (U-13)

Of course, if one were to read every article in a reflective way, there would never be enough time for that. However, I have learned to browse issues so quickly that I can select these things. Of course, some issues may go unnoticed but anyway, I have developed a kind of filter for issues that I find interesting or uninteresting. (E-1)

These approaches support the assumption that the filtering strategy carried out in a disciplined way may provide an effective method of coping with the glut of information. Interestingly, the latter mentioned interviewee (E-1) strengthened his argument by referring to the consequences of less disciplined information seeking. If the individual craves all kinds of information, the problem of information overload will certainly be there and the information seeker will suffer from it.

The filtering strategy also manifested itself in the selection of topics that are intentionally left unnoticed when reading newspapers, for example. Many of the interviewees in both groups reported that they skip the sports news. News related to recurrent violent events such as the political conflicts in the Middle East may also be ignored. They can even be perceived as boring and therefore relegated to the peripheral region of relevance.

Just those television news, the reports on the war in Lebanon and such things. I will not take them, I will put them aside. Let's just take Lebanon as an example, whatever is happening there. It has simply become an uninteresting topic because there is nothing new in it. Of course, I may quickly browse some news about it but usually I only glance at the headlines. (U-10)

The filtering approach drew on specific criteria by which information use, for example, reading newspaper articles will be stopped. In most cases, these criteria pertained to the extent to which the information content extracted from the information source is able to meet the personal or situational interests of the reader. Often, the information provided by headlines and leaders appeared to be decisive in this respect.

Often, when reading newspapers, I just have a look at the headlines and turn the page if they are uninteresting. I browse the paper but never read every article. So, I tend to take a superficial approach. Of course, I get interested if I find a topic personally interesting. On the other hand, I may become interested if there is an issue that somehow affects the lives of people I know. (U-1)

Sometimes, however, the filtering approach was found to be problematic because important things may go unnoticed. This may cause a guilty conscience, indicating that ultimately, the strategies for coping with information overload are sensitive from the moral point of view. The moral obligations behind the ideal of an informed citizen may be hidden, but nevertheless, they may affect the ways in which the consequences of the filtering approach are reflected.

> In fact, this happens only in the case of articles I know I should really have read. However, the article may be difficult and I may be so tired that I cannot read up on that topic. Afterwards, I may feel guilty and think that anyway, I should have been persistent and ploughed through it. (E-5)

On the other hand, such self-accusations tend to be temporary. Usually, they are not strong enough to motivate the queuing approach, that is, to store the unread journals or magazines and return to them at a less busy time. Referring to objective factors such as time constraints may also soothe a guilty conscience. As one of the participants put it, "I simply don't have more time for it, and so I have no distress about this" (E-17). At the end of the day, an unread article rarely causes harm to anyone in non-work contexts.

> I'm not accountable to anyone else. I have no need to explain my reading to other people because I read solely for myself. Work issues are different in this sense. (E-15)

> In my view, I monitor daily issues well enough. I have no need to know everything about everything. This is simply because I'm not interested in all kinds of issues like trade unions negotiating wages for the next year. I may just notice: aha, a paper mill has been closed down. However, that specific event does not distress me particularly much. (U-5)

The Withdrawal Strategy

Another coping strategy was withdrawal from the information supply by minimizing the number of information sources used daily. Compared to the filtering approach, the withdrawal strategy was seldom mentioned among the interviewees. Those favoring this approach attempted to protect themselves from excessive information bombardment in order to retain their peace of mind. These motives were personal and often affectively colored.

> Well, I tend to close my ears. I don't read all kinds of rubbish and I don't believe all the stuff that I read. Anyway, we can absorb only a minor part of all the information available to us. There may be a kind of self-protection instinct be-

hind this, you cannot read endlessly. It may be reported in the media that 200 people have died in floods. Of course, this is cruel but you just have to let it be as it is. When you get the feeling that there are too many things like these, you simply stop reading the newspapers. (U-16)

One of the environmental activists (E-7) had adopted a strictly selective approach by abandoning television and the daily newspaper although she could financially afford them. This was mainly due to the fact that she had become tired of television news reporting shocking and painful issues like recurrent wars and famine in Africa. To protect herself from the flood of anxiety-causing news, she narrowed down her monitoring to listening to a few carefully selected radio programs; sometimes she also obtained information through personal sources such as her daughter.

Well, in my view, decisions like these are healthy for human beings if you want to exist as a person. Perhaps there are persons of other kinds, but . . . (E-7)

The withdrawal strategy was also employed in a less categorical way by defining more precisely the specific information sources that are avoided.

I have restrained it (information overload). For example, I have made it clear that I will not accept direct ads, be they provided by telephone or sent to my mailbox. (E-16)

The withdrawal strategy was also grounded on the assumption that most of the issues causing anxiety go beyond the individual's capacity to provide help to the suffering people discussed in the media. Since the flood of daily news reminds people painfully of the ultimate powerlessness of the individual media user, the frustration may be relieved by screening out things that cannot be fixed.

Some time ago I realized that I have my own life here and now and that other things are outside there. If you get deeply interested in the problems in Africa and tsunamis in Asia and other horrible things occurring all over the world, so you may. . . . I don't know what other people think about this approach, whether they take those issues seriously or not. But anyway, you cannot be in your right mind if you begin to think about these issues too much. In one way or another, you have to exclude them. (E-9)

Since the filtering and withdrawal strategies are ideal approaches, they may rarely manifest themselves in pure forms. For example, the filtering strategy resulting in the skipping of news that endlessly reports on the political conflicts in the Middle East may also have been interpreted as a withdrawal approach because it aims at avoiding information on an affective basis, rather than using it in a selective way. Thus, depending on the nature of the interest at hand in monitoring everyday events in specific situations, the information seekers may emphasize the role of affective and cognitive factors differently, in order to cope with information overload. This suggests that these strategies complement each other and that in practice information seekers employ a mixed strategy to cope with information overload. Since the individual information seeker is not able to use all the information sources that are available daily, a withdrawal strategy of some kind becomes a practical necessity, often on a habitual basis. The abundance of information available in the information sources selected makes it necessary to employ a filtering strategy: read the best and skip the rest.

Discussion

Information overload is a controversial issue that has seldom been investigated as a factor affecting everyday information seeking and use. This section fills this gap by shedding new light upon the nature of information overload in everyday contexts. The study is unique in that it provides empirical knowledge about the ways in which people cope with information overload when monitoring everyday events through the media.

The study revealed opposing views on the significance of information overload. On the one hand, it was recognized as a real problem afflicting information seeking particularly in the networked environments. On the other hand, it was claimed that the problems caused by overload are overestimated and that in the end they constitute a quasi problem. In this respect, the present study supports the findings of David Bawden and his associates[71] and Tonya Tidline[72] suggesting that the phenomena of information overload may be associated with mythical assumptions and that many information seekers do not experience information overload as a problem. This may be because people have learned to live with the overload and are less likely to complain about it; it has become an accepted state.[73] However, this view does not necessarily imply a fatalistic stand on information overload. In contrast, there seems to be a real need to cope with it by employing diverse strategies.

Two major approaches for coping with information overload were identified among the environmental activists as well as the unemployed people. The filtering strategy is based on the need to focus on the most useful information by systematically weeding out useless material from sources chosen for use, particularly in networked environments. Since this approach emphasizes the significance of systematic and disciplined judgment of information content, it is in accord with the ideal of a cognitively oriented rational information seeker. In contrast, the withdrawal strategy is primarily driven by affective factors emphasizing the personal need to shelter oneself from the excessive bombardment of information. Keeping the number of daily information sources to a minimum carries out this strategy. Interestingly, these approaches run parallel with coping strategies by which people try to master, tolerate, reduce, or minimize stressful events.[74] On the one hand, problem-solving strategies represent efforts to do something active to alleviate stressful circumstances; the filtering approach is characteristic of this strategy. On the other hand, emotion-focused strategies involve efforts to regulate the emotional consequences of stressful or potentially stressful events; the withdrawal approach runs parallel with this strategy.

However, the strategies for coping with stressful events in general or information overload in particular may rarely appear in the ideal form. In practice, the coping strategies contain elements of the withdrawal as well as the filtering approach. Necessarily, information seekers have to focus on a few information sources and only a part of the information available in these sources may be taken into closer consideration. Thus, ultimately, the filtering approach as well as the withdrawal strategy share the idea of satisficing, suggesting that people tend to stop information seeking at the point where a "good enough" solution has been found with regard to their information needs or interests at hand.

These strategies have similarities with those identified by Miller.[75] In particular, *filtering,* defined by Miller as the systematic omission of certain categories of information and *approximation,* defined as cutting categories of discrimination because there is no time to be precise, are characteristic of the filtering approach identified in this study, while *escape* comes close to the withdrawal approach. On the other hand, those monitoring everyday events through the media are rarely interested in approaches such as *queuing* (postponing information seeking to a later time). For example, there appeared to be little interest in consulting newspapers that had remained unread during the holidays. Naturally, this may be explained by the specific context of this study, that is, seeking and use of orienting information. Moreover, since orienting information is primarily sought for personal needs and the individual is morally accountable only to himself or herself for the sufficiency of this activity, the sense of duty with regard to disciplined seeking of information tends to be weaker than in work-related settings.

NOTES

1. Ross J. Todd, "Utilization of Heroin Information by Adolescent Girls in Australia: A Cognitive Analysis," *Journal of the American Society for Information Science* 50, no. 1 (1999).

2. Ching-chih Chen and Peter Hernon, *Information Seeking: Assessing and Anticipating User Needs* (New York: Neal-Schuman, 1982), 56.

3. Elfreda A. Chatman, "Life in a Small World: Applicability of Gratification Theory to Information-Seeking Behavior," *Journal of the American Society for Information Science* 42, no. 6 (1991).

4. Patrick Wilson, *Second-Hand Knowledge: An Inquiry into Cognitive Authority* (Westport, Conn.: Greenwood Press, 1983).

5. B. J. Fogg and Hsiang Tseng, "The Elements of Computer Credibility," *Proceedings of the SIGCHI Conference on Human Factors in Computing Systems: The CHI is the Limit, 15–20 May, 1999* (Pittsburgh, Pa.: Association for Computing Machinery, 1999), 80–81. http://portal.acm.org/citation.cfm?coll=GUIDE&dl=GUIDE&id=303001 (10 May 2007).

6. Miriam J. Metzger et al., "Credibility for the 21st Century: Integrating Perspectives on Source, Message, and Media Credibility in the Contemporary Media Environment," in *Communication Yearbook*. Vol. 27, ed. Pamela J. Kalbfleisch (Mahwah, N.J.: Lawrence Erlbaum, 2003); Soo Young Rieh and David R. Danielson, "Credibility: A Multidisciplinary Framework," in *Annual Review of Information Science and Technology*. Vol. 41, ed. Blaise Cronin (Medford, N.J.: Information Today, Inc., 2007).

7. Wilson, *Second-Hand Knowledge*.

8. Wilson, *Second-Hand Knowledge*, 10, 13–14.

9. Wilson, *Second-Hand Knowledge*, 15.

10. Wilson, *Second-Hand Knowledge*, 18.

11. Wilson, *Second-Hand Knowledge*, 146–47.

12. Wilson, *Second-Hand Knowledge*, 142–43.

13. Pamela J. McKenzie, "Justifying Cognitive Authority Decisions: Discursive Strategies of Information Seekers," *Library Quarterly* 73, no. 3 (2003).

14. McKenzie, "Justifying Cognitive Authority," 267, 281–82.

15. Soo Young Rieh, "Judgment of Information Quality and Cognitive Authority in the Web," *Journal of the American Society for Information Science and Technology* 53, no. 2 (2002).

16. Rieh, "Judgment of Information Quality," 146.

17. Rieh, "Judgment of Information Quality," 146.

18. Rieh, "Judgment of Information Quality," 153.

19. Rieh, "Judgment of Information Quality," 158.

20. Johan Olaisen, "Information Quality Factors and Cognitive Authority of Electronic Information," in *Information Quality: Definitions and Dimensions*, ed. Irene Wormell (London: Taylor Graham, 1990).

21. Olaisen, "Information Quality Factors," 92.

22. Olaisen, "Information Quality Factors," 92.

23. C. Nadine Wathen and Jacquelyn Burkell, "Believe It or Not: Factors Influencing Credibility on the Web," *Journal of the American Society for Information Science and Technology* 53, no. 2 (2002), 135.

24. Fogg and Tseng, "The Elements of Computer," 80.

25. Rieh, "Judgment of Information Quality."

26. Wilson, *Second-Hand Knowledge*.

27. Spiro Kiousis, "Public Trust or Mistrust? Perceptions of Media Credibility in the Information Age," *Mass Communication and Society* 4, no. 4 (2001); Metzger et al., "Credibility for the 21st Century."

28. Kiousis, "Public Trust," 382.

29. Metzger et al., "Credibility for the 21st Century," 306.

30. Andrew J. Flanagin and Miriam J. Metzger, "Perceptions of Internet Information Credibility," *Journal of Mass Communication Quarterly* 77, no. 3 (2000); Thomas J. Johnson and Barbara K. Kaye, "Cruising Is Believing? Comparing Internet and Traditional Sources on Media Credibility Measures," *Journal of Mass Communication Quarterly* 75, no. 2 (1998); Thomas J. Johnson and Barbara K. Kaye, "Webelievability: A Path Model Examining How Convenience and Reliance Predict Online Credibility," *Journal of Mass Communication Quarterly* 79, no. 3 (2002); Wolfgang Schweiger, "Media Credibility—Experience or Image? A Survey on the Credibility of the World Wide Web in Germany in Comparison to Other Media," *European Journal of Communication* 15, no. 1 (2000); Wathen and Burkell, "Believe It or Not."

31. Schweiger, "Media Credibility," 49–51.

32. Schweiger, "Media Credibility," 53–54.

33. Flanagin and Metzger, "Perceptions of Internet."

34. Flanagin and Metzger, "Perceptions of Internet," 524–25.

35. Flanagin and Metzger, "Perceptions of Internet," 531.

36. Nicholas J. Burbules, "Paradoxes on the Web: The Ethical Dimensions of Credibility," *Library Trends* 49, no. 3 (2001), 450.

37. Burbules, "Paradoxes on the Web," 448.

38. Flanagin and Metzger, "Perceptions of Internet," 517.

39. Burbules, "Paradoxes on the Web," 447.

40. Flanagin and Metzger, "Perceptions of Internet."

41. Burbules, "Paradoxes on the Web."

42. Metzger et al., "Credibility for the 21st Century," 303–4.

43. Chatman, "Life in a Small World."

44. McKenzie, "Justifying Cognitive Authority."

45. Tonya J. Tidline, "The Mythology of Information Overload," *Library Trends* 47, no. 3 (1999).

46. Angela Edmunds and Anne Morris, "The Problem of Information Overload in Business Organisations: A Review of Literature," *International Journal of Information Management* 20, no. 1 (2000).

47. David Bawden, "Digital Literacies: A Review of Concepts," *Journal of Documentation* 57, no. 2 (2001).

48. David Bawden, Clive Holtham, and Nigel Courtney, "Perspectives on Information Overload," *Aslib Proceedings* 51, no. 8 (1999), 249.

49. David K. Allen and M. Shoard, "Spreading the Load: Mobile Information and Communications Technologies and Their Effect on Information Overload," *Information Research* 10, no. 2 (2005). http://InformationR.net/ir/10-2/paper227.html (10 May 2007); David K. Allen and Tom D. Wilson, "Information Overload: Context and Causes," *The New Review of Information Behaviour Research* 4 (2003); Edmunds and

Morris, "The Problem of Information Overload"; Martin J. Eppler and Jeanne Mengis, "The Concept of Information Overload: A Review of Literature from Organization Science, Accounting, Marketing, MIS, and Related Disciplines," *The Information Society* 20, no. 5 (2004).

50. Richard S. Wurman, *Information Anxiety* (New York: Doubleday, 1989).

51. Richard S. Wurman, Loring Leifer, and David Sume, *Information Anxiety 2* (Indianapolis, Ind.: QUE, 2001), 14.

52. Georg Simmel, "The Metropolis and Mental Life," in *The Sociology of Georg Simmel*, ed. Kurt H. Wolff (New York: Free Press, 1964). http://condor.depaul.edu/~dweinste/intro/simmel_M&ML.htm (10 May 2007).

53. George A. Miller, "Information Input Overload," in *Self-Organizing Systems*, ed. M. C. Yovits (Washington, D.C.: Spartan Books, 1962).

54. George A. Miller, "The Magic Number Seven, Plus Minus Two: Some Limits on Our Capacity for Processing Information," *The Psychological Review* 63, no. 2 (1956).

55. Miller, "Information Input Overload."

56. Patrick Wilson, "Unused Relevant Information in Research and Development," *Journal of the American Society for Information Science* 46, no. 1 (1995), 46.

57. Edmunds and Morris, "The Problem of Information Overload."

58. Edmunds and Morris, "The Problem of Information Overload," 23.

59. Ofer Bergman, Ruth Beyth-Marom, and Rafi Nachmias, "The User-Subjective Approach to Information Management Systems," *Journal of the American Society for Information Science and Technology* 54, no. 9 (2003); Jenni Ingham, "E-Mail Overload in the UK Workplace," *Aslib Proceedings* 55, no. 3 (2003); Maureen L. Mackenzie, "Storage and Retrieval of E-Mail in a Business Environment: An Exploratory Study," *Library and Information Science Research* 24, no. 4 (2002).

60. Harry Bruce, William Jones, and Susan Dumais, "Information Behaviour That Keeps Found Things Found," *Information Research* 10, no. 1 (2004). http://InformationR.net/ir/10-1/paper207.html (10 May 2007); William Jones, "Finders, Keepers? The Present and Future Perfect in Support of Personal Information Management," *First Monday* 9, no. 3 (2004). http://www.firstmonday.org/issues/issue9_3/jones/index.html (10 May 2007).

61. Bo Reimer, *The Most Common of Practices: On Mass Media Use in Late Modernity* (Stockholm: Almqvist & Wiksell International, 1994).

62. Eppler and Mengis, "The Concept of Information Overload," 338.

63. Orrin E. Klapp, *Overload and Boredom: Essays on the Quality of Life in the Information Society* (Westport, Conn.: Greenwood Press, 1986).

64. Wurman, *Information Anxiety*.

65. David Shenk, *Data Smog: Surviving the Information Glut* (San Francisco, Calif.: Harper Edge, 1998).

66. C. E. Wilson, "Information Discrimination: A Human Habit," *Canadian Journal of Information Science* 1, no. 1 (1976), 59.

67. Denise E. Agosto, "Bounded Rationality and Satisficing in Young People's Web-Based Decision Making," *Journal of the American Society for Information Science and Technology* 53, no. 1 (2002), 17. [*Satisficing*, a word of Scottish origin, is a

blend of sufficing and satisfying. The concept was elaborated on by Herbert Simon in the context of the theory of bounded rationality.]

68. Agosto, "Bounded Rationality"; Jennifer Berryman, "What Defines 'Enough' Information? How Policy Workers Make Judgements and Decisions During Information Seeking: Preliminary Results from an Exploratory Study," *Information Research* 11, no. 4 (2006). http://InformationR.net/ir/11-4/paper266.html (10 May 2007); Lisl Zach, "When Is 'Enough' Enough? Modeling the Information-Seeking and Stopping Behavior of Senior Arts Administrators," *Journal of the American Society for Information Science and Technology* 56, no. 1 (2003).

69. Klapp, *Overload and Boredom.*

70. Tidline, "The Mythology of Information Overload."

71. Bawden, Holtham, and Courtney, "Perspectives on Information Overload," 250–51.

72. Tidline, "The Mythology of Information Overload."

73. Edmunds and Morris, "The Problem of Information Overload," 26.

74. Susan Folkman and Richard S. Lazarus, "An Analysis of Coping in Middle-Aged Community Sample," *Journal of Health and Social Behavior* 21 (September 1980).

75. Miller, "Information Input Overload"; Wilson, "Unused Relevant Information," 46.

Chapter Seven

Practices of Information Sharing

Finally, we review information sharing as a mode of everyday information practices. Information sharing is a significant constituent of these practices, but has not been widely researched. The terminology varies among researchers; information scientists tend to prefer the concept of *information sharing*, while particularly in the context of knowledge management studies, the concept of *knowledge sharing* is also used.[1] Often, however, these concepts are used synonymously. Because the main context of the present study is information practices, it is logical to use the concept of information sharing.

The study of information sharing is important since it sheds light upon the communicative aspects of everyday information practices. Secondly, these studies deepen our understanding of information encountering[2] and information seeking "by proxy,"[3] defined as receiving information sought by other people. In general, information sharing may be understood as a set of activities by which information is provided:

> to others, either proactively or upon request, such that the information has an impact on another person's (or persons') image of the world . . . and creates a shared, or mutually compatible working, understanding of the world.[4]

In the broadest sense, information sharing may include providing information, receiving information provided by other people, confirming receipt of the information, and confirming that the information is jointly understood. Thus, the process of information sharing incorporates two major aspects, that is, giving information to others to be shared, and receiving information that has been given for this purpose. The next section focuses on the former aspect.

APPROACHES TO INFORMATION SHARING

The questions of information sharing deal with the ways in which people use their knowledge or intellectual capital communicatively, for example, by drawing on contact networks. From this perspective, information sharing is a major characteristic of actors such as opinion leaders and gatekeepers in both work-related contexts[5] and non-work contexts.[6] In work-related contexts, the issues of information sharing have primarily been discussed as a factor of collaborative information retrieval or seeking. Sanna Talja and Preben Hansen's article on information sharing provides an excellent review of these studies.[7]

In a work-related context, David Constant and his colleagues found that the motives for giving technical advice vary widely, ranging from altruistic intentions to help other people, to occasional and less affectively based incentives to pass on information that may elicit interest among the recipients.[8] On the other hand, the norms of generalized reciprocity seem to direct the provision of help by sharing information. These norms emerge when people have a positive regard for the social system in which requests for help are embedded and show respect for it through offering help. Importantly, these norms sustain kindness as a social institution and lead people who can provide help to do so. Since the present study concentrates on information sharing occurring in non-work contexts, the work-related studies will not be reviewed here.

The studies on social capital provide a useful starting point to review the issues of information sharing. In general, social capital refers to networks, norms, trust, and mutual understanding that bind together the members of human networks and communities and enable participants to act together more effectively to pursue shared objectives.[9] From the perspective of social capital, information exists as an embedded resource or an opportunity in social networks, and in general, the use of the resources is directed by the obligations to reciprocate.[10] However, since social capital may be approached at social, organizational (corporate), group (team), and individual levels, there is no consensus about the definition of this concept or the ways in which social capital should be measured.[11]

When looking at the issues of information sharing in particular, it is useful to approach the phenomena of social capital in terms of social networks. In a study of these networks, attention is devoted to the strength, density, direction, and context of links, ties, contacts, connections, and ways of resource exchange that constitute the social networks.[12] Mark Granovetter's theory of the strength of weak ties exemplifies this research tradition.[13] According to him, strong tie relationships occur among people who are similar in many respects; these people may not have dissimilar information. When information is unavailable through strong ties, for example, family members, people may obtain it through weak ties—relationships characterized as absent or infrequent contact, lack of emotional closeness, and no history of reciprocal services. Thus, relative strangers can sometimes offer an advantage over friends and colleagues on obtaining useful information. Importantly, weak ties may function as "local bridges" in that they connect individuals situated in different social networks; weak ties can offer people access to resources that are not found in their strong tie relationships.

By drawing on this distinction, social capital can be seen as either bonding or bridging.[14] Bonding social capital is characterized by dense, multifunctional ties, specific reciprocity, and strong but localized trust. Capital of this type may be available, for example, in ethnic fraternal organizations providing social and psychological support for less fortunate members of the community. In essence, these networks serve the everyday needs of "getting by." What is characteristic of the bridging social capital is the weak ties[15] described by Granovetter, broader identity and reciprocity. Thus, bridging networks are better for linkage, for external assets, and information diffusion and sharing. These networks are outward looking and cover people across diverse social divides, primarily serving the needs of "getting ahead." Civil movements and associations for environmental protection may exemplify social capital of this type.

In the tradition of ELIS studies, there are a few empirical studies exploring the issues of information sharing, although not necessarily in such explicit terms as social capital and social networks drawing on strong and weak ties. Elfreda A. Chatman[16] in the mid-1980s conducted some of the earliest studies on information sharing. She explored the ways in which women, enrolled in a subsidized employment program, shared information. Of the participants, those identified as opinion leaders engaged in more information exchange than nonopinion leaders. However, the majority of the shared information was directed outside the work environment, for example, to friends and family. In particular, sharing information about available jobs was not shared widely because it may lessen one's own chances for permanent employment.

In another study characterizing the impoverished information world of low-skilled workers, Chatman examined the information needs and information-seeking behavior of female janitors at a university.[17] It appeared that they had a narrow, concrete, and local view of the world, restricted to familiar social milieus. Thus, information originating outside of this "small world" was not of great interest to them. Although the janitors expressed a number of information-needs concerning, for example, career opportunities and coping in everyday life, they did not engage in active information seeking and sharing in order to improve their situation. Primarily, family members and other people perceived to be reliable in character were trusted as information sources and everyday problems were shared with them. Poor people living in a small world appeared to be engaged in self-protective behavior because talking too openly about one's problems to fellow workers might mean a risk. If the supervisors knew of the problems they were having, that information would be used against them with the result that the job would be lost.

Chatman also identified self-protective behavior among the residents of a retirement community.[18] Since the respondents feared institutionalization or becoming dependent on their children, they chose to appear healthier than they were. Consequently, they avoided risk-taking by not telling anyone about declining health concerns, thus not seeking or sharing information or gaining emotional support from others. However, some information sharing took place in areas deemed less risky from the perspective of self-protection.[19] First, generalized information about everyday events was shared in order to engage in daily conversation or stay informed about localized happenings. Second, within an appropriate standard or norm, advice was asked about everyday issues involving no great risk of revealing one's health problems. The worries originating from these problems were shared only with professional caretakers.

The studies on diverse information grounds conducted by Karen Fisher and her associates draw more explicitly on the studies of social capital.[20] The construct of information grounds is particularly relevant for the study of information sharing, since these grounds stand for everyday contexts for this activity. It is characteristic of information grounds, such as a foot clinic, that people gather at them for a primary, instrumental purpose besides information sharing and that people engage in formal and informal information sharing, and information flow occurs in many directions.[21]

These features of information grounds were identified, for example, in Karen Pettigrew's study focusing on information sharing at a foot clinic.[22] She observed seniors as they received foot care from nurses. The study drew on Granovetter's[23] ideas of the strength of weak ties by hypothesizing that the nurses provide the seniors with human services information that the seniors could not obtain from other network members.

The study revealed that nurses were bridging weak ties by playing an important role in linking seniors with local services because they provided information in a caring manner that seniors associated with strong ties. The nurses used three interrelated strategies for giving information. First, the "depending on the situation" strategy occurred when the manner of information giving depended on the perceived importance of the senior's need in a specific situation. Second, the "planting nuggets" or "providing food for thought" strategy occurred when a nurse gave only a small amount of information or just mentioned an idea in anticipation of a future need. Third, the "working up the referral—reinforcement and building trust" strategy was used when the senior already had a concrete need for help.[24]

It appeared that information needs were rarely stated as direct requests, but instead emerged subtly as nurses and seniors shared their situations with one another and chitchatted. The topics of incidents related to information sharing varied widely, and they included, for example, shopping, health and personal care, recreation, social activities, transportation, and income maintenance.[25] Sometimes, however, the seniors made use of casual interactions to question the nurse about his or her knowledge of a particular area in which the senior might be experiencing difficulty.[26] This suggests that information sharing may give rise to occasionally seeking information. On the other hand, information may also be shared in the context of information encountering, because the information received this way may be passed on to others.

One of the studies on information grounds explored how new immigrants in Queens, New York, used their coping skills and the literacy programs run by Queens Public Library to share information.[27] The study showed that the immigrants share information in multiple directions often as a part of social interaction and that topics of information could arise quite serendipitously as well as through the literacy program's various subjects. Another survey drawing on telephone interviews showed that people favor information grounds using diverse criteria.[28] However, a common denominator was the opportunity to share common interests or needs, and the feeling as if other people understood their needs, and that these people may be trusted. For example, a health care facility can provide opportunities to talk with people having similar life experiences. Many of the interviewees described their churches as places where they could find like-minded people with the same values and the same type of concerns.

Julie Hersberger has also discussed the issues of information sharing by drawing on the ideas of social capital, more specifically, from the viewpoint of strong or weak ties.[29] Her study focusing on homeless populations revealed, for example, that the social networks of these people tend to be small, sparse, and unconnected. Problems concerning housing, employment, and healthcare for children were areas where risk of exposure concerning true problems was not a consideration when seeking or sharing information.[30] On the other hand, information seeking or sharing concerning domestic violence, substance abuse, legal issues, and bad credit were seen as problematic topics. The homeless people were less willing to share information with other shelter residents than with the shelter staff, due to the negative consequences outweighing any benefits. Interestingly, many of the findings were in line with the propositions of the theory of information poverty developed by Chatman.[31]

Information may also be shared in the context of information encountering or incidental information seeking, because the information received this way may be forwarded to others. Information sharing based on these motives has much in common with "information seeking by proxy"[32] identified by Pamela McKenzie, that is, information is received without seeking since someone else looks for information and shares it with others on their own initiative. In a survey focusing on the ways in which university students share information encountered on the web, Sanda Erdelez and Kevin Rioux found that the most frequently used methods of sharing were writing an e-mail and e-mail forwarding.[33] Information was also shared by copying and pasting a URL hyperlink to useful information in an e-mail message. As to the content of information, the students most often shared entertainment and personal types of information and sometimes shared work or study related information. Overall, the findings of this study suggest that the Internet provides an instantaneous and fairly effortless tool for sharing information. Naturally, the flip side of this development may be the growth of information overload and the devaluation of "information gifts" obtained by forwarding e-mail messages.

THE EMPIRICAL STUDY

The literature review suggests that information sharing is a multifaceted phenomenon that draws on the availability of social capital. Social capital manifests itself in social networks, norms, trust, and mutual understanding; information sharing may be based on the use of social networks that are connected by strong and weak ties. Information grounds stand for major contexts of information sharing. Expectations of reciprocity may affect the motives of information giving. On the other hand, many factors such as self-protective behavior and secrecy may hamper it.

However, earlier studies have devoted insufficient attention to questions such as what motivates people to provide non-work information in these contexts, for example, within contact networks drawing on strong and weak ties. To fill this gap, the present study addresses the following research questions:

- From the viewpoint of information giving, what are the major motives of sharing non-work information among the environmental activists and the unemployed people?
- To what extent do expectations of reciprocity affect the motives for information sharing in this context?

The process of information sharing incorporates two aspects, that is, "giving information for the purpose of sharing" and "receiving information that has been given to be shared." The present study primarily approaches information sharing from the viewpoint of "giving information." This is simply because the interviewees were not able to recall in detail how they had used information received in individual situations. By contrast, they found it easier to describe the ways in which they—more or less intentionally—gave information to others to be shared.

The interviewees were encouraged to characterize their experiences and ways to share information, in particular, the strategies employed in information sharing. Overall, the research setting was based on a comparative approach since it was hypothesized that the environmental activists would be more active in sharing information than the unemployed people would be. This assumption drew on the findings of Chatman suggesting that unemployed people would be more vulnerable to factors such as alienation, which may cause information poverty.[34]

DAILY CONTEXTS OF INFORMATION SHARING

Almost all the interviewees were able to recall situations in which they had given information to others. However, the narratives of these situations given by the unemployed people were shorter and less nuanced than those provided by the environmental activists. Some of the participants in both groups pointed out that these situations tended to be trivial, for example, chitchatting in the cafeteria with friends. The topics of discussion also tended to be mundane, and usually contained nothing dramatic.

> All kinds of good rumors are told. While playing Trivial Pursuit we talk about recipes, picking berries, what we are going to do in the fall, and so on. Then, we may talk about cleaning and stain removal, if someone happens to know a good method for it. (U-16)

As this quotation suggests, the topics may also originate from problem-solving situations. For example, a friend may call and say that her child is complaining of an earache: "should we go see the doctor or would it be better to wait for a while because the pain may stop?" On the other hand, as one of the interviewees (E-6) put it, information sharing may simply mean a "reciprocal comparison of opinions." At the workplace, during lunch, or a coffee break, may provide opportunities to share experiences related to daily work concerns or non-work topics of miscellaneous kinds. Often, the topics of discussion originate from events reported in the media, particularly television. A newspaper article or a startling documentary shown on television may also provide an opportunity for information sharing.

Finally, the meetings of environmental associations provide forums for sharing information. For example, the local association of Friends of the Earth organizes meetings every second week. It appeared that the unemployed people seldom participated in the activities of civic associations; only one of the interviewees (U-7) referred to such forums as an opportunity to create contact networks. This suggests that overall, the unemployed people were fairly passive in this respect; their contact networks mainly consisted of strong ties such as friends and acquaintances.

The interviewees were also asked to characterize their contact network from the viewpoint of sharing information, as well as opportunities to share everyday concerns and questions within this network in order to get help or advice in problematic situations. Most participants felt that their contact networks had been broadened within the last five to ten years. One of the interviewees (E-5) described the change as "dramatic," due to the substantial growth of the number of people belonging to his contact network. Some interviewees felt that as they grew older, their life experiences gave them the confidence to provide help to others. All of the networks underwent changes, as new members had come in and some had left for various reasons, for example, moving to another city.

> Well, more people are coming in all the time. On the other hand, it (the contact network) has become more specialized according to my interests. In a way, my acquaintances tend to come from the same circles. (E-12)

Overall, the contact networks were found as significant information resources and central starting points of information sharing. Although the interviewees did not explicitly refer to social capital, its importance was implied as a prerequisite of information sharing and seeking.

> In my view, they (contact networks) are extremely important. The longer I have participated in organizational activities, the more convinced I have become of the fact that ultimately, everything will be based on personal relationships. The official way of decision-making or official structures merely stand for the surface layer. Real decision-making is often based on personal relationships. (E-2)

One of the strengths of information obtained from human sources is that they provide experience-based interpretation of the objects of actual interest. In this way, these sources may substantially complement and specify information received from other sources.

For example, I may need a new television set. However, I have no competence to evaluate all kinds of technical properties. Another example: computers. I know nothing about them. So, my friends and acquaintances who know more can explain these things to me. (U-3)

Such contact networks form the natural context for information sharing. The phenomena of information sharing were deemed complex, because they tend to be situationally sensitive. One of the interviewees (E-18) described her experiences of information sharing in an analytic way.

It (information sharing) manifests itself in so many things, it is different for different people. For example, when I talk with someone close to me, I tell him or her what I personally think at the moment. If I talk with my friends, parents and so on, I take another viewpoint and they know it is me, and they can filter information from that perspective. In the context of mailing lists, information sharing means forwarding messages and telling other people, for example, that I have visited somewhere and here are my notes about my experiences and that I will answer questions if anyone happens to be interested to know more about my visit. In turn, I may be overjoyed if someone tells me something valuable. (E-18)

The importance of information given to others may also vary according to the topic. As one of the interviewees (U-12) put it, the sharing of information related to solving specific problems is often valued more than merely "chitchatting on the happenings of the world in general."

MOTIVES FOR INFORMATION GIVING

Compared to the unemployed people, the environmental activists were able to provide more detailed explanations of their motives for information giving. This is partly because they were more active in contributing to the activities of civic associations. In both groups, however, information was often provided based on altruistic motives that remained unspecific. Information was given to people articulating an information need, as well as to those potentially interested in the topic, but posing no specific questions. In both groups, there appeared to be altruistic motives that drew on the principles of "gift economy."

They (contact networks) are very important. In fact, I have a lot of friends who have been unemployed every now and then. In particular, there are women among them; every now and then they have a job. So, it is easy to talk with them about the things they are doing at that time, it is easy to share experiences. (U-4)

> If I happen to know about things that may be of interest to my friends, I may
> share it. If I have something that others do not know, I'm pleased to share it,
> even though the individual is a relative stranger and I may only know his or her
> name. (E-13)

Interestingly, most participants recognized the fact that information sharing is
a two-way activity: information is both given and received. In general, the interviewees were not willing to hold on to information for egoistic reasons; information sharing was found to be an emotionally rewarding experience for
both information givers and receivers. Often, the altruistic motive of information giving originated from encountering similar problems and ways to
seek solutions to them.

> For example, my recent case dealing with the apartment has inspired much talk
> among my friends. I told them what happened to me and explained the way
> things went. They in turn described their experiences and their ways of putting
> things like this in order. It was terrific to hear how they had resolved these prob-
> lems. So, this way you come to recognize that you are not the only one in the
> world struggling with such problems. In any case, it (information sharing) pro-
> vides you with peer support of some kind. (U-13)

However, information giving does not necessarily lead to a positive feedback.
Particularly those actively distributing information within environmental associations may encounter criticism, and the information sharers may be perceived as "wiseguys." This problem may be faced in various forums of information sharing, ranging from chatting during a coffee break to advocating
one's views in the networked forums.

> I guess some people may get a little bit angry if you are going to preach at them.
> Some people may not be interested in knowing things you have in your mind,
> while others don't like the way you present things. Anyway, if I'm sure that the
> recipient will benefit from what I know, I will go on. (E-9)

> If someone happens to encounter health problems, for example, I'm very eager
> to help and start seeking information for them. Not all people always like it, for
> example, my sisters may get angry about it! (E-8)

The latter quote exemplifies another major motive for information giving:
this activity serves the ends of information seeking "by proxy."[35] In this case,
information is sought in order to be shared through strong ties: the recipients
are people who are known to have an information need but no access to specific information sources. Naturally, the altruistic motives discussed are also
present in this case, although information giving is more strongly driven by

the desire to provide an answer to a specific question. Information giving may also serve the common interests related to hobbies, for example.

> This is important among like-minded people who love similar kinds of music, movies, books, and so on. For example, we may recommend books to each other: "recently, I read this book, it is good and worth reading." I also subscribe to a movie magazine and tell others if there happen to be articles on good movies, the cast, and so on. (U-16)

Information seeking by proxy may also benefit people who are not able to monitor daily events, for example, environmental debates. In these cases, information giving is closely connected with helping people to solve concrete problems.

> I may help people to fill out forms or other things required by the officials. For example, I have helped an immigrant family for several years. I have checked all kinds of papers never seen before, for example, forms that are needed when you apply for a residence permit, unemployment benefits, or social insurance. In my view, immigrant families with little command of the Finnish language are unable to manage such things. On the other hand, there is reciprocity in this because some day they may help me in another issue. (U-17)

In addition to altruism, information giving may also be based on duty-driven needs. The people elected to positions of trust in environmental associations exemplified this motive most clearly. In itself, the existence of this motive is not surprising, since their specific role triggers expectations of actively giving information to the members of the associations. Information may be provided face-to-face or by telephone, but in many cases, information was given by using mailing lists. Interestingly, these people found it difficult to differentiate between the roles of "information giver," "information distributor," or "information intermediary."

> In a way, it is difficult to assess my role as an "information giver." Maybe I'm a "virtual influential person" because I extensively use e-mail and contribute to diverse mailing lists and monitor them. In addition, I distribute or pass on information that may be of interest for some people, even though I may not find a specific piece of information as personally interesting. This is because I have adopted the role of an information intermediary. I just want to share issues that I find important. (E-17)

This example suggests that information sharing does not always occur only between two individuals, that is, from one to another, but also from one to many. In addition, information giving driven by one's duty may occur at an

organizational level because information is distributed to other associations active in environmental issues. Information giving of this kind may
also serve the needs of cooperation, for example, to draft a joint appeal to
regional decision-makers.

EXPECTATIONS OF RECIPROCITY IN INFORMATION GIVING

Most interviewees felt that overall; information giving rests on expectations
of reciprocity, although the extent to which reciprocity is attained tends to
vary from one person to another. However, despite predominantly positive
experiences of information sharing, it may be difficult to attain reciprocity in
giving and receiving information. This is because people's areas of interest
differ as do their range of experiences and the breadth of knowledge. In addition, people's abilities and social skills to give information may vary, likewise their interests, degree of enthusiasm, and ways of using time.

> It (information sharing) is not a fifty-fifty affair. This is because there are peo-
> ple who can provide me with a lot of information; on the other hand, I'm not
> sure whether I'm able to give to them very much. But then there are people who
> are unable to find out things and I will share information with them. So, this is
> a funny story, a totality of things that is not based on fifty-fifty. But anyway I
> may receive equally much compared to what I give to others. (U-13)

Most interviewees in both groups felt that giving and receiving information is
seldom balanced; usually, people obtain more than they are able to give. This
is characteristic of people who in face-to-face situations prefer to "listen to
what others have to say," rather than personally contributing to the ongoing
discussion (U-2). Particularly if information is provided through networked
forums such as mailing lists, it is not realistic to expect that all participants
would be able to reciprocate equally. These expectations may only be met occasionally.

The interviewees took a critical stance on the view that information sharing should be based on cost/benefit calculations in order to guarantee the balance between giving and receiving useful information. However, many participants felt it difficult to discuss this issue at a general level because the ratio
of giving and receiving information varies situationally, depending on the
topic under discussion, as well as the interests of people asking questions, and
commenting on each other's views. The obligation to reciprocate was not
seen as an absolute requirement and the absence of reciprocity did not
markedly weaken the motives of information giving. Individuals unable to
contribute equally will not necessarily be excluded from contact networks.

However, although total reciprocity is not expected, the value of information sharing is enhanced if the participants can provide different viewpoints.

> Reciprocity is seldom realized when talking with different people. Rather, there are people from whom I take information and then some other people to whom I give it. I don't believe that we exchange information; rather, we get something different out of this process. We can call it "exchange," but not in the sense that you would give and receive the same thing. (E-8)

It appeared, however, that information giving may sometimes be directed by personal cost/benefit calculations. Particularly in the networked forums, the motive for giving important ideas to unknown people may be weaker compared to face-to-face discussion with like-minded friends. The nature of networks drawing on strong ties may be a factor here because friends who are expected to reciprocate may be favored. In cases of substantive material benefits, the personal cost/benefit calculations seem to become even more obvious.

> Well, it depends on the case. People who chatter about all they know are stupid. In particular, if there is a question about looking for a job, I may not necessarily call my friend X and let her know that there is a vacant post, if I'm going to apply for that particular job. Of course, I would be very quiet about it. On the other hand, if I happen to hear something about another job that does not interest me, I may let others know, too. (U-18)

This suggests that in individual situations, the motives for giving information may depend more on the specific content of information and the degree to which the recipients are trusted, rather than the emotional rewards obtained from altruistic attempts to help people. The more delicate or personal issues discussed, the stricter the criteria used in the selection of the recipients of information.

> Well, there are reliable people and with them you can share sensitive information, too. There is no risk in talking about issues that should not be leaked out to others, for example, the nesting place of the white-backed woodpecker. (E-11)

This suggests that information giving may sometimes be restricted by the "self-preservation instinct." Particularly in work-related contexts, it may be better not to provide sensitive information to outsiders. While the example of referring to the risks associated with revealing the nesting place of a rare and timid bird may sound fairly innocent, this "instinct" may be useful in non-work contexts, particularly if the giving of sensitive information draws on weak ties.

DISCUSSION

Information sharing stands for a significant process through which social capital is put into use. In general, the empirical findings support the view that, like social capital in general, information giving draws on networks, norms, trust, and mutual understanding that bind together the members of human networks.

The empirical study showed that information sharing might manifest itself in various forms, ranging from face-to-face chitchatting to submitting messages to networked forums. Among the environmental activists, as well as the unemployed people, the topics of shared information varied considerably, ranging from hobbies to daily concerns (e.g., health problems). In contrast to the unemployed people, the motives of information sharing among the environmental activists were strongly oriented by a common interest in the activities of civic organizations. They provide a basis for the development of weak ties that may be used in information seeking and sharing. Thus, information may also be shared with relative strangers, through mailing lists in particular. For example, individuals elected to positions of trust in associations are a good example of information sharers of the latter type. In comparison, the practices of information sharing among the unemployed people mainly drew on the use of strong ties (friends and acquaintances), while the role of the networked forums such as mailing lists appeared to be insignificant. The findings support Karen Fisher and Charles Naumer's[36] proposition that information grounds can occur in any type of temporal setting and are predicated on the presence of individuals. Information giving occurred both proactively and upon request. Thus, information giving also serves the ends of encountering information[37] and information seeking by proxy.[38]

Three major motives for information giving were identified: first, serendipitous altruism to provide help to other people, second, pursuit of the ends of seeking information by proxy, and third, duty-driven needs characteristic of people elected to positions of trust. Because information giving was mainly driven by altruistic motives, there were no particular expectations of reciprocity. Altruism[39] seems to be a major motive of information giving in work-related contexts, too. This suggests that information giving is not primarily based on cost/benefit calculations concerning the relationship between information given to others versus information obtained and that much of information giving draws on kindness as a social institution. Particularly in the networked forums, the expectations of high reciprocity seem to be unrealistic, since the participants may differ substantially with regard to their level of knowledge, interest in the topic, as well as time that can be allocated to reciprocate with an "information gift." However, in the case of sensitive information, information giving tends to be restricted by calculations of the risk of information leakage against the benefits derived from the personally rewarding experience of providing important information to others. Interestingly, self-protective behavior of this kind was also identified by Chatman.[40] She found that talking too openly about job opportunities or health concerns may mean a risk because other people can play upon one's openheartedness.

NOTES

1. Gunilla Widén-Wulff and Mariam Ginman, "Explaining Knowledge Sharing in Organizations through the Dimensions of Social Capital," *Journal of Information Science* 30, no. 5 (2004), 5; Jen-Te Yang, "Job-Related Knowledge Sharing: Comparative Case Studies," *Journal of Knowledge Management* 8, no. 3 (2004).

2. Sanda Erdelez, "Information Encountering: A Conceptual Framework for Accidental Information Discovery," in *Information Seeking in Context*, eds. Pertti Vakkari, Reijo Savolainen, and Brenda Dervin (London: Taylor Graham, 1997).

3. Pamela J. McKenzie, "A Model of Information Practices in Accounts of Everyday Life Information Seeking," *Journal of Documentation* 59, no. 1 (2003).

4. Diane H. Sonnenwald, "Challenges in Sharing Information Effectively: Examples from Command and Control," *Information Research* 11, no. 4 (2006). http://informationr.net/ir/11-4/paper270.html (10 May 2007).

5. Thomas J. Allen, *The Differential Performance of Information Channels in the Transfer of Technology* (Cambridge: Massachusetts Institute of Technology, 1966).

6. John Agada, "Inner-City Gatekeepers: An Exploratory Survey of Their Information Use Environment," *Journal of the American Society for Information Science* 50, no. 1 (1999); Elfreda A. Chatman, "Opinion Leadership, Poverty, and Information Sharing," *Reference Quarterly* 26, no. 3 (1987).

7. Sanna Talja and Preben Hansen, "Information Sharing," in *New Directions in Human Information Behavior*, eds. Amanda Spink and Charles Cole (Berlin: Springer, 2005); Sanna Talja, "Information Sharing in Academic Communities: Types and Levels of Collaboration in Information Seeking and Use," *The New Review of Information Behaviour Research* 3 (2002); Jonathan Foster, "Collaborative Information Seeking and Retrieval," in *Annual Review of Information Science and Technology*. Vol. 40, ed. Blaise Cronin (Medford, N.J.: Information Today, Inc., 2006).

8. David Constant, Lee Sproull, and Sara Kiesler, "The Kindness of Strangers: On the Usefulness of Electronic Weak Ties for Technical Advice," in *Culture of the Internet*, ed. Sara Kiesler (Mahwah; N.J.: Lawrence Erlbaum, 1997), 306–7.

9. Widén-Wulff and Ginman "Explaining Knowledge Sharing," 449; Nan Lin, *Social Capital: A Theory of Social Structure and Action* (Cambridge, UK: Cambridge University Press, 2001); Tom Schuller, Stephen Baron, and John Field, "Social Capital: A Review and Critique," in *Social Capital: Critical Perspectives*, eds. Stephen Baron, John Field, and Tom Schuller (Oxford, UK: Oxford University Press, 2000).

10. Julie Hersberger, "Everyday Information Needs and Information Sources of Homeless Parents," *The New Review of Information Behaviour Research* 2 (2001), 100.

11. Lin, *Social Capital*; Robert D. Putnam, *Bowling Alone: The Collapse and Revival of American Community* (New York: Simon & Schuster, 2000).

12. Hersberger, "Everyday Information Needs," 96–98.

13. Mark Granovetter, "The Strength of Weak Ties," *American Journal of Sociology* 78, no. 6 (1973); Mark Granovetter, "The Strength of Weak Ties: A Network Theory Revisited," *Sociological Theory* 1 (1983).

14. Putnam, *Bowling Alone*, 22–23.

15. Granovetter, "The Strength of Weak Ties."

16. Chatman, "Opinion Leadership."

17. Elfreda A. Chatman, "The Information World of Low-Skilled Workers," *Library and Information Science Research* 9, no. 4 (1987); Elfreda A. Chatman, "Life in a Small World: Applicability of Gratification Theory to Information-Seeking Behavior," *Journal of the American Society for Information Science* 42, no. 6 (1991).

18. Elfreda A. Chatman, *The Information World of Retired Women* (Westport, Conn.: Greenwood Press, 1992).

19. Elfreda A. Chatman, "The Impoverished Life-World of Outsiders," *Journal of the American Society for Information Science* 47, no. 3 (1996).

20. Karen E. Fisher et al., "Something Old, Something New: Preliminary Findings from an Exploratory Study about People's Information Habits and Information Grounds," *Information Research* 10, no. 2 (2005). http://InformationR.net/ir/10-2/paper223.html (10 May 2007); Karen E. Fisher and Charles M. Naumer, "Information Grounds: Theoretical Basis and Empirical Findings on Information Flow in Social Settings," in *New Directions in Human Information Behavior*, eds. Amanda Spink and Charles Cole (Dordrecht, The Netherlands: Springer, 2005).

21. Fisher and Naumer, "Information Grounds," 98–99.

22. Karen E. Pettigrew, "Waiting for Chiropody: Contextual Results from an Ethnographic Study of the Information Behaviour among Attendees at Community Clinics," *Information Processing and Management* 35, no. 6 (1999); Karen E. Pettigrew, "Lay Information Provision in Community Settings: How Community Health Nurses Disseminate Human Services Information to the Elderly," *Library Quarterly* 70, no. 1 (2000).

23. Granovetter, "The Strength of Weak Ties."

24. Pettigrew, "Lay Information Provision," 68–71.

25. Pettigrew, "Waiting for Chiropody," 806.

26. Pettigrew, "Waiting for Chiropody," 812.

27. Karen E. Fisher, Joan C. Durrance, and Marian B. Hinton, "Information Grounds and the Use of Need-Based Services by Immigrants in Queens, New York: A Context-Based, Outcome Evaluation Approach," *Journal of the American Society for Information Science and Technology* 55, no. 8 (2004).

28. Fisher et al., "Something Old, Something New."

29. Julie Hersberger, "A Qualitative Approach to Examining Information Transfer via Social Networks among Homeless Populations," *The New Review of Information Behaviour Research* 4 (2003).

30. Julie Hersberger, "Are the Economically Poor Information Poor? Does the Digital Divide Affect the Homeless and Access to Information," *The Canadian Journal of Information and Library Science* 27, no. 3 (2002), 58.

31. Chatman, "The Impoverished Life-World."

32. McKenzie, "A Model of Information Practices."

33. Sanda Erdelez and Kevin Rioux, "Sharing Information Encountered for Others on the Web," *The New Review of Information Behaviour* 1 (2000).

34. Chatman, "Opinion Leadership."; Chatman, "Life in a Small World."

35. McKenzie, "A Model of Information Practices."

36. Fisher and Naumer, "Information Grounds."

37. Erdelez, "Information Encountering."

38. McKenzie, "A Model of Information Practices."

39. Constant, Sproull, and Kiesler, "The Kindness of Strangers."

40. Chatman, *The Information World*; Chatman, "Life in a Small World."

Chapter Eight

Concluding Remarks

In an information-intensive world characterized by reflective modernization, everyday information practices become even more central to people's daily lives. As the information environment becomes increasingly complex with a growing number of information sources competing for our attention, the ways in which the value of information is judged becomes increasingly important for making sense of the daily life world. To master their destinies in conditions of reflexive modernization, people have to engage in continuous monitoring of daily events, through the media in particular. Daily problem solving is increasingly dependent on the critical selection and use of information sources.

This study approaches information practices in the context of the daily life world by drawing on the ideas of social phenomenology. The main idea is the perspectivist view of a life world that is structured to regions of relevance according to the interests of the actor. This approach is constitutive of the definition of information source horizon indicating the ways in which people put information sources in an order of preference while seeking orienting or problem-specific information. The perspectivist view proposed by social phenomenology can also be understood in temporal terms. Information practices have their own past in the biographically based experiences of information seeking, use, and sharing. These practices also have their own present, manifesting themselves in situationally bound opportunities and constraints of information seeking, use, and sharing. Finally, information practices orient to the future, driven by the goals of information seeking, use, and sharing that serve the ends of furthering everyday projects.

Another major source of conceptual inspiration, that is, a practice turn in the social sciences, provided ideas to thematize information seeking, use, and sharing as socially and culturally affected sets of action that constitute practices. The integration of the ideas of social phenomenology and these practice theories opened up an alternative perspective to approach issues that have so far been discussed predominantly in terms of "information behavior." This book suggests that the "practice turn" is possible in information studies, too, and that information seeking, use, and sharing can be perceived as deeply contextualized "perspectivist practices."

Drawing on the ideas of social phenomenology and practice theories, the model of everyday information practices was developed. The model suggests that information seeking, use, and sharing become meaningful in the context of furthering everyday projects of various kinds. More specifically, one's stock of knowledge forms the necessary basis of information seeking, use, and sharing that serve the ends of pursuing everyday projects. The accomplishment of information practices may also refine one's stock of knowledge and thus provide a more nuanced repertoire of typifications for use by the actor pursuing everyday projects. Moreover, the model suggests that everyday information practices are driven by the actor's teleoaffective structure, particularly his or her interests in furthering everyday projects. Importantly, these interests structure the subject areas of daily life into an order of importance or regions of relevance. These preferences, in turn, are reflected in the construction of information source horizons.

Since everyday projects are oriented to the future, it is also characteristic of everyday information practices that they are temporally sensitive. Seeking orienting information may be conceived of as a generic project that represents a lifelong endeavor, while information seeking serving the ends of change or pursuit projects may have a shorter temporal perspective. Everyday projects may be constituted of specific tasks that are performed within episodes of varying length. Everyday information practices can also be accomplished in spatial contexts since information seekers, users, and sharers have to cross physical distance in order to access information sources. However, the growing use of networked sources has reduced the meaning of spatial factors since the Internet may be seen as a "placeless" source of information. The spatial factors are constitutive of everyday information practices since the construction of regions of relevance in general, as well as information source horizons and information pathways in particular, draws on the principle of "the closer the better" or "first things first." Overall, this suggests that everyday information practices are spatiotemporally sensitive, and thus, profoundly contextual.

The study showed that information seeking is a major mode of everyday information practice. Seeking orienting, as well as problem-specific information tends to be dependent on habitual action; in most cases, information seeking practices are directed by the principles of "good enough" or "satisficing." The selection (acceptance or rejection) of information sources occurs in the context of information source horizons, and the accepted sources are accessed in a context-specific order indicated by the information pathway. The empirical analysis demonstrated that the criteria of information content, as well as availability and accessibility of information are of crucial importance while seeking orienting or problem-specific information. The dominance of the criteria pertaining to information content supports the assumption that information seeking is oriented by the subject field of everyday projects; primarily, the actor expects that the information is topically relevant. Other preference criteria, such as availability and accessibility, are of lesser importance, although they may be influential in specific situations in which information seeking is constrained by lack of time, for example.

As noted, it is characteristic of everyday information seeking practices that they tend to be oriented by the principles of "good enough" and "satisficing." Overall, in everyday information seeking, the role of routines and habits are more significant than has earlier been assumed. Thus, everyday information seeking practices tend to change quite slowly; this reflects the established nature of the life world and the pivotal role of the "natural attitude" toward the daily world. Despite this inertia, these practices do undergo changes, although they do not manifest themselves in a dramatic way.

This assumption may be supported by Pertti Alasuutari's view on the role of routines in daily life.[1] Routines are crucially important and even necessary for the performance of everyday actions because the actors cannot stop to reflect on all the steps that they take daily. On the other hand, routines are reflected on to some extent and the constant interplay between routines and reflexivity can pave the way for the change of routines. This transformation becomes evident if we look at the ways in which the Internet gradually changed the routines and habits of everyday-life information seeking since the late 1990s. The Internet has established its position among the central sources of information. However, the networked sources complement, but do not replace other sources in the seeking of both orienting and problem-specific information.

The principle of "good enough" is apparently also constitutive of information use practices. The principle is reflected in the ways in which people assess media credibility and cognitive authority and develop strategies to cope with information overload. The present study showed that the strategies of filtering and avoiding information are becoming more significant, as information overload grows. Apparently, people use these strategies in a complementary way. Given the constraints of information use such as lack of time, the strategy of "read the best and skip the rest" is often a necessity. However, a highly selective use of information may give rise to nagging moral questions as to whether the stock of knowledge has been augmented enough in order to further one's everyday projects. In the context of life world, however, other people such as friends rarely ask such moral questions, since information users are primarily accountable only to themselves. On the other hand, the issues of "good enough" are social and cultural since the sufficiency of one's stock of knowledge may be "tested" in everyday situations in which other people ask for help to solve a problem.

This suggests that information use is closely connected to the practice of information sharing. In general, it stands for information actions by which people contribute to their stocks of knowledge based on mutual interests and thus, solidarity. The empirical study showed that information giving is primarily driven by motives of serendipitous altruism. This indicates that despite the centrality of values characteristic of individualism in our society, the importance of solidarity is still recognized and people are willing to support each other's everyday projects. However, cost/benefit calculations of reciprocity and thus, egoistic motives may also direct information giving. The empirical study of information sharing indicated the importance of contact networks for getting by in everyday life, whether these networks consisted of weak or strong ties. Information sharing is not an isolated component of everyday information practices because it may broaden one's source repertoire. In this way, information sharing may affect the construction of information source horizons and thus information seeking and information use.

Because this is the first study elaborating on the characteristics of everyday information practices in particular; there remains a need for further research, both conceptual and empirical. Since this book draws on a rather small convenient sample of environmental activists and unemployed people, further research is needed to elaborate the practices of information seeking, use, and sharing by focusing on other population groups in order to obtain comparative data. The conceptual issues of everyday information practices may be elaborated on by making use of the studies produced by practice theorists. There is also a need to analyze further the tradition of social phenomenological research in order to elaborate on the picture of the life world concerning issues of information seeking, use, and sharing.

Within information studies, comparative studies may be conducted to analyze how the model of everyday information practices is related to approaches such as the normative theory of behavior developed by Elfreda A. Chatman.[2] This is intriguing, since there are areas of common interest. Chatman provides a compelling case of the ways in which social and cultural factors such as norms determine daily information seeking, use, and sharing in the specific context of "small world." Importantly, Chatman's research project epitomizes an ambitious attempt to use the repertoire of social scientific theories and ethnographic approaches to enhance our understanding of information seeking practices. This book shares this research interest, even though the model of everyday practices draws on different concepts, placing less emphasis on the norms and rule-bound forces that direct the practices of everyday information seeking. Although Chatman refers to "information behavior," not information practices, and draws mainly on the ideas of functionalist sociology, the conceptual and terminological differences should not be seen as a barrier to a comparative theoretical discussion.

Another theoretically interesting framework is that provided by the approach to "information grounds" developed by Karen Fisher and colleagues.[3] In particular, it thematizes the spatiotemporal factors of information practices, and thereby pays attention to the contextually sensitive nature of everyday information environments. The analytic studies on the ways in which moral conceptions affect information practices would provide a significant starting point to explore the ways in which people construct their information seeking practices as "good enough."[4] The concept of everyday information practices can also be explained by looking at issues of personal information management in a mundane context. Jenna Hartel's study of the ways in which cooks place favorite recipes into files and folders provides an intriguing example of the practice of personal information management.[5] Finally, nonwork information practices should be compared to information practices characteristic of work-related contexts.[6] Studies such as these would open up opportunities to specify the picture of information practices in both contexts and cross-fertilize the ideas to develop a genuinely contextualist approach to information practice.

NOTES

1. Pertti Alasuutari, *Social Theory and Human Reality* (London: Sage, 2004).

2. Elfreda A. Chatman, "Framing Social Life in Theory and Research," *The New Review of Information Behaviour Research* 1 (2000).

3. Karen E. Fisher and Charles M. Naumer, "Information Grounds: Theoretical Basis and Empirical Findings on Information Flow in Social Settings," in *New Directions in Human Information Behavior*, eds. Amanda Spink and Charles Cole (Dordrecht, The Netherlands: Springer, 2005).

4. Kimmo Tuominen, "Whoever Increases His Knowledge Merely Increases His Heartache: Moral Tensions in Heart Surgery Patients' and Their Spouses' Talk about Information Seeking," *Information Research* 10, no. 1 (2004). http://InformationR .net/ir/10-1/paper202.html (10 May 2007).

5. Jenna Hartel, "The Serious Leisure Frontier in Library and Information Science: Hobby Domains," *Knowledge Organization* 30, nos. 3–4 (2003).

6. Sanna Talja and Preben Hansen, "Information Sharing," in *New Directions in Human Information Behavior*, eds. Amanda Spink and Charles Cole (Berlin: Springer, 2005).

Bibliography

Agada, John. "Inner-City Gatekeepers: An Exploratory Survey of Their Information Use Environment." *Journal of the American Society for Information Science* 50, no. 1 (1999), 74–85.

Agosto, Denise E. "Bounded Rationality and Satisficing in Young People's Web-Based Decision Making." *Journal of the American Society for Information Science and Technology* 53, no. 1 (2002), 16–27.

Agosto, Denise E., and Sandra Hughes-Hassell. "Toward a Model of the Everyday Life Information Needs of Urban Teenagers, Part 1: Theoretical Model." *Journal of the American Society for Information Science and Technology* 57, no. 10 (2006), 1394–1403.

———. "Toward a Model of the Everyday Life Information Needs of Urban Teenagers, Part 2: Empirical Model." *Journal of the American Society for Information Science and Technology* 57, no. 11 (2006), 1418–26.

Alasuutari, Pertti. *Social Theory and Human Reality*. London: Sage, 2004.

Allen, David K., and M. Shoard, "Spreading the Load: Mobile Information and Communications Technologies and Their Effect on Information Overload." *Information Research* 10, no. 2 (2005). http://InformationR.net/ir/10-2/paper227.html (10 May 2007).

Allen, David K., and Tom D. Wilson. "Information Overload: Context and Causes." *The New Review of Information Behaviour Research* 4 (2003), 31–44.

Allen, Thomas J. *The Differential Performance of Information Channels in the Transfer of Technology*. Cambridge: Massachusetts Institute of Technology, 1966.

Altheide, David L. "The Sociology of Alfred Schutz." In *Existential Sociology*, edited by Jack D. Douglas et al., 133–52. Cambridge: Cambridge University Press, 1977.

Bagozzi, Richard P., Zeynep Gürhan-Canli, and Joseph H. Priester. *The Social Psychology of Consumer Behavior*. Buckingham, UK: Open University Press, 2002.

Bar-Ilan, Judit, et al. "The Role of Information in a Lifetime Process: A Model of Weight Maintenance by Women over Long Time Periods." *Information Research* 11, no. 4 (2006). http://InformationR.net/ir/11-4/paper263.html (10 May 2007).

Barnes, Barry. "Practices as Collective Action." In *The Practice Turn in Contemporary Theory*, edited by Theodore R. Schatzki, Karin Knorr Cetina, and Eike von Savigny, 17–27. London: Routledge, 2001.

Barry, Carol L., and Linda Schamber. "User's Criteria for Relevance Evaluation: A Cross-Situational Comparison." *Information Processing and Management* 34, no. 2–3 (1998), 219–36.

Bawden, David. "Digital Literacies: A Review of Concepts." *Journal of Documentation* 57, no. 2 (2001), 218–59.

Bawden, David, Clive Holtham, and Nigel Courtney. "Perspectives on Information Overload." *Aslib Proceedings* 51, no. 8 (1999), 249–55.

Beck, Ulrich, Anthony Giddens, and Scott Lash. *Reflexive Modernization: Politics, Tradition and Aesthetics in the Modern Social Order*. Cambridge, UK: Cambridge University Press, 1994.

Belkin, Nicholas, N. R. Oddy, and H. M. Brooks. "ASK for Information Retrieval, Part 1: Background and Theory." *Journal of Documentation* 38, no. 2 (1982), 61–71.

Bennett, Tony. "The Invention of the Modern Cultural Fact: Towards a Critique of the Critique of Everyday Life." In *Contemporary Culture and Everyday Life*, edited by Elizabeth B. Silva and Tony Bennett, 21–36. Durham, UK: Sociologypress, 2004.

Bergman, Ofer, Ruth Beyth-Marom, and Rafi Nachmias. "The User-Subjective Approach to Information Management Systems." *Journal of the American Society for Information Science and Technology* 54, no. 9 (2003), 872–78.

Berman, Yitzhak. "Discussion Groups on the Internet as Sources of Information: The Case of Social Work." *Aslib Proceedings* 48, no. 2 (1996), 31–36.

Berryman, Jennifer. "What Defines 'Enough' Information? How Policy Workers Make Judgements and Decisions during Information Seeking: Preliminary Results from an Exploratory Study." *Information Research* 11, no. 4 (2006). http://InformationR.net/ir/11-4/paper266.html (10 May 2007).

Bourdieu, Pierre. *Distinction: A Social Critique of the Judgement of Taste*. London: Routledge, 1984.

——. *The Logic of Practice*. Cambridge, UK: Polity Press, 1990.

Bruce, Harry. *The User's View of the Internet*. Lanham, Md.: Scarecrow Press, 2002.

Bruce, Harry, William Jones, and Susan Dumais, "Information Behaviour That Keeps Found Things Found." *Information Research* 10, no. 1 (2004). http://InformationR.net/ir/10-1/paper207.html (10 May 2007).

Budd, John M. "Phenomenology and Information Studies." *Journal of Documentation* 61, no. 1 (2005), 44–59.

Bull, Michael. *Sounding Out the City: Personal Stereos and the Management of Everyday Life*. Oxford, UK: Berg, 2000.

Burbules, Nicholas J. "Paradoxes on the Web: The Ethical Dimensions of Credibility." *Library Trends* 49, no. 3 (2001), 441–53.

Camic, Charles. "The Matter of Habit." *American Journal of Sociology* 91, no. 5 (1986), 1039–87.

Carey, James W. *Communication as Culture: Essays on Media and Society*. Boston: Unwin Hyman, 1989.

Case, Donald O. *Looking for Information: A Survey of Research on Information Seeking, Needs and Behavior*. San Diego, Calif.: Academic Press, 2002.

——. "Information Behavior." In *Annual Review of Information Science and Technology*. Vol. 40, edited by Blaise Cronin, 293–327. Medford, N.J.: Information Today, Inc., 2005.

Certeau, Michel de. *The Practice of Everyday Life*. Berkeley: University of California Press, 1984.

Chaney, David. *Cultural Change and Everyday Life*. Houndmills, Hampshire, UK: Palgrave, 2002.

Chatman, Elfreda A. "The Information World of Low-Skilled Workers." *Library and Information Science Research* 9, no. 4 (1987), 265–83.

——. "Opinion Leadership, Poverty, and Information Sharing." *Reference Quarterly* 26, no. 3 (1987), 341–53.

——. "Life in a Small World: Applicability of Gratification Theory to Information-Seeking Behavior." *Journal of the American Society for Information Science* 42, no. 6 (1991), 438–49.

——. *The Information World of Retired Women*. Westport, Conn.: Greenwood Press, 1992.

——. "The Impoverished Life-World of Outsiders." *Journal of the American Society for Information Science* 47, no. 3 (1996), 193–206.

——. "A Theory of Life in the Round." *Journal of the American Society for Information Science* 50, no. 3 (1999), 207–17.

——. "Framing Social Life in Theory and Research." *The New Review of Information Behaviour Research* 1 (2000), 3–17.

Chen, Ching-chih, and Peter Hernon. *Information Seeking: Assessing and Anticipating User Needs*. New York: Neal-Schuman, 1982.

Choo, Chun Wei. *The Knowing Organization: How Organizations Use Information to Construct Meaning, Create Knowledge and Make Decisions*. 2nd ed. New York: Oxford University Press, 2006.

——. "Information Seeking in Organizations: Epistemic Contexts and Contests." *Information Research* 12, no. 2 (2007). http://InformationR.net/ir/12-2/paper298.html (10 May 2007).

Constant, David, Lee Sproull, and Sara Kiesler. "The Kindness of Strangers: On the Usefulness of Electronic Weak Ties for Technical Advice." In *Culture of the Internet*, edited by Sara Kiesler, 303–22. Mahwah, N.J.: Lawrence Erlbaum, 1997.

Cook, Scott D. N., and John Seely Brown. "Bridging Epistemologies: The Generative Dance between Organizational Knowledge and Organizational Knowing." *Organization Science* 10, no. 4 (1999), 381–400.

Corbin, Juliet M., and Anselm L. Strauss. *Unending Work and Care: Managing Chronic Illness at Home*. San Francisco, Calif.: Jossey-Bass Publishers, 1998.

Costelloe, Timothy M. "Between the Subject and Sociology: Alfred Schutz's Phenomenology of the Life-World." *Human Studies* 19, no. 3 (1996), 247–66.

Courtright, Christina. "Context in Information Behavior Research." In *Annual Review of Information Science and Technology*. Vol. 41, edited by Blaise Cronin, 273–306. Medford, N.J.: Information Today, Inc., 2007.

Cox, Ronald R. *Schutz's Theory of Relevance: A Phenomenological Critique.* The Hague, The Netherlands: Martinus Nijhoff, 1978.

Dant, Tim. *Knowledge, Ideology and Discourse: A Sociological Perspective.* London: Routledge, 1991.

Dervin, Brenda. "An Overview of Sense-Making Research: Concepts, Methods and Results to Date." Paper presented at the annual meeting of the International Communication Association, Dallas, Tex., May 1983.

———. "On Studying Information Seeking Methodologically: The Implications of Connecting Metatheory to Method." *Information Processing and Management* 35, no. 6 (1999), 727–50.

Dervin, Brenda, and Micheline Frenette. "Sense-Making Methodology: Communicating Communicatively with Campaign Audiences." In *Sense-Making Methodology Reader: Selected Writings of Brenda Dervin*, edited by Brenda Dervin and Lois Foreman-Wernet, 233–49. Cresskill, N.J.: Hampton Press, 2003.

Dervin, Brenda, and Michael Nilan. "Information Needs and Uses." In *Annual Review of Information Science and Technology*, Vol. 21, edited by Martha E. Williams, 3–33. White Plains, N.Y.: Knowledge Industry Inc., 1986.

Dervin, Brenda, et al. *The Development of Strategies for Dealing with the Information Needs of Urban Residents Vol. 1: Citizen Study.* Washington, D.C.: U.S. Department of Health, Education, and Welfare. Office of Libraries and Learning Resources, 1976.

Dreher, Jochen. "The Symbol and the Theory of the Life-World: The Transcendences of the Life-World and Their Overcoming by Signs and Symbols." *Human Studies* 26, no. 2 (2003), 141–63.

Durrance, Joan C. *Armed for Action: Library Response to Citizen Information Needs.* New York: Neal-Schuman, 1984.

Edmunds, Angela, and Anne Morris. "The Problem of Information Overload in Business Organisations: A Review of Literature." *International Journal of Information Management* 20, no. 1 (2000), 17–28.

Ellen, Debbie. "Telecentres and the Provision of Community-Based Access to Electronic Information in Everyday Life in the UK." *Information Research* 8, no. 2 (2003). http://InformationR.net/ir/8-2/paper146.html (10 May 2007).

Elveton, Roy. "Lebenswelt (Lifeworld)," in *The Literary Encyclopedia.* http://www.litencyc.com/php/stopics.php?rec=true&UID=1539 (10 May 2007).

Encyclopedia Britannica Online. "Human Behaviour." http://search.eb.com/eb/article-9110429 (10 May 2007).

Endress, Martin. "Introduction: Alfred Schutz and Contemporary Social Theory and Social Research." In *Explorations of the Life-World: Continuing Dialogues with Alfred Schutz*, edited by Martin Endress, George Psathas, and Hisashi Nasu, 1–15. Dordrecht, The Netherlands: Springer, 2005.

———. "Reflexivity, Reality and Relationality: The Inadequacy of Bourdieu's Critique of the Phenomenological Tradition in Sociology." In *Explorations of the Life-World. Continuing Dialogues with Alfred Schutz*, edited by Martin Endress, George Psathas, and Hisashi Nasu, 51–74. Dordrecht, The Netherlands: Springer, 2005.

Eppler, Martin J., and Jeanne Mengis. "The Concept of Information Overload: A Review of Literature from Organization Science, Accounting, Marketing, MIS, and Related Disciplines." *The Information Society* 20, no. 5 (2004), 325–44.

Erdelez, Sanda. "Information Encountering: A Conceptual Framework for Accidental Information Discovery." In *Information Seeking in Context,* edited by Pertti Vakkari, Reijo Savolainen, and Brenda Dervin, 412–21. London: Taylor Graham, 1997.

Erdelez, Sanda, and Kevin Rioux. "Sharing Information Encountered for Others on the Web." *The New Review of Information Behaviour* 1 (2000), 219–33.

Felski, Rita. "The Invention of Everyday Life." *New Formations* 39 (1999), 15–31.

Fishbein, Martin, and Icek Ajzen. *Belief, Attitude, Intention and Behavior: An Introduction to Theory and Research.* Reading, Mass.: Addison-Wesley, 1975.

Fisher, Karen E., Joan C. Durrance, and Marian B. Hinton. "Information Grounds and the Use of Need-Based Services by Immigrants in Queens, New York: A Context-Based, Outcome Evaluation Approach." *Journal of the American Society for Information Science and Technology* 55, no. 8 (2004), 754–66.

Fisher, Karen E., Sanda Erdelez, and Lynne McKechnie. "Preface." In *Theories of Information Behavior*, edited by Karen E. Fisher, Sanda Erdelez, and Lynne McKechnie, xix–xxii. Medford, N.J.: Information Today, Inc., 2005.

Fisher, Karen E., et al. "Something Old, Something New: Preliminary Findings from an Exploratory Study about People's Information Habits and Information Grounds." *Information Research* 10, no. 2 (2005). http://InformationR.net/ir/10-2/paper223.html (10 May 2007).

Fisher, Karen E., and Charles M. Naumer. "Information Grounds: Theoretical Basis and Empirical Findings on Information Flow in Social Settings." In *New Directions in Human Information Behavior*, edited by Amanda Spink and Charles Cole, 93–111. Dordrecht, The Netherlands: Springer, 2006.

Flanagan, John C. "The Critical Incident Technique." *Psychological Bulletin* 51, no. 4 (1954), 327–59.

Flanagin, Andrew J., and Miriam J. Metzger. "Perceptions of Internet Information Credibility." *Journal of Mass Communication Quarterly* 77, no. 3 (2000), 515–40.

Fogg, B. J., and Hsiang Tseng. "The Elements of Computer Credibility." In *Proceedings of the SIGCHI Conference on Human Factors in Computing Systems: The CHI Is the Limit,* May, 15–20 1999, 80–87. Pittsburgh, Pa.: Association for Computing Machinery (ACM), 1999. http://portal.acm.org/citation.cfm?coll=GUIDE&dl=GUIDE&id=303001 (10 May 2007).

Folkman, Susan, and Richard S. Lazarus. "An Analysis of Coping in Middle-Aged Community Sample." *Journal of Health and Social Behavior* 21 (September 1980), 219–39.

Foster, Jonathan. "Collaborative Information Seeking and Retrieval." In *Annual Review of Information Science and Technology*. Vol. 40, edited by Blaise Cronin, 329–56. Medford, N.J.: Information Today, Inc., 2006.

Fry, Jenny. "Scholarly Research and Information Practices: A Domain Analytic Approach." *Information Processing and Management* 42, no. 1 (2006), 299–316.

Gardiner, Michael E. *Critiques of Everyday Life*. London: Routledge, 2000.

Giddens, Anthony. *The Constitution of Society: Outline of a Theory of Structuration.* Cambridge, Mass.: Polity Press, 1984.

———. *The Consequences of Modernity.* Cambridge, Mass.: Polity Press, 1990.

———. *Modernity and Self-Identity: Self and Society in the Late Modern Age.* Cambridge, Mass.: Polity Press, 1991.

Graham, George. "Behaviorism," in *Stanford Encyclopedia of Philosophy.* http:// plato.stanford.edu/entries/behaviorism/ (10 May 2007).

Granovetter, Mark. "The Strength of Weak Ties." *American Journal of Sociology* 78, no. 6 (1973), 1360–80.

———. "The Strength of Weak Ties: A Network Theory Revisited." *Sociological Theory* 1 (1983), 201–33.

Habermas, Jürgen. *The Theory of Communicative Action, Part 2: Lifeworld and System: A Critique of Functionalist Reason.* Cambridge, Mass.: Polity Press, 1992.

Harris, Roma M., and Patricia Dewdney. *Barriers to Information: How Formal Help System Fail Battered Women.* Westport, Conn.: Greenwood Press, 1994.

Hartel, Jenna. "The Serious Leisure Frontier in Library and Information Science: Hobby Domains." *Knowledge Organization* 30, nos. 3–4 (2003), 228–38.

———. "Information Activities and Resources in an Episode of Gourmet Cooking." *Information Research* 12, no. 1 (2006). http://InformationR.net/ir/12-1/paper282 .html (10 May 2007).

Heeren, John. "Alfred Schutz and the Sociology of Common-Sense Knowledge." In *Understanding Everyday Life: Toward the Reconstruction of Sociological Knowledge*, edited by Jack D. Douglas, 45–56. London: Routledge & Kegan Paul, 1973.

Hektor, Anders. *What's the Use? Internet and Information Behavior in Everyday Life.* Linköping, Sweden: Linköping University, 2001.

Hersberger, Julie. "Everyday Information Needs and Information Sources of Homeless Parents." *The New Review of Information Behaviour Research* 2 (2001), 119–34.

———. "Are the Economically Poor Information Poor? Does the Digital Divide Affect the Homeless and Access to Information?" *Canadian Journal of Information and Library Science* 27, no. 3 (2002), 45–63.

———. "A Qualitative Approach to Examining Information Transfer via Social Networks among Homeless Populations." *The New Review of Information Behaviour Research* 4 (2003), 63–78.

Hogan, Timothy P., and Carole P. Palmer. "'Information Work' and Chronic Illness: Interpreting Results from a Nationwide Survey of People Living with HIV/AIDS." In Proceedings of the Annual Meeting of the American Society for Information Science and Technology, Charlotte, N.C., October 28–November 2, 2005. (CD-ROM). Volumes/ASIS05/papers/150/150_paper.html (10 May 2007).

Hujanen, Erkki. *Lukijakunnan rajamailla. Sanomalehden muuttuvat merkitykset arjessa* [On the Fringes of Readership: The Changing Meanings of Newspaper in Everyday Life]. Jyväskylä, Finland: University of Jyväskylä, 2007. http://julkaisut .jyu.fi/?id=978-951-39-2730-1 (10 May 2007).

Ingham, Jenni. "E-Mail Overload in the UK Workplace." *Aslib Proceedings* 55, no. 3 (2003), 166–80.

Ingwersen, Peter, and Kalervo Järvelin. *The Turn: Integration of Information Seeking and Retrieval in Context.* Dordrecht, The Netherlands: Springer, 2005.

JESSE. "Listserv Discussion on Information Behavior, December 1999." http://listserv .utk.edu/cgi-bin/wa?A1=ind9912&L=jesse (10 May 2007).

Johnson, J. David. *Information Seeking: An Organizational Dilemma.* Westport, Conn.: Quorum Books. 1996.

———. "On Contexts of Information Seeking." *Information Processing and Management* 39, no. 5 (2003), 735–60.

Johnson, J. David, et al. "Fields and Pathways: Contrasting or Complementary Views of Information Seeking." *Information Processing and Management* 42, no. 2 (2006), 569–82.

Johnson, John M. "Ethnomethodology and Existential Sociology." In *Existential Sociology,* edited by Jack D. Douglas et al., 153–74. Cambridge: Cambridge University Press, 1977.

Johnson, Thomas J., and Barbara K. Kaye. "Cruising Is Believing? Comparing Internet and Traditional Sources on Media Credibility Measures." *Journal of Mass Communication Quarterly* 75, no. 2 (1998), 325–40.

———. "Webelievability: A Path Model Examining How Convenience and Reliance Predict Online Credibility." *Journal of Mass Communication Quarterly* 79, no. 3 (2002), 619–42.

Jones, William. "Finders, Keepers? The Present and Future Perfect in Support of Personal Information Management." *First Monday* 9, no. 3 (2004). http://www.first monday.org/issues/issue9_3/jones/index.html (10 May 2007).

Julien, Heidi E., and David Michels. "Intra-Individual Information Behaviour in Daily Life." *Information Processing and Management* 40, no. 3 (2004), 547–62.

Kari, Jarkko. *Information Seeking and Interest in the Paranormal: Toward a Process Model of Information Action.* Tampere, Finland: University of Tampere, 2001. http://acta.uta.fi/pdf/951-44-5134-1.pdf (10 May 2007).

Kari, Jarkko, and Reijo Savolainen. "Toward a Contextual Model of Information Seeking on the Web." *The New Review of Information Behaviour Research* 4 (2003), 155–75.

Kelly, Diane. "Measuring Online Information Seeking in Context, Part 2: Findings and Discussion." *Journal of the American Society for Information Science and Technology* 57, no. 14 (2006), 1862–74.

King, Anthony. "Thinking with Bourdieu against Bourdieu: A 'Practical' Critique of the Habitus." *Sociological Theory* 18, no. 3 (2000), 417–33.

Kiousis, Spiro. "Public Trust or Mistrust? Perceptions of Media Credibility in the Information Age." *Mass Communication and Society* 4, no. 4 (2001), 381–403.

Klapp, Orrin E. *Overload and Boredom: Essays on the Quality of Life in the Information Society.* Westport, Conn.: Greenwood Press, 1986.

Knorr Cetina, Karin. "Objectual Practice." In *The Practice Turn in Contemporary Theory,* edited by Theodore R. Schatzki, Karin Knorr Cetina, and Eike von Savigny, 175–88. London: Routledge, 2001.

Krikelas, James. "Information-Seeking Behavior: Patterns and Concepts." *Drexel Library Quarterly* 19, no. 6 (1983), 5–20.

Lave, Jean. "The Practice of Learning." In *Understanding Practice: Perspectives on Activity and Context*, edited by Seth Chaiklin and Jean Lave, 3–32. Cambridge, Mass.: Cambridge University Press, 1993.

Leckie, Gloria J. "General Model of Information Seeking of Professionals." In *Theories of Information Behavior*, edited by Karen E. Fisher, Sanda Erdelez, and Lynne McKechnie, 158–63. Medford, N.J.: Information Today, Inc., 2005.

Leontev, Alexei N. "Activity and Consciousness." In *Philosophy in the USSR: Problems of Dialectical Materialism*, 180–202. Moscow: Progress Publishers, 1977. http://www.marxists.org/archive/leontev/works/1977/leon1977.htm (10 May 2007).

——. *Activity, Consciousness, and Personality*. Englewood Cliffs, N.J.: Prentice-Hall, 1978. http://www.marxists.org/archive/leontev/works/1978/index.htm (10 May 2007).

Lin, Nan. *Social Capital: A Theory of Social Structure and Action*. Cambridge, Mass.: Cambridge University Press, 2001.

Lincoln, Yvonna S., and Egon G. Guba. *Naturalistic Inquiry*. Newbury Park, Calif.: Sage, 1985.

Lynch, Michael. "Theorizing Practice." *Human Studies* 20, no. 2 (1997), 335–44.

——. "Ethnomethodology and the Logic of Practice." In *The Practice Turn in Contemporary Theory*, edited by Theodore R. Schatzki, Karin Knorr Cetina, and Eike von Savigny, 131–48. London: Routledge, 2001.

Mackenzie, Maureen L. "Storage and Retrieval of E-Mail in a Business Environment: An Exploratory Study." *Library and Information Science Research* 24, no. 4 (2002), 357–72.

Marcella, Rita, and Graeme Baxter. "The Information Needs and the Information-Seeking Behaviour of a National Sample of the Population in the United Kingdom, with Special Reference to Needs Related to Citizenship." *Journal of Documentation* 55, no. 2 (1999), 159–83.

McKenzie, Pamela J. "Justifying Cognitive Authority Decisions: Discursive Strategies of Information Seekers." *Library Quarterly* 73, no. 3 (2003), 261–88.

——. "A Model of Information Practices in Accounts of Everyday Life Information Seeking." *Journal of Documentation* 59, no. 1 (2003), 19–40.

Meadow, Charles T., and Weijing Yuan. "Measuring the Impact of Information: Defining the Concepts." *Information Processing and Management* 33, no. 6 (1997), 697–714.

Mele, Alfred R. *Springs of Action: Understanding Intentional Behavior*. Oxford, UK: Oxford University Press, 1992.

Metzger, Miriam J., et al. "Credibility for the 21st Century: Integrating Perspectives on Source, Message, and Media Credibility in the Contemporary Media Environment." In *Communication Yearbook*. Vol. 27, edited by Pamela J. Kalbfleisch, 293–335. Mahwah, N.J.: Lawrence Erlbaum, 2003.

Miller, George A. "The Magic Number Seven, Plus Minus Two: Some Limits on Our Capacity for Processing Information." *The Psychological Review* 63, no. 2 (1956), 81–97.

———. "Information Input Overload." In *Self-Organizing Systems*, edited by M. C. Yovits, 61–88. Washington, D.C.: Spartan Books. 1962.

Moores, Shaun. *Media and Everyday Life in Modern Society*. Edinburgh: Edinburgh University Press, 2000.

Morgan, David. "Everyday Life and Family Practices." In *Contemporary Culture and Everyday Life*, edited by Elizabeth B. Silva and Tony Bennett, 37–51. Durham, UK: Sociologypress, 2004.

Ng, Kwong Bor. "Towards a Theoretical Framework for Understanding the Relationship between Situated Action and Planned Action Models of Behavior in Information Retrieval Contexts: Contributions from Phenomenology." *Information Processing and Management* 38, no. 5 (2002), 613–26.

Nguyen, An, and Mark Western. "The Complementary Relationship between the Internet and Traditional Mass Media: The Case of Online News and Information. *Information Research* 11, no. 3 (2006). http://InformationR.net/ir/11-3/paper259.html (10 May 2007).

Olaisen, Johan. "Information Quality Factors and Cognitive Authority of Electronic Information." In *Information Quality: Definitions and Dimensions*, edited by Irene Wormell, 91–121. London: Taylor Graham, 1990.

Olsson, Michael. "Beyond 'Needy' Individuals: Conceptualizing Information Behavior," in Proceedings of the Annual Meeting of the American Society for Information Science and Technology, Charlotte, N.C., October 28–November 2, 2005 (CD-ROM). File:///Volumes/ASIST/papers/61/61_paper.html (10 May 2007).

Orlikowski, Wanda J. "Knowing in Practice: Enacting a Collective Capability in Distributed Organizing." *Organization Science* 13, no. 3 (2002), 249–73.

Østerlund, Carsten, and Paul Carlile. "Relations of Practice: Sorting through Practice Theories in Knowledge Sharing in Complex Organizations." *The Information Society* 21, no. 2 (2005), 91–107.

Oxford English Dictionary. "Action." http://dictionary.oed.com (10 May 2007).

———. "Activity." http://dictionary.oed.com (10 May 2007).

Palmer, Carole L. "Structures and Strategies of Interdisciplinary Science." *Journal of the American Society for Information Science* 50, no. 3 (1999), 242–53.

Palmer, Carole L, and Laura J. Neumann. "The Information Work of Interdisciplinary Humanities Scholars: Exploration and Translation." *Library Quarterly* 72, no. 1 (2002), 85–117.

Parker, Edwin B., and William J. Paisley. *Patterns of Adult Information Seeking*. Stanford, Calif.: Stanford University, Institute for Communication Research, 1966.

Pettigrew, Karen E. "Waiting for Chiropody: Contextual Results from an Ethnographic Study of the Information Behaviour among Attendees at Community Clinics." *Information Processing and Management* 35, no. 6 (1999), 801–17.

———. "Lay Information Provision in Community Settings: How Community Health Nurses Disseminate Human Services Information to the Elderly." *Library Quarterly* 70, no. 1 (2000), 47–85.

Pettigrew, Karen E., Raya Fidel, and Harry Bruce. "Conceptual Frameworks in Information Behavior." In *Annual Review of Information Science and Technology*.

Vol. 36, edited by Martha E. Williams, 43–78. Medford, N.J.: Information Today, Inc., 2001.

Prigoda, Elena, and Pamela J. McKenzie. "Purls of Wisdom: A Collectivist Study of Human Information Behaviour in a Public Library Knitting Group." *Journal of Documentation* 63, no. 1 (2007), 90–114.

Putnam, Robert D. *Bowling Alone: The Collapse and Revival of American Community*. New York: Simon & Schuster, 2000.

Reimer, Bo. *The Most Common of Practices: On Mass Media Use in Late Modernity*. Stockholm: Almqvist & Wiksell International, 1994.

Rice, Ronald E., Maureen McCreadie, and Shan-Ju Chang. *Accessing and Browsing Information and Communication*. Cambridge: MIT Press, 2001.

Rieh, Soo Young. "Judgment of Information Quality and Cognitive Authority in the Web." *Journal of the American Society for Information Science and Technology* 53, no. 2 (2002), 145–61.

———. "On the Web at Home: Information Seeking and Web Searching in the Home Environment." *Journal of the American Society for Information Science and Technology* 55, no. 8 (2004), 743–53.

Rieh, Soo Young, and David R. Danielson. "Credibility: A Multidisciplinary Framework." In *Annual Review of Information Science and Technology*. Vol. 41, edited by Blaise Cronin, 307–64. Medford, N.J.: Information Today, Inc., 2007.

Savolainen, Reijo. "Everyday Life Information Seeking: Approaching Information Seeking in the Context of Way of Life." *Library and Information Science Research* 17, no. 3 (1995), 259–94.

———. "The Role of the Internet in Information Seeking: Putting the Networked Services in Context." *Information Processing and Management* 35, no. 6 (1999), 765–82.

———. "Seeking and Using Information from the Internet: The Context of Non-Work Use." In *Exploring the Contexts of Information Behaviour*, edited by Tom D. Wilson and David K. Allen, 356–70. London: Taylor Graham, 1999.

———. "Living Encyclopedia or Idle Talk? Seeking and Providing Consumer Information in an Internet Newsgroup." *Library and Information Science Research* 23, no. 1 (2001), 67–90.

———. "Enthusiastic, Realistic and Critical: Discourses of Internet Use in the Context of Everyday Life Information Seeking." *Information Research* 10, no. 1 (2004). http://InformationR.net/ir/10-1/paper198.html (10 May 2007).

———. "Information Use as Gap-Bridging: The Viewpoint of Sense-Making Methodology." *Journal of the American Society for Information Science and Technology* 57, no. 8 (2006), 1116–25.

———. "Media Credibility and Cognitive Authority: The Case of Seeking Orienting Information." *Information Research* 12, no. 3 (2007). http://InformationR.net/ir/12-3/paper319.html (10 May 2007).

———. "Motives for Giving Information in Non-Work Contexts and the Expectations of Reciprocity: The Case of Environmental Activists," a paper presented in the annual meeting of the American Society for Information Science and Technology, Milwaukee, Wisc., October 18–25, 2007 http://www.asis.org/proceedings.html (12 February 2008).

———. "Information Behavior and Information Practice: Reviewing the Umbrella Concepts of Information Seeking Studies." *Library Quarterly* 77, no. 2 (2007), 109–32.

———. "Filtering and Withdrawing: Strategies for Coping with Information Overload in Everyday Contexts." *Journal of Information Science* 33, no. 5 (2007), 611–21.

———. "Information Source Horizons and Source Preferences of Environmental Activists: A Social Phenomenological Approach." *Journal of the American Society for Information Science and Technology* 58, no. 12 (2007), 1709–19.

———. "Source Preferences in the Context of Seeking Problem-Specific Information." *Information Processing and Management* 44, no. 1 (2008), 274–93.

Savolainen, Reijo, and Jarkko Kari, "Placing the Internet in Information Source Horizons: A Study of Information Seeking by Internet Users in the Context of Self-Development." *Library and Information Science Research* 26, no. 4 (2004), 415–33.

———. "Facing and Bridging Gaps in Web Searching." *Information Processing and Management* 42, no. 2 (2006), 519–37.

Schatzki, Theodore R. "Practices and Actions: A Wittgensteinian Critique of Bourdieu and Giddens." *Philosophy of Social Sciences* 27, no. 3 (1997), 283–308.

———. "Introduction: Practice Theory." In *The Practice Turn in Contemporary Theory*, edited by Theodore R. Schatzki, Karin Knorr Cetina, and Eike von Savigny, 1–14. London: Routledge, 2001.

———. "Practice Mind-ed Orders." In *The Practice Turn in Contemporary Theory*, edited by Theodore R. Schatzki, Karin Knorr Cetina, and Eike von Savigny, 42–55. London: Routledge, 2001.

Schatzki, Theodore R., Karin Knorr Cetina, and Eike von Savigny, eds. *The Practice Turn in Contemporary Theory*. London: Routledge, 2001.

Schuller, Tom, Stephen Baron, and John Field. "Social Capital: A Review and Critique." In *Social Capital: Critical Perspectives*, edited by Stephen Baron, John Field, and Tom Schuller, 1–38. Oxford, UK: Oxford University Press, 2000.

Schutz, Alfred. *Collected Papers 1: The Problem of Social Reality*, edited by Maurice Natanson. The Hague, The Netherlands: Martinus Nijhoff, 1962.

———. *Collected Papers 2: Studies in Social Theory*, edited by Arvid Brodersen. The Hague, The Netherlands: Martinus Nijhoff, 1964.

———. *Collected Papers 3: Studies in Phenomenological Philosophy*, edited by Ilse Schutz. The Hague, The Netherlands: Martinus Nijhoff, 1966.

———. *The Phenomenology of the Social World*. Evanston, Ill.: Northwestern University Press, 1967.

———. *Reflections on the Problem of Relevance*, edited by Richard M. Zaner. New Haven, Conn.: Yale University Press, 1970.

———. "Appendix: The Notebooks." In *Alfred Schutz and Thomas Luckmann, The Structures of the Life-World (Vol. 2)*, 159–324. Evanston, Ill.: Northwestern University Press. 1989.

Schutz, Alfred, and Thomas Luckmann. *The Structures of the Life-World (Vol. 1)*. Evanston, Ill.: Northwestern University Press, 1973.

———. *The Structures of the Life-World (Vol. 2)*. Evanston, Ill.: Northwestern University Press, 1989.

Schweiger, Wolfgang. "Media Credibility—Experience or Image? A Survey on the Credibility of the World Wide Web in Germany in Comparison to Other Media." *European Journal of Communication* 15, no. 1 (2000), 37–59.

Shenk, David. *Data Smog: Surviving the Information Glut.* San Francisco, Calif.: Harper Edge, 1998.

Shenton, Andrew K., and Pat Dixon. "Issues Arising from Youngsters' Information-Seeking Behavior." *Library and Information Science Research* 26, no. 2 (2004), 177–200.

Silverstone, Roger. *Television and Everyday Life.* London: Routledge, 1994.

Simmel, Georg. "The Metropolis and Mental Life." In *The Sociology of Georg Simmel*, edited by Kurt H. Wolff. New York: Free Press, 1964. http://condor.depaul.edu/~dweinste/intro/simmel_M&ML.htm (10 May 2007).

Solomon, Paul. "Discovering Information Behavior in Sense Making, Part 2: The Social." *Journal of the American Society for Information Science* 48, no. 12 (1997), 1109–26.

———. "Information Mosaics: Patterns of Action That Structure." In *Exploring the Contexts of Information Behaviour*, edited by Tom D. Wilson and David K. Allen, 150–85. London: Taylor Graham, 1999.

Sonnenwald, Diane H. "Evolving Perspectives of Human Information Behaviour: Contexts, Situations, Social Networks and Information Horizons." In *Exploring the Contexts of Information Behaviour*, edited by Tom D. Wilson and David K. Allen, 176–90. London: Taylor Graham, 1999.

———. "Challenges in Sharing Information Effectively: Examples from Command and Control." *Information Research* 11, no. 4 (2006). http://informationr.net/ir/11-4/paper270.html (10 May 2007).

Sonnenwald, Diane H., Barbara M. Wildemuth, and Gary T. Harmon. "A Research Method to Investigate Information Seeking Using the Concept of Information Horizons: An Example from a Study of Lower Socio-Economic Students' Information-Seeking Behaviour." *The New Review of Information Behaviour Research* 2 (2001), 65–86.

Sundin, Olof, and Jenny Johannison. "The Instrumentality of Information Needs and Relevance." In *CoLIS 2005*, edited by Fabio Crestani and Ian Ruthven, 107–18. Berlin: Springer, 2005.

Swidler, Ann. "What Anchors Cultural Practices?" In *The Practice Turn in Contemporary Theory*, edited by Theodore R. Schatzki, Karin Knorr Cetina, and Eike von Savigny, 74–92. London: Routledge, 2001.

Talja, Sanna. "Information Sharing in Academic Communities: Types and Levels of Collaboration in Information Seeking and Use." *The New Review of Information Behaviour Research* 3 (2002), 143–59.

———. "The Domain Analytic Approach to Scholar's Information Practices." In *Theories of Information Behavior*, edited by Karen E. Fisher, Sanda Erdelez, and Lynne McKechnie, 123–27. Medford, N.J.: Information Today, Inc., 2005.

Talja, Sanna, and Preben Hansen. "Information Sharing." In *New Directions in Human Information Behavior*, edited by Amanda Spink and Charles Cole, 113–34. Berlin: Springer, 2005.

Taylor, Robert S. *Value-Added Process in Information Systems.* Norwood, N.J.: Ablex, 1986.

——. "Information Use Environments." In *Progress in Communication Sciences.* Vol. 10, edited by Brenda Dervin, 217–55. Norwood, N.J.: Ablex, 1991.

Thévenot, Laurent. "Pragmatic Regimes Governing the Engagement with the World." In *The Practice Turn in Contemporary Theory*, edited by Theodore R. Schatzki, Karin Knorr Cetina, and Eike von Savigny, 56–73. London: Routledge, 2001.

Thivant, Eric. "Information Seeking and Use Behaviour of Economists and Business Analysts." *Information Research* 10, no. 4 (2005). http://InformationR.net/ir/10-4/paper234.html (10 May 2007).

Tidline, Tonya J. "The Mythology of Information Overload." *Library Trends* 47, no. 3 (1999), 485–506.

Todd, Ross J. "Utilization of Heroin Information by Adolescent Girls in Australia: A Cognitive Analysis." *Journal of the American Society for Information Science* 50, no. 1 (1999), 10–23.

Tombros, Anastasios, Ian Ruthven, and Joemon M. Jose. "How Users Assess Web Pages for Information Seeking." *Journal of the American Society for Information Science and Technology* 56, no. 4 (2005), 327–44.

Toms, Elaine G. "What Motivates the Browser?" In *Exploring the Contexts of Information Behaviour*, edited by Tom D. Wilson and David K. Allen, 191–207. London: Taylor Graham, 1999.

Tuominen, Kimmo. "Whoever Increases His Knowledge Merely Increases His Heartache: Moral Tensions in Heart Surgery Patients' and Their Spouses' Talk about Information Seeking." *Information Research* 10, no. 1 (2004). http://InformationR.net/ir/10-1/paper202.html (10 May 2007).

Tuominen, Kimmo, Sanna Talja, and Reijo Savolainen. "The Social Constructionist Viewpoint to Information Practices." In *Theories of Information Behavior*, edited by Karen E. Fisher, Sanda Erdelez, and Lynne McKechnie, 328–33. Medford, N.J.: Information Today, Inc., 2005.

Turner, Stephen. *The Social Theory of Practices: Tradition, Tacit Knowledge and Presuppositions.* Cambridge, UK: Polity Press, 1994.

——. "Bad Practices: A Reply." *Human Studies* 20, no. 2 (1997), 345–56.

——. "Throwing Out the Tacit Rule Book: Learning and Practices." In *The Practice Turn in Contemporary Theory*, edited by Theodore R. Schatzki, Karin Knorr Cetina, and Eike von Savigny, 120–30. London: Routledge, 2001.

Wagner, Wolfgang, and Nicky Hayes. *Everyday Discourse and Common Sense: The Theory of Representations.* Houndmills, Hampshire, UK: Palgrave, 2005.

Warner, Edward, Ann D. Murray, and Vernon E. Palmour. *Information Needs of Urban Citizens: Final Report.* Washington, D.C.: U.S. Department of Health, Education and Welfare, Office of Education, Bureau of Libraries and Learning Resources, 1973.

Wathen, C. Nadine, and Jacquelyn Burkell. "Believe It or Not: Factors Influencing Credibility on the Web." *Journal of the American Society for Information Science and Technology* 53, no. 2 (2002), 134–44.

Wathen, C. Nadine, and Roma Harris. "An Examination of the Health Information Seeking Experiences of Women in Rural Ontario, Canada." *Information Research* 11, no. 4 (2006). http://InformationR.net/ir/11-4/paper267.html (10 May 2007).

Wersig, Gernot, and Gunter Windel. "Information Science Needs a Theory of Information Actions." *Social Science Information Studies* 5, no. 1 (1985), 11–23.

Widén-Wulff, Gunilla, and Mariam Ginman. "Explaining Knowledge Sharing in Organizations through the Dimensions of Social Capital." *Journal of Information Science* 30, no. 5 (2004), 448–58.

Williamson, Kirsty. "Discovered by Chance: The Role of Incidental Information Acquisition in an Ecological Model of Information Use." *Library and Information Science Research* 20, no. 1 (1998), 23–40.

———. "Ecological Theory of Human Information Behavior." In *Theories of Information Behavior*, edited by Karen E. Fisher, Sanda Erdelez, and Lynne McKechnie, 128–32. Medford, N.J.: Information Today, Inc., 2005.

Wilson, C. E. "Information Discrimination: A Human Habit." *Canadian Journal of Information and Library Science* 1, no. 1 (1976), 59–63.

Wilson, George. "Action," in *Stanford Encyclopedia of Philosophy*. http://plato.stanford .edu/entries/action (10 May 2007).

Wilson, Patrick. *Public Knowledge, Private Ignorance: Toward a Library and Information Policy*. Westport, Conn.: Greenwood Press, 1977.

———. *Second-Hand Knowledge: An Inquiry into Cognitive Authority*. Westport, Conn.: Greenwood Press, 1983.

———. "Unused Relevant Information in Research and Development." *Journal of the American Society for Information Science* 46, no. 1 (1995), 45–51.

Wilson, Tom D. "On User Studies and Information Needs." *Journal of Documentation* 37, no. 1 (1981), 3–15.

———. "Information Behaviour: An Interdisciplinary Perspective." In *Information Seeking in Context*, edited by Pertti Vakkari, Reijo Savolainen, and Brenda Dervin, 39–49. London: Taylor Graham, 1997.

———. "Human Information Behaviour." *Informing Science* 3, no. 2 (2000), 49–56. http://www.inform.nu/Articles/Vol3/v3n2p49-56.pdf (10 May 2007).

———. "Alfred Schutz: Phenomenology and Research Methodology for Information Behaviour Research." *The New Review of Information Behaviour Research* 3 (2002), 71–81.

———. "A Re-Examination of Information Seeking Behaviour in the Context of Activity Theory." *Information Research* 11, no. 4 (2006). http://InformationR.net/ir/ 11-4/paper260.html (10 May 2007)

Wurman, Richard S. *Information Anxiety*. New York: Doubleday, 1989.

Wurman, Richard S., Loring Leifer, and David Sume. *Information Anxiety 2*. Indianapolis, Ind.: QUE, 2001.

Yang, Jen-Te. "Job-Related Knowledge Sharing: Comparative Case Studies." *Journal of Knowledge Management* 8, no. 3 (2004), 118–26.

Zach, Lisl. "When Is 'Enough' Enough? Modeling the Information-Seeking and Stopping Behavior of Senior Arts Administrators." *Journal of the American Society for Information Science and Technology* 56, no. 1 (2005), 23–35.

Index

accessibility, 62–63, 99–102, 107, 115, 117–20, 127–30, 134, 141–42
accuracy, 118
act(s), 20, 27
action(s), 2; agency and, 18; basic, 25; behavior and, 11n18, 22–23, 45–47; chain of, 21, 27; communicative, 70n68; defined, 20, 24; as doings and sayings, 25–26, 30, 34n94, 50, 64; freedom of, factors determining, 51; future and, 53; goals and, 20, 21, 25–30; habitual, 23, 30; information use and, 7; intention and, 46, 47, 48; interests and, 29, 30; knowledge and, 20; pleasurability of, 30; practices and, 17–20, 23, 24, 25; priority to, 20; projects and, 27–30; prompting and responding to performing, 34n94; reasons and, 19, 22; resources as determinants of, 18–19; rules as determinants of, 18–19, 28, 66; situated and planned, 11n18; social phenomenology and, 21; stock of knowledge and, 26–28, 30, 34n94, 66; theory of, 46; values and, 28–29. *See also* information actions; information seeking actions; social action
actionable directions, 27
active scanning, 38, 114

active search, 44
active seeking, 38
activities: defined, 20–21, 24, 47; habitual, 42; institutionalization of, 41–42; motives for, 21, 25–26; practices in relation to, 20–21, 23, 24, 41. *See also* information activities; information activity practices
activity theory, 21, 24
affectivity, 28, 29
agency, 18
Ajzen, Icek, 22
alienation, 189
Allen, Thomas J., 37–38
altruism, 8, 9, 191–93, 196, 204
anxiety. *See* information anxiety
approximation, 177
Armed for Action: Library Response to Citizen Information Needs (Durrance), v
attention, 43–44, 56, 90
attitudes, 22, 26
availability, 74n105, 75n112, 92, 95, 99–102, 107, 115, 117–18, 127–30, 141–42, 148n69

Barnes, Barry, 24
Barry, Carol L., 147n69
basic actions, 25

221

About the Author

Reijo Savolainen is professor in the Department of Information Studies, University of Tampere, Finland. He has been actively involved in researching everyday-life information seeking (ELIS) since the early 1990s. Studies he has conducted in this field have focused on the ELIS practices of various groups such as teachers, industrial workers, people interested in self-development, environmental activists, and the unemployed. He has more than 100 publications in national and international forums in the field of information and library studies.